OTHER BOOKS BY AXEL MADSEN

Nonfiction

The Sewing Circle: Female Stars Who Loved Other Women

Stanwyck: The Life and Times of Barbara Stanwyck

Chanel: A Woman of Her Home

Sonia Delaunay: The Painter of the Lost Generation

Silk Roads: The Asian Adventures of Clara and André Malraux

Gloria and Jose: The Star-Crossed Love Affair of Gloria Swanson and Joe Kennedy

Cousteau: A Biography

60 Minutes: The Power and Politics of America's Most Popular Show

Private Power

Living for Design: The Yves Saint-Laurent Story

John Huston: A Biography

Hearts and Minds: The Uncommon Journey of Jean-Paul Sartre and Simone de Beauvoir

Malraux: A Biography

William Wyler: The Authorized Biography

Billy Wilder

Fiction

Unisave

Borderlines

The Deal Maker

The Deal Maker

How William C. Durant
Made General Motors

AXEL MADSEN

John Wiley & Sons, Inc.
New York • Chichester • Weinheim • Brisbane
• Singapore • Toronto

Copyright © 1999 by Madsen & Associates, Inc.
All rights reserved

Published by John Wiley & Sons, Inc.
Published simultaneously in Canada

This publication is designed to provide accurate and authorita-
tive information in regard to the subject matter covered. It is
sold with the understanding that the publisher is not engaged in
rendering professional services. If professional advice or other
expert assistance is required, the services of a competent
professional person should be sought.

Photo credits: The photographs appearing in this book are
courtesy of the Kettering/GMI Alumni Foundation
of Industrial History, Flint, Michigan.
Frontispiece photo: William C. Durant, circa 1908

Library of Congress Cataloging-in-Publication Data:
Madsen, Axel.
    The deal maker : how William C. Durant made General Motors /
Axel Madsen.
        p.   cm.
    Includes bibliographical references and index.
    ISBN 0-471-28327-4 (cloth : alk paper)
    1. Durant, William Crapo, 1861–1947. 2. General Motors
Corporation—History. 3. Businesspeople—United States—Biography.
I. Title.
HD9710.U52D855   1999
338.7'6292'092—dc21
[B]   99-11639

10 9 8 7 6 5 4 3 2

To Carol and Richard Gagnon

Contents

Contents

The Funeral

Two hundred former associates and persons prominent in the industry gathered at the Episcopal Calvary Church on Manhattan's Park Avenue South and
Twenty-first Street. Reverend Samuel M. Shoemaker read
from Romans, chapter 8. There was no eulogy. Perhaps the
long life of William C. Durant was too hard to sum up. In its
obituary the day before, the *New York Times* had called the
founder of General Motors a manipulative genius, spoken of
the vast enterprise he originated, and described him as a
man who had made and lost several fortunes. It said nothing of his foresight, and his willingness to take risks that
had accelerated the dawn of the automobile age. Lowell
Thomas was more generous in his broadcast that morning.
He called Durant a fabulous figure.

Durant's first million had come easily enough.* Serious

*Figures are given in vintage dollars. To get a sense of values (and
inflation) since 1900, the reader should multiply by 17. The average weekly earnings in the United States were $9.70. A gallon of

1

money—and those who possessed it—never intimidated him. During his golden years, he bought companies at the rate of one every three weeks. To go after new targets made for boldness, and kept him ahead of his own brainstorms. The *Detroit Free Press*'s Malcolm W. Bingay, who knew all the automotive pioneers, said that with Durant all superlatives were understatements. "The world for him was just a hickory nut which he, and he alone, knew how to crack. Durant never thought in dollars and cents. Always in millions."

The chancel rail and the coffin were banked with lilies of the valley, roses, and gladioli. The organist played Dykes's *Lead, Kindly Light*. Catherine L. Durant daubed her eyes. She was flanked by Winfred Murphy, who had been her husband's longtime personal secretary, and by Aristo Scrobogna, the young Italian immigrant who had started as a caretaker and became indispensable during the last difficult years. At the funeral, Murphy recalled an incident back in Michigan in 1908 that summed up the spirit of the man they were mourning. Because they had missed the Pere Marquette Railroad local to Detroit and didn't want to miss the Detroit–New York express, Durant had decided to drive the 65 miles to Detroit. They were halfway down the gravel highway when they were caught behind a tractor pulling a wagon stacked so high and wide with hay it obscured everything. Durant gunned the car and veered through a ditch. "What was that?" Murphy shouted when a loud snap signaled a broken spring leaf.

"Never mind," the boss had yelled, pulling out of the ditch ahead of the hay wagon. "We're still running."

gasoline was six cents, a pound of sugar cost 4 cents, a dozen eggs 14 cents. Source: Federal Reserve Library, Philadelphia, and *The Economist*. For the inflation value after 1913, see http://woodrow. mpls.rfb.fed.us.

Impatience had been a lifelong trait. Scrobogna remembered how Durant in his eighties had chafed at his own diminished capacities and lack of attention from others, how hard Durant had exercised to recover from a stroke, and how he told former colleagues to keep working.

Durant's socialite daughter, Margery, had come down from New Canaan, Connecticut, with her husband, Fitzhugh Green, who with Charles Lindbergh had coauthored the first book on Lindbergh's historic flight across the Atlantic. To Margery, "Pops" had been a constant in her agitated life, and she had written a book about him. Mrs. Eddie Rickenbacker, as the newspaper dutifully noted, was also among the mourners. It was more than thirty years before that Adelaide Frost had divorced Durant's playboy son Clifford and on the rebound married America's World War I flying ace. Cliff had died ten years earlier.

William Crapo Durant had touched all those who assembled that Tuesday morning, March 20, 1947, to see him to his grave. Frederick A. Aldrich had known the deceased since the horse-drawn buggy days. Willie or Billy, as everybody called the boss back in 1889, had offered Aldrich $12 a week to join the Flint Road Cart Company. In 1908, Durant had rewarded Fred and his brother Ralph with $10,000 for setting up a meeting with the Cadillac people in Detroit. That had been money wisely spent, since the Cadillac division pulled the fledgling General Motors through several rough spots. Billy, said his old friends from Flint, had a tendency to soar high, wide, and handsome. Fred was one of the few men who could bring him down to earth. Billy had made Fred secretary-treasurer of Stirling and Chevrolet Motors. Willie didn't care for titles himself. "Elect me janitor or office boy," he said when offered the Flint Road Cart presidency by his partner Dallas Dort. Dallas had died in 1928. The following year, Durant lost most of his fortune in the Wall Street crash. His wealth, as the *New York Times* told its readers in its obituary, had been $120 million before the 1929 Wall Street crash; his assets, when he declared bankruptcy in 1936, $250.

In the pew behind Aldrich was George E. Daniels. This former Harvard law graduate was an early believer in the importance of automobiles. He had left the bar to become a Buick manager in Philadelphia, and Durant had made him the first interim president of GM.

K. T. Keller outranked Aldrich, Daniels, and the rest of the automotive phalanx. The chief executive officer of Chrysler Corporation had endured Durant's insensitivity to the needs of subordinates and benefited from the way he showered them with wealth. They had met in 1916, when Durant decided to pay Walter Chrysler $10,000 a month and a yearly bonus of half a million to run the Buick division. Keller had been a young production engineer back then, fiercely loyal to Chrysler but in awe of their soft-spoken boss who loved to operate in the midst of hurricanes. Durant had promoted Keller to vice president of Chevrolet and general manager of the Canadian division of General Motors before losing him to Chrysler.

∽o∼

At the dawn of the twentieth century, the automobile had quickened the pulse of shirtsleeve entrepreneurs and fired public imagination. Prime among the informal and confident can-do entrepreneurs was William Crapo Durant. He was not a pioneer tinkering in a greasy workshop. He was the man inventors turned to, the one who knew how to raise money for their sputtering and temperamental dreamworks.

Style was all. With his trademark smile and personal charisma, Durant created excitement. He dominated meetings by the intensity of what he had to say even when he was the last to speak. Walter Chrysler said Durant had the most winning personality, that he could coax a bird right down out of a tree.

He made some bad guesses, but his sharp sense of timing and opportunity allowed him to make nervy decisions. J. Pierpont Morgan, who had refused to underwrite the birth of what was now America's foremost carmaker and the largest privately owned industrial organization, had called him "an unstable visionary." Durant's nonchalant approach to vast amounts of money always scared financiers and bankers.

The muscular capitalism of his time worshiped ruthless, self-made men, entrepreneurs who disdained common folk and fought tradition and mediocrity. Not so Durant. Gracious and loyal, he played checkers with elevator operators. Insofar as he could, he made sure friends and followers prospered along with him. He was devoted to his mother, spoiled his two children, and cried shamelessly watching Raymond Massey play Abraham Lincoln on a New York stage. He was a man of boundless enthusiasm. His lifelong optimism, ironically, was also responsible for his downfall. He could not abide failure. To bolster and vindicate his financial constructs and keep share prices from falling, he bought his own company's shares.

Intuition served him well. While Henry Ford's big idea was to turn the car into a necessity, Durant believed people wanted choice. Where Ford imagined hundreds of thousands of Model Ts rolling off assembly lines until, as he told his wife, streets would be four-deep in traffic, Durant sensed people would want variety, and that carmakers might have to sell on credit. Ford came up with the moving assembly line in 1913 after visiting Chicago slaughterhouses where cow carcasses were carried down a line. Five years earlier, Durant invented vertical integration. Where Ford backed into mass production to satisfy demand, Durant scaled up the industry itself.

ം◦ം

During its formative years, GM's center of gravity was wherever Durant was, and he had been in constant motion. It drove bankers and organization men crazy. He scheduled meetings without regard for clocks, summoning people to 1:30 A.M. get-togethers, but was always the first to arrive in the office in the morning, natty and smiling. He believed that monopoly and control destroyed initiative and often led to abuse of power. He liked to say that if he controlled the car business, the public would very likely get what he cared to build. With competition, people would get what they wanted, because if he didn't supply it somebody else would. He knew how to sell a salesman a career, and realized cars would advertise themselves on the street and at the curb. He was the first to develop a sales organization on a North American scale.

Durant's Promethean years were marked by epic struggles with financiers. He depended on only a few sources of big money to finance the exploding business, and pitted himself against forces he underestimated or refused to consider. In hindsight, the moneymen would emphasize the amateurishness of his ride through the industry. Not that their vision was particularly provident. Where Ford and Durant saw untapped riches in selling affordable automobiles to every household, Morgan and other grandees of the purse saw too many cars chasing too few rich men. Even when Americans started buying tens of thousands of cars every year, bankers tightened credits and recalled loans at the slightest slump in car sales. The bankers' unease was understandable. In 1909, when there were nearly 300 carmakers, 18 new firms began building automobiles. In 1910, 18 went belly up, and only one entered the fray.

Both Ford and Durant—they were born two years apart, and Ford died a month after Durant—tried to keep control by working longer and harder themselves. Ford was too big a stockholder of Ford Motor Company to be cast aside, but corporate arthritis set in. During the Flaming Twenties, innovations were introduced by others. Lack of ample financial resources and Durant's own inattention contributed to the slow demise of Durant Motors in the late 1920s. In his own mind, the collapse of Durant Motors and his earlier loss of the stewardship of General Motors were both failures of nerve, failures of confidence, by others.

The ranking absentee at the funeral was Alfred Pritchard Sloan. Corporate needs had kept the CEO from coming to New York. General Motors was retooling for peace after the war effort that saw the company design fighter and bomber planes and build tanks, trucks, and airplanes. Durant had acquired the young MIT graduate in 1917 when purchasing the Hyatt Roller Bearing Company, and had seen him become his successor. Sloan had harbored deep skepticism about the Durant leadership, and was exasperated and alarmed by the dynamic and autocratic style, the visions and hunches of Durant—and Henry Ford. Sloan retained Durant's decentralized structure, the autonomous Buick, Cadillac, Pontiac, Oldsmobile, GMC, and various other divisions, but perfected a rigid system of command and control. The GM he built was a conglomerate that, independent of the whims of one man, could run itself.

Sloan's respect for GM's founder was nevertheless considerate and on occasion poignant. He believed that when GM was hours away from collapsing in 1920, Durant had tried single-handedly to prop up the stock out of pride and confidence in the future. In 1940, when Durant was approaching eighty and largely forgotten, Sloan invited him to the rollout of General Motors's 25 millionth car. On that occasion, Sloan led Durant by the hand to the front of the platform and introduced him to the 5,000 guests. "Too often," said Sloan, "we fail to recognize the creative spirit."

Reverend Shoemaker read from Romans, chapter 8.

"The Spirit itself beareth witness with our spirit, that we are the children of God. And if children, then heirs, heirs of God, and joint-heirs with Christ; if so be that we suffer with Him, that we may be also glorified together." From John, chapter 14, he read: "Peace I leave with you, my peace I give unto you."

Pachelbel's *When in the Hour of Utmost Need* accompanied the coffin to the hearse on Park Avenue. The private burial was at Woodlawn Cemetery in the Bronx.

1

‿〇◟

The Man

illiam Crapo Durant was the Great Gatsby of carmaking. His tale is a can-do story of a time when America was upsizing, not downsizing. With such latter-day players as Ted Turner, Andy Grove, Steve Jobs, and John Malone, he belongs to the charmed circle of Americans who, in a span of less than two decades, built wholly new industries. His story tells of the uneasy alliances struck again and again between inventors and capital, the built-in conflict between prime movers and bean counters, between innovation and control of innovation.

He was a small man of a trim 120 pounds, too short to be called dashing (he stood just under 5 feet 8 inches tall), but with soft, handsome features. His manners were cultivated and friendly, and he was usually easy to approach. When he was forty-eight, a Detroit news reporter wrote that he radiated intense and controlled energy:

> There are no harsh lines in his face, no note of the autocrat in his speech or act. In fact, he is a man of extreme reticence. He has the modesty, which frequently

accompanies tenacity of purpose. Yet there is something about him that makes you feel that here is an extraordinarily virile personality . . . Probably his eyes are Mr. Durant's most distinctive features. They are brown, frank eyes, shrewd, but not the shrewdness of the eye that tries to read you just to find what is in the back of your head . . . bright and gleaming eyes and yet with a feminine softness. The face is the face of an idealist, the planner, the dreamer but the dreamer of realizable dreams.

As a friend said, he was never happy unless he was hanging to a windowsill by his fingertips. He swept through meals, eating what was set before him with neither praise nor complaint. He took little notice of his daughter and son, Margery and Cliff, when they were children, and spoiled them when they were adults. He hated exercise, and kept his office windows closed most of the time. Always in need of a secretary or just someone to talk to during his incessant travels, he would take journalists along on dashes to see his mother at the family summer home on Lake Michigan. He did not encourage familiarity, but when he held marathon work sessions in Flint reporters knew they could catch him sipping coffee at an all-night restaurant. He was always good for a story. Lee Dunlap, the general manager of the Pontiac division, likened the boss's visits to "the visitation of a cyclone":

> He would lead his staff in, take off his coat, begin issuing orders, dictating letters, and calling the ends of the continent on the telephone, talking in his rapid, easy way to New York, Chicago, San Francisco. That sort of thing was less common than it is now; it put most of us in awe of him. Only the most phenomenal memory could keep his deals straight; he worked so fast that the records were always behind.

He was good with words, and knew how to listen. "Assume that the man you are talking to knows as much or more than you do," he advised his salesmen. "Do not talk too much. Give the customer time to think. In other words, let the customer sell himself." He was both a visionary sketching glories in thin air, and a hard-nosed industrialist. To buy companies and consolidate the industry, he took out the equivalent of home-equity loans on existing assets. "What a man!" wrote Jacob H. Newmark, who for twenty-five years was Durant's advertising chief. "What an actor! What a life! What a fighter!"

He loved power and itched to achieve big things, although not at any cost. There was a craving for approval deep in his psyche. His single-minded work methods created friction, but he couldn't bear feeling hated or even disliked. In cases where he had reason to deal harshly with associates and underlings, he was the first to seek accommodation and compromise. He basked in people's gratitude and quietly did more for others than many high-profile philanthropists. He was a soft touch when it came to friends and collaborators, but had no gift or taste for becoming a patron of the arts. His incurable optimism made him hope for the best and never prepare for the worst. He wrestled repeatedly with business cycles, and was surprised each time a downturn hit.

❧

Durant was the grandson of Michigan's governor, Henry Howland Crapo. He was also the son of that Victorian rarity—a divorced woman. He grew up loved and coddled, but with the memory of a father whose name was best left unmentioned in the parlors of his mother's principled and successful family. His mother's nurturing, his good looks, and his energetic charm turned him into Flint's eligible bachelor. At twenty-four, he married Clara Pitt, a ticket agent's daughter who assumed her husband's status in Flint society. She bore him two children. For twenty years, she was the dutiful wife while her husband made his first serious money and erected ever more dizzying business constructs.

Breathtaking success and a wandering eye made him divorce Clara and, in less than seemly circumstances, marry a nineteen-year-old woman who today would be called a trophy wife. The marriage took, however. Catherine Lederer was a shy woman who despite their wealth never hit the gossip columns. Darling Muddie, as he called her, made him take time out—to enjoy a palatial villa on the New Jersey shore, to see Europe and the playgrounds of Miami Beach. But unlike his younger Wall Street acquaintance and fellow stock speculator Joseph P. Kennedy, Billy had little taste for the sporting life. Catherine decorated their Fifth Avenue apartment and their grand retreat in Deal, New Jersey, in glitzy opulence. Their dinner and weekend guests, however, were not members of the Park Avenue limousine crowd, but other auto executives and their wives.

Flint forgave him for living in New York. The Michigan town of his childhood, youth, and early success regarded him as a native son, although he was born in Boston. Flint's citizens thought he was the most exciting man. Associates didn't refer to him as "the boss," but as "the Man." They would say, "The Man wants it done this way" or "The Man was pleased." When he was in his eighties and running a bowling alley, he never sat down on the job, but tended affably to his customers.

He both loathed and believed in the raw Darwinian capitalism that characterized so much of industry a hundred years ago. He both deplored and profited from the anarchy of production. With a foresight unmatched by Henry Ford, he understood the need to consolidate. But the country then was ambivalent about cartels. Three years after he folded a half dozen companies into General Motors in 1908, the Supreme Court broke up John D. Rockefeller's Standard Oil. Durant wondered if he might be next. But it

Durant in his sixties

wasn't until twenty years after he died that Washington's trustbusters looked askance at GM's 64 percent market share—and then decided to go after International Business Machines instead. Twenty years after that, nimbler imports and Detroit's inbred arrogance had reduced GM's North American market share to less than 30 percent.

He was a lifelong Republican. In April 1929 he went

to Washington and, at a late night meeting at the White House, warned President Herbert Hoover that a ruinous depression was inevitable if the Federal Reserve Board didn't stop trying to curtail brokerage loans. In the summer of 1929, Billy had $6 million in bonds in a safe-deposit vault for the purpose of providing Catherine and himself with an annuity. Before the paperwork was done, Wall Street crashed. Although he was heavily leveraged in stocks, he refused to panic. As with earlier misfortunes, he forced himself to see the positive side, and, in public, to be on the side of the angels. America would survive, he said, because Americans were optimistic, progressive, and living in "an age of big things." In response to margin calls, he put up the entire $6 million, and lost it all. Hoover should have taken his advice, he said. Two years later he caused a stir by announcing he would vote for Franklin D. Roosevelt.

Promoters, schemers, and mad scientists knew he was receptive to new things and had money galore. They tripped over each other to propose every conceivable invention. Some of them got through to him and sold him an idea. The electric icebox he named Frigidaire was a winner, the walk-behind Samson farm tractor a dud. He was quick to change management when car sales sagged. He would appear at the headquarters of the drooping division, fire the sales group wholesale, and personally take charge. He would focus on setting things right, but tire of it after a few days. Soon, a new face would take over.

He could never forget that the bankers got the best of him. In an unfinished and never-published autobiography he began writing shortly after his eightieth birthday, he wrote with some bitterness:

My work has been interesting, my friends legion. Naturally, I have suffered at times, as every man must suffer whose motives are misunderstood and whose confidence betrayed.

2

❧

Rebecca's Boy

Billy Durant was a mother's boy. In his adult years, his many ventures spared him little time for Rebecca Crapo Durant, but he never stopped doting on her. She, on her side, wrote to him every day. He called her death, at ninety-one, the "first real sorrow of my life."

Rebecca was what midwestern society dreaded, a woman approaching forty with a failed marriage behind her, when, in 1872, she moved in with her sister and brother-in-law, bringing along her fifteen-year-old daughter and ten-year-old son. Her sister Rhoda's choice of a husband had been wiser, and together Dr. and Mrs. James Willson put up Rebecca and her two children.

Uncle Jim was everything Willie's father was not. At sixteen, Willson had left his parents' farm in Canada to seek his fortune in the late 1840s California gold rush. Illness forced him back East. In Olean, New York, he became a photographer. Later, he found his vocation at the University of Michigan medical school. He was twenty-three when he graduated and set up practice in Flint. When the Tenth

Michigan marched off to the Civil War under a colonel who had twice been the mayor of Flint, Dr. Willson went along as their surgeon. Not yet forty, he was a pillar of Flintian society, organizer of the Genesee County Savings Bank, a member of the county agricultural society, and a trustee of the Presbyterian church. Willie grew up with Uncle Jim as a forceful and straightforward model, and with pained memories of a disavowed father.

It had all looked promising when William Clark Durant married Rebecca on Thanksgiving Day, 1855. Durant was the son of a New Hampshire tavern owner. A long line of Revolutionary War veterans, civil servants, a Supreme Court justice, and college professors stretched back to François Durant, a French Calvinist who, to escape Catholic persecution, fled to the New World in 1650. Not that Puritan New England proved more tolerant. William's great-great-grandfather, John Durant of Billerica, Massachusetts, died in Cambridge jail on October 17, 1692, accused of witchcraft. Like so many nineteenth-century families, illness and death had taken William's father, a brother, and sister before he was ten. His mother, Ann Christy Durant, had died while he was still in his twenties. William had moved from his hometown of Lempster, New Hampshire, to Boston, where life coursed richer and, he was sure, opportunities knocked. He became a clerk at the National Webster Bank in 1853, and seems to have met Rebecca while collecting warrants for timberlands in Michigan. He was twenty-seven years old and a clerk at the Webster Bank when he came calling on her. As a part-time stockbroker, however, he had made some money, and possessed a gift for painting his future in confident strokes.

The Crapo family (pronounced CRAY-po) also traced its origins to colonial New England and back to early French settlers. The original name was Crepaud, and family legend had it that on his way to Boston, the forefather had shipwrecked at Buzzards Bay. Safely on shore, Peter Crepaud married Penelope White, granddaughter of Resolved White, one of the original Mayflower Pilgrims. Their son Peter, who was a freeholder of Dartmouth and Freetown, Massachusetts, and a soldier in the French and Indian War, changed the surname to Crapo, and married Mary West of Freetown. Their son Jesse married Phoebe Howland, a descendant of John Howland, an early settler of Plymouth.

Jesse and Phoebe led a hardscrabble existence as farmers in Dartmouth, Massachusetts. Their son Henry Howland Crapo escaped the farm by becoming the village schoolteacher. At twenty-one, he married Mary Ann Slocum, a descendant of Giles Slocum of Somerset, England, who had settled in Portsmouth, Rhode Island, in 1637. Henry and Mary Ann moved to New Bedford, where Mary Ann bore him a son and nine daughters. To feed his brood, he started in real estate, worked as an accountant, was elected town clerk and tax collector, published a business

(From left to right) Henrietta, Rhoda, Wilhelmina on her father's knee, Mary M., Mary Ann Slocum Crapo, William Wallace, Emma, Rebecca, Lucy Ann, Sarah, and Lydia

directory, and became the secretary of an insurance company. His son, William Wallace Crapo, became a lawyer and a politician in New Bedford and, to his sisters, a support they could count on.

It was in Michigan that Rebecca's father had made his fortune and in turn become mayor of Flint and governor of Michigan. Henry Howland Crapo had convinced two New Bedford associates to be his partners in buying a huge tract of pineland in Michigan. The price was $150,000 (in 1854 money), but simply by cutting the timber the trio would net $30,000 a year, and once the tract was cleared, the arable land would be worth a million. It had all worked, but for ten years Henry struggled to make payments on his own $50,000 assessment.

He was fifty-one and facing bankruptcy when he volunteered to go out to Michigan and set up a lumbering operation. Logging was done in the winter, and logs, each branded with its owner's initial, were floated downstream in the spring. The Flint River ran north and emptied into Lake Huron in Saginaw Bay. The settlement that took its name from the river had sprung up thirty years earlier as a fur-trading post. By the time Henry came to Flint, it already had six sawmills. He decided he would be the owner of the seventh.

In 1858, Henry brought out Mary Ann and their unmarried daughters, and sold his interest in the pinelands, although he kept scattered pieces of real estate. The Civil War was good for lumber prices, and he joined a syndicate that built an 18-mile railway spur from Holly and gave Flint's lumberyards year-round access to markets.

Nine-tenths of Flint's population was from New York and New England. As noted in the social registry of Genesee County, of which Flint was the seat, the citizens of Flint were people who "brought with them the advanced ideas of the favored communities from which they came upon the subjects of education and religious observances." In 1860,

Henry accepted the Republican nomination for mayor, and won the election. Two years later, he went to the Michigan senate. In 1864, he won the governorship, and was re-elected two years later.

Rebecca was his favorite daughter, and in letters and one visit to Boston he followed the newlyweds as they set up their household. There were hints at business possibilities between Henry, his son William, and Rebecca's husband. A year after the marriage, Rebecca gave birth to a girl. They christened her Rebecca, but everybody called her Rosa or Rosy. Willie followed on December 8, 1861.

∽∘∾

The Crapos were a family where success was hard earned. By virtue of his lowly position and dabbling in stocks, William Durant knew he did not belong, yet he could not help being fascinated by his father-in-law's money. Old Henry's hard work had made him rich, but he had taken chances, invested, and faced bankruptcy. Why couldn't the old man help a son-in-law do the same? We know that William Durant's suggestions of business dealings with his father-in-law and brother-in-law never materialized. What irritated the Crapos was that Durant was not inclined to work hard yet felt entitled to life's richer rewards. The summer Rebecca was pregnant with Willie and paid a long visit to her family in Flint, her husband took a three-week vacation in the White Mountains of New Hampshire. When Henry ever so gently scolded his son-in-law in a letter, William canceled his upcoming visit to Michigan and demanded that Rebecca and baby Rosy return to Boston.

During a visit two years later when William, Rebecca, and the children came out, he clashed with his father-in-law. After the Durants returned East, Henry wrote to his son William Wallace back in New Bedford:

When Durant was here I thought he was too much im-
bued with a mania for stock speculation, and my advice
to him was to go back into the Bank and hold on to his
place there, and be careful about committing himself
wholly and entirely to the troubled and uncertain seas
of stock speculation, which I regard like every other system of gambling when pursued as a profession.

William should have listened to the advice. The ledgers
of R. G. Dun & Company (the precursor of Dun and Brad-
street) recorded in terse language the Dostoevskian descent
of William, his younger brother James C. Durant, and a
partner named Hastings. In a May 19, 1865, entry, an
anonymous Dun employee wrote:

It is very difficult if not impossible to place them [Du-
rant and Hastings]. They are great speculators & do risky
business, have a good many friends, said to have 25,000
shares of Water Power (they & friends) at 40, plus other
dubious operations. May come out right.

A June 12, 1866, entry noted that the brothers Durant
"lost good deal of money," adding "J. C. D[urant] is not
known to bring any strength to the firm, considered quite
weak and not reliable. Brokers would require collateral
on any time transactions." Five months later, William and
James Durant were described as being "weak in Cr[edit]
but seem to have money at command from some quarter."

Willie was five the following year when his father,
surly, defeated, yet arrogant, parked wife and children
with his in-laws while he scouted northern Michigan for
business opportunities. When he returned to Flint from
his swing through the Upper Peninsula, Henry Crapo was
dying of what son-in-law Jim Willson diagnosed as blad-
der stones, aggravated by a blood clot in one eye that left
the patriarch partially blind. Willie and Rosy sat mutely
at their grandfather's dinner table while the grown-ups

clashed, their father angrily lashing out and Grandpa Crapo staring across the table with his one good eye while their mother sat biting her lips in humiliation.

Before the Durants returned to Boston, Henry Crapo thrust a hundred-dollar bill into his daughter's hand behind her husband's back. After they left, he wrote to his son that Durant would no doubt land in the gutter soon:

> He has been so intoxicated here as to have a regular drunken jab with Rebecca at the table before us all, so that we felt it the best course to leave them one by one to avoid a scene. Poor Rebecca. Her visit was not half out, and has been spoiled by him, and she has gone home almost broken hearted.
>
> His mind now seems to run into going into some saloon, where he thinks that he can make piles of money. Since here he has tried to buy out some beer establishment in Pine Run. He can't think of any business worthy of his attention unless it has speculation, not to say gambling in it, or what is equally captivating to him—either whiskey or beer, etc., in some form. You cannot name any small, but reputable business that would enable him to maintain his family decently and lay up something every year, which he will not at once spurn.
>
> . . . And if he comes to you as I presume he will, you must be decided. Let him know distinctly that he must change his course or expect nothing from me; for if I have ultimately to take care of his family I shall do so without any copartnership in the matter with him.

We do not know what Willie thought of such scenes. What we do know is that Rebecca smothered him in protective affection to the point where Rosy, four years his senior, grew resentful. Willie was the center of attention and adoration. He was seven when he was taken to a parade honoring President Ulysses S. Grant in Boston. Rebecca thought him "a quick little chap" in his Little Lord Fauntleroy black velvet suit and red cap. Years later in a

Sister Rosy at seventeen

note to Willie, she would recall thinking that he might never be president, but "he will always be his mother's good boy, I am sure."

Her father also showed a marked preference for her son. Willie would remember his grandfather ordering his elderly mare hitched to his shay, and the two of them trotting out to look at sheep. In deteriorating health and bedridden, Henry wrote to his eight-year-old grandson:

My dear little grandson, 'Willie' C. Durant,
Grandpa has received both of his very good letters and is very proud of them as he is of his noble boy. Grandpa has not been outdoors in about seven months and has

not "set up" more than 6 or 8 times a few hours at a time—in all that period . . . I am very glad indeed that you like your Michigan sled and wagon, and hope you will have a great deal of pleasure playing with them.

Henry Howland Crapo died three months later, lamenting to the end that his estate was not adequate for Mary Ann and the nine daughters. His son William came out for the funeral, and at the obligatory family reunion and lawyers' appointments saw to it that his sisters' interests were not neglected and that their mother was provided for.

After the final breakup with William Durant in 1869, Rebecca and her children's stay with Rhoda and the doctor was mercifully short. When Mary Ann died in 1875 and the Crapo estate was settled, William Crapo and his nine sisters discovered they were rich. Each received $189,000, or, as William told Rebecca in a letter, "with good handling and the absence of ill fortune this figure in time may be increased to a round $200,000" ($3.5 million in today's money). Rebecca had enough assets to live independently. She bought a large house across the street from her sister and brother-in-law. It was one of the first homes in Flint wired for electricity.

∽∘∾

Willie entered the brand-new Flint High School, and spent four uneventful years learning the fundamentals of 1880s education. Flint had grown to a population of 4,000 and the community was proud of the spired high school building that had cost $80,000. Close by was the library, which had cost $60,000 and to which Governor Crapo had contributed. Willie's scholastic ratings were good to excellent with the exception of French, an elective, which earned him his lowered grades. He learned to play the cornet well enough to join the local band. Flint had its field of dreams, and Willie joined the Flint Athletics, one of the town's two baseball teams. The Athletics elected their pitcher, catcher, and manager, and sixteen-year-old Willie was named manager. Once, after a game at the Fair Grounds, Rebecca gave a supper for both teams.

Willie saw his mother flourish as a single woman.

With its sawmills and woodworking plants that transformed lumber into sashes, doors, pails, tubs, furniture, chairs, buggies, wagons, and sleighs, Flint vigorously pursued commerce. The town was not without culture, however, and Rebecca gave herself to its arts. The town had four weekly newspapers—the *Flint Journal* went daily in 1883. There were steamboat excursions in addition to one band and two singing societies that entertained at political and church functions. Rebecca gave musicales and dances, and was a leading figure in the First Presbyterian Church, one of Flint's ten churches. She vied with her sister Rhoda for soirees, and gave parties for the Kettle Drum Society

Rebecca Crapo Durant

and the Married People's Club. The soirees were held from seven to eleven, with refreshments. "Among those who had spacious homes for these brilliant affairs were Dr. J. C. Willson and Mrs. R. C. Durant," a chronicler noted in the *Golden Jubilee* of Flint, Michigan, in 1905.

There seems to have been at least one attempt by William Durant to reconcile. The year Rebecca left him, he wrote to her. She forwarded the letter to her brother, apparently to ask for his advice on how to answer. William Wallace Crapo wrote back that he, too, had received a letter from her former husband, a letter "full of excuses—very humble and full of the most solemn promises. It is hardly worth while to send it to you." We do not know whether Rebecca or her brother answered William Durant. He lived in Detroit in the 1870s, and was listed in the city directory as a clerk. He turned to his mother's family and found employment for a while with the Christy Brothers, wholesalers and dealers in lumber, laths, and shingles. When William Crapo served in the Massachusetts House of Representatives, he received a plea from his former brother-in-law, asking if he could help with a clerkship. In 1877, Durant tried Crapo once more, asking to help him earn an agent's commission in the sale of land in Michigan's Upper Peninsula to another party. He was "very anxious," he wrote, " so as to make something as [he] needed it."

There is no record whether William Durant appeared at Rosy's wedding in Flint in 1875. Perhaps to escape her mother's preference for her brother, nineteen-year-old Rosy married Dr. John Willett. After that William Durant disappeared. In her book on the history of the Chevrolet car, Beverly Rae Kimes would write that young Billy hired detectives to find his father. Much can be read into this teenager's search for a father rejected by his mother and her family, but there is no mention of such sentiments in surviving records. Billy was twenty-two when William Clark Durant died in 1883.

3

❦

Testing the Waters

No disgrace greeted Willie when he quit school at seventeen, one year short of finishing high school. Uncle Jim might have been a doctor, but in that time academic pursuits weighed less than mettle, competence, and a knack for grasping opportunities. Flint was optimistic and progressive, a town of skilled labor, capital, and management talent, a community of people who could build, organize, and adapt. Willie might be the late Governor Crapo's grandson, the nephew of Dr. Willson, and the son of the respected Mrs. Durant, but there were really only two avenues open to a young man fresh out of school—to start a vigorous apprenticeship on a shop floor or to begin in an office or behind a counter.

It was the production of carriages and wagons that had moved Flint from sawmills to manufacturing and turned the town into an enterprising center of commerce. There were five vehicle companies in town, all locally owned. One wagon maker was George Henry Sturt, an Englishman who had arrived in 1857 with his father. Sturt's wife had upholstered the seat cushions of the early models of the Sturt

26

wagons, cutters, and sleighs. Abner Randall, a trained machinist and metalworker who served as a member of the high school board, ran a ten-man workshop, while the brothers William and Sidney Stewart had recently started making carriage parts in rented premises.

The most impressive shop, William A. Paterson's three-story brick factory at the corner of Sixth and Saginaw, was the town's showpiece. Like Uncle Jim, Paterson was a Canadian who had left a farm in Ontario, dirt poor, in 1838, and apprenticed himself to a carriage maker. For five years he had been a journeyman, traveling with his tools through New England and the South, before hearing of Flint and its carriage works. With $500 he had come to town, started a shop, and worked alongside his hired hands until the business began to pay. Flint elected him mayor, and he was one of the founders of the Union Trust & Savings Bank. Once during a run on the bank, he took a train to Detroit and borrowed large sums of cash on his personal note. Upon his return, he elbowed his way through the crowd, and in a voice that carried through the building asked a clerk to record his huge deposit. The crowd scattered and the run was over. In an unpublished manuscript on the industrial history of Flint, Frank M. Rodolf would write that Paterson, although a Presbyterian, hammered out a new iron cross when the new Episcopalian church needed an iron cross to top the steeple. By the century's last decades, younger men were challenging Paterson. In 1882, Josiah Begole and George Walker poured $100,000 into an existing sawmill and transformed it into the Flint Wagon Works, the fifth vehicle company in town.

∽⚬∾

Tradition in industrious Flint demanded that even sons of first families start out, if only ever so briefly, in overalls.

Durant at twenty-one

On the appointed day, Willie reported to the foreman of the Crapo sawmill. Perhaps Rebecca feared her son might catch a cold working outdoors because he showed up wrapped from neck to ankles in a woolen snowsuit. The foreman examined the swaddled boy, and after telling him to take off his outer garment, sent him over to pile lumber. The pay was seventy-five cents a day.

Willie stacked lumber at the mill only for a short while. For another $3 a week, he became a nighttime seller of patent medicine made by a local drugstore, and then quit the sawmill job when he found a second selling job, this time as a traveling cigar salesman. His employer, George T. Warren, was skeptical when young Durant asked for $2 a day in travel expenses. After a two-day swing to Port Huron, Michigan, Willie came back with orders for 22,000 cigars. Warren was flabbergasted. Easy, explained Willie. He had convinced Port Huron storekeepers to bypass the local wholesaler and order directly from Warren's Flint factory.

William Crapo Durant had found his calling.

∽o∽

The characteristics of the later Durant, who didn't so much overpower people as leave them with a lasting impression of who he was, were already conspicuous. He was a handsome if diminutive youth, with short-clipped hair, big brown eyes, a prominent but aquiline nose, sensual lips, and a winning smile. He possessed a knack for projecting unswerving confidence, but had none of the caricatured salesman's backslapping, condescension, or oily fast talk. Yet contemporaries would remember him for what he was selling. All who knew him agreed he was convincing, but in a soft-spoken way, and that he knew how to be patient.

For a while he worked for Warren, earning $25 a week and replacing three other salesmen. Next he sold real estate, then worked as a bookkeeper for the local water company, where he graduated to the service department, handling complaints and winning new customers. Selling fire insurance was next. Fires were the plague of Flint. Wooden workshops, lit by oil lamps and located next to coal-fired furnaces and blacksmiths' forges, went up in flames with agonizing frequency. Billy saw an opportunity here, and, in a partnership with a school chum, I. Wixom Whitehead, set up a fire insurance agency. His next try as a self-employed entrepreneur was as part owner of the Casino roller-skating rink, where Flint's youngsters and young couples disported themselves on Saturday nights.

He was twenty-three and still living at home when Rebecca thought it was time he find a wife. "Wm. C. Durant" was described as among the town's eligible bachelors in a local newspaper's 1884 New Year's Eve edition:

Inasmuch as tomorrow begins the Leap Year, when the young gentlemen are supposed to take a back seat and allow the young ladies to do the gallant—to take the young men to the theater and other places of amusement, to see them to the front gate of their residences at 2 A.M., to do the "proposing." etc., we publish below a partial list of the marriageable and desirable young men of this city, who have to the present time successfully withstood the effects of the fair sex.

It would be another year and a half before Willie found a wife.

On June 17, 1885, he married Clara Pitt. Not much is known about his first wife. Clara was a comely young woman with pretty blue eyes and bobbed, blonde hair. She was the daughter of Ralph S. Pitt, a ticket agent of the Flint and Pere Marquette Railroad. "If it was considered a match somewhat beneath the grandson of the railroad's former president," Bernard A Weisberger would write a century later, "no one was indiscreet enough to say so, and perhaps no one thought so. Dynastic matches were not in fashion in little Flint, and even as the daughter of a minor official, Clara had respectability, which was the true god of the domestic hearth."

The newlyweds spent a brief honeymoon that began in Detroit and continued to New York City. Upon their return, they moved into a spacious house of their own on Fourth Avenue and Garland Street, a few blocks from Rebecca's.

Willie was twenty-five and Clara was expecting their first child when a ride down Saginaw Street in a buggy not made in Flint led to colossal changes for him and his hometown. He was late for a board meeting at the waterworks that morning in September 1886 when, at the corner of Kearsley and Saginaw, John Alger, a friend who worked at the Bussey hardware store, offered him a ride.

Clara Pitt Durant

As the horse giddyapped down Saginaw, Willie discovered his seat had none of the hard bouncing and shaking that usually went with a ride in a light cart. Instead, it swayed easily up and down and side to side. Upon closer inspection, he realized the seat rode on top of springs that moved freely around shafts. Every farmer's son, he decided, would want one of these carts.

Alger told him that the slight, graceful-looking cart was made in Coldwater, halfway across Michigan toward the Indiana border. The next day, Willie was on the train to Coldwater. He spent the night in a hotel across from the Coldwater railway station, and the following morning poked his head inside the shop of William Schmedlin and Thomas O'Brien.

Schmedlin and O'Brien were men in their fifties. They were less than overwhelmed by the young fast talker from Flint, who told them he didn't have much money but wanted to buy into their business because he had ridden in one of the carts and found the vehicle more than promising. Schmedlin and O'Brien turned him down as the third partner in their modest enterprise. But when Durant asked how much they wanted for the business, their answer came quickly. Fifteen hundred dollars. And would that include the patent for the seat? It would.

What made them agree was Willie's forthrightness. He didn't have $1,500, he told them, but thought he could raise the money. They agreed to give him five days. Together the trio walked over to Schmedlin and O'Brien's lawyer, who drew up a bill of sale and an assignment of the patent for the seat, both of which were deposited in Schmedlin and O'Brien's local bank.

Twenty-four hours later, Willie was back on Saginaw Street, wondering how to raise the money. Because he feared being compared with his father, he didn't dare ask his cousin Will Orrell, who headed the First National Bank of Flint. Nor did he want to apply at the Genesee County Savings Bank, which Uncle Jim Willson had helped establish. That left him Robert J. Whaley, the president of the Citizens Bank of Flint. After hearing him out, Whaley walked him to a cashier and ordered the employee to issue a ninety-day note for $2,000. An hour later, Willie acquired a partner, when his friend Josiah Dallas Dort, the manager of James Bussey's hardware store, asked if Willie would sell him a half interest for $1,000. Dort was a young man with a flourishing handlebar mustache, a year older than Willie. He was born in Inkster, a suburb of Detroit, and after attending the Michigan teaching school in Ypsilanti had found business more exciting than pedagogy. Durant and Dort had met a year earlier and called each other Billy and Dallas.

Their handshake partnership was formalized on September 28, 1886, when they opened a business account in the name of W. C. Durant and J. Dallas Dort. Within a

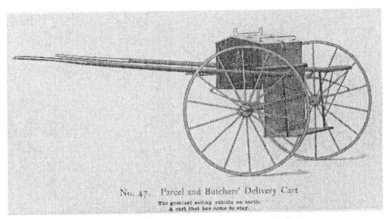

No. 47. Parcel and Butchers' Delivery Cart

The greatest selling vehicle on earth.
A cart that has come to stay.

"Greatest selling vehicle on earth," a D & D cart

week the contents of the Schmedlin and O'Brien shop and one finished cart were put on a railway car in Coldwater and shipped to Flint's Pere Marquette depot. The two young entrepreneurs transferred their assets to a small building they had rented.

4

✌︎o✌︎

D & D

From the beginning, Dort supervised the making of their renamed Flint Road Cart Company vehicles, and Durant sold them. They were so good at it that in fourteen years they became the largest producers of horse-drawn vehicles in the United States.

With the one cart built in Coldwater, Durant had headed for a state fair in Wisconsin. He demonstrated his cart with such enthusiasm to the judges that they gave it a blue ribbon—the beginning of the Flint Road Cart Company's "Famous Blue Ribbon Line"—and took orders for 600 carts. Back in Flint, he and Dallas had no way of filling the orders. They solved that problem by having William Paterson, the town's leading manufacturer, build the carts for them at wholesale.

The deal lasted until Paterson caught on. When he discovered the boys were selling the carts at double his prices, he began telling customers they could buy the same vehicles cheaper by dealing directly with him. Durant and

Durant *(left)* and Dort at the Flint depot

Dort countered that only *their* carts came with the spring-loaded seat. Still, they had no choice but to take over an idle cotton mill, hire their own workers, and start production themselves.

During their first year, they made and sold about 4,000 sprightly carts at $22 each. They discovered that Paterson was no real threat. While the veteran wagon maker and Flint's other cart and buggy builders sold their vehicles to farmers they had known for years, Billy sought out middlemen to become dealers. Calculating costs and margins if Dort and Durant stepped up production, they quickly saw they needed to expand. To make sure there was a market for their entire stepped-up inventory, they decided to advertise. Advertising led to still more sales.

The Flint Road Cart Company was a year old when Clara bore Billy a daughter. They named her Margery after

Clara's mother. Three years later, their second, and last, child, Russell Clifford—Cliff to everybody—was born. A family photo of Clara, Margery, and baby Cliff shows Margery inheriting her mother's blonde curls and her father's dark eyes.

∽o∾

Durant showed a knack for spotting talent. Charles H. Bonbright, who came to Flint after selling farm equipment in Des Moines, Iowa, Muncie, Indiana, and Chicago, became the head of the sales department. Fred Hohensee was hired to oversee the shop floor, and Fred Aldrich became the youthful office manager. Durant was not above raiding other companies for talent. From a carriage plant in nearby Davison, he hired a young foreman named Alexander Brownell Cullen Hardy, known as A. B. C. Hardy, to run a new Diamond Buggy subsidiary. Hardy was sitting down to a Thanksgiving Day turkey dinner in 1896 when Willie called and offered him the job. The dinner got cold as Hardy immediately took the train to Flint to talk it over. Six months later, Diamond Buggy tripled its profits. A. B. C. was good at fixing problems, at straightening out production and sales bottlenecks. Within two years, he was Durant's deputy surrogate when Willie was out of town. Hardy was a tireless worker, but unlike the boss, his capacity for work was not limitless. To his irritation, Durant had a way of tracking him down by telephone whenever Hardy managed to get away.

It was on his own shop floor that Durant found the most amazing talent. Charles W. Nash was a laborer who in 1890 began working for the Flint Road Cart Company as a blacksmith. He was twenty-six years old and had behind him a Dickensian childhood. Born on an Illinois farm and orphaned at six, he was placed with a farm family which was supposed to feed and lodge him, allow him three months of schooling every year, and, on his twenty-first birthday, send him into the world with a suit of clothes and $100. The family worked him so hard that he ran away when he was twelve, reckoning that he was old enough to fend for himself. His adolescence was spent in grinding poverty, wandering from farm to farm as an itinerant laborer. Later, when he became president of General Motors, people would tease him, "Charlie, please show us the first nickel you ever earned. You've got it hidden somewhere." He did. He couldn't help it.

He was twenty years old and managing a farm outside Flint for $20 a month when he married. The backbreaking farm work was too much for his wife, and they moved into town, where he took a job in a store. Until he started working for Willie and Dallas, he had never earned more than $300 a year.

Charlie made sure the boss noticed him. When Durant passed the forge, Charlie told him it was a waste of time to have him, Nash, pound iron. Instead, the company should buy a $25 power hammer that could do more pounding in a day than Charlie could do in a month. Durant okayed the expense and moved Charlie to a drill press where cart braces were shaped. The next time Billy came through the shop, Charlie had mechanized the press with overhead springs and a foot pedal that allowed him to have his hands free.

Nash advanced to stuffing buggy cushions and soon had the trimming department straightened out. In short order he rose to Hohensee's rank, then outstripped him to become general superintendent. "He was as steady and careful as Mr. Durant was brilliant and daring—or reckless, as you may choose to call it," Alfred Sloan would write in his memoirs.

Durant was a bundle of energy. His pace was almost terrifying. He pretended not to know what time it was, and kept working until the day's job was done. His vitality, allure, and gusto were the driving force behind an expansion that, in 1892, led to the first subsidiary. The Webster Vehicle Company was set up in an abandoned farm machinery plant to build light spring wagons. Two years later, he established the Victoria Vehicle Company to make a new line of conveyances, and, no doubt to his mother's satisfaction, bought Grandpa Crapo's old sawmill. In 1895, the partners found the Flint Road Cart name too parochial and renamed their company the Durant-Dort Carriage Company. Webster and Victoria were subsidiaries, soon known as Durant-Dort plants No. 2 and No. 3. In 1898, in a move that got them in over their heads, they made their first out-of-town acquisition, buying the Imperial Wheel Company in Jackson, Michigan.

Jackson was no outlying Genesee County hamlet, but a town south of Lansing, 80 miles from Flint. Jackson was called the birthplace of the Republican Party for the 1854 mass meeting "under the oaks," which had brought together Whigs, Democrats, and Free-Soilers. The town's foremost industry was wheelwrighting. The new Durant-Dort acquisition was a distant second to Jackson's mighty Hayes Wheel Company. Still, it produced more than 50,000 sets of wheels, more than the D & D plants 1, 2, and 3 needed. To justify the investment, Billy took to the road and sold 140,000 sets of wheels to other cart builders.

Billy's initiative and self-confidence turned Durant-Dort Carriage Company into the North American leader. He accomplished this by lowering his costs, and by reducing the number of models. By standardizing production, he set up a system of component suppliers, and marketed farm and urban vehicles that even defied the depression of 1893.

The D & D operations, including the final assembly, were downtown along the northside of Flint River on Water Street, the hub of industry since the sawmill days. Heating steel rods in blast ovens and hammering them into axles was a noisy process. After James Whiting, the superintendent at Paterson's Flint Wagon Works, told Billy that making axles in the middle of town was deafening, D & D bought the 220-acre Hamilton farm two miles north of the city and erected a new plant. Durant responded to scuttlebutt of a syndicate cornering the linseed oil market by inventing a new subsidiary, the Flint Varnish Works. Rumors of a trust bent on controlling the manufacture of steel axles had him rush to West Virginia to buy axle-making machinery, and set up the Flint Axle Works.

"By sharpness of intellect, exceptional marketing skills and willingness and capacity to work eighteen- and twenty-hour days for long periods," automobile historian Richard Crabb would write, "Durant had, in less than twenty years, marketed several times the number of horse-drawn vehicles sold by the Velie Works at Moline, Illinois, the Studebaker Brothers at South Bend, Indiana, the Fisher Family Carriage Works at Norwalk, Ohio, or any of the other builders of wagons, carts, buggies or carriages."

The whims of fashion accounted for D & D's only setback, which came the year they decided to manufacture bicycles. Their bikes were smart enough, but as they began marketing them the bicycle fad declined.

The wages at D & D varied between $4 and $10 a week, with foremen earning $20. Work hours were from 7:30 A.M. to 5:30 P.M. six days a week. The atmosphere in the parlorlike main offices with its rolltop desks, wicker chairs, and potted ferns was familial. Durant, Dort, Hardy, Aldrich, Hohensee, and Nash were all neighbors. Billy was, of course, always on sales tours, but there was no doubt he was the head of the family, especially after Dort took two years off to take his ailing wife to a dry climate. Hardy took Dort's place, but hated Durant's indomitable management style so much that he and his wife took an extended trip to Europe in early 1900 to get out of the boss's telephone range. In Paris, he took in L'Exposition industrielle and fell in love with horseless carriages. He flagged down motorists so he could get a ride, and crawled under the humming machines to see how they were made. When he returned to Flint in 1901, he went to Durant and Dort. "Get out of the carriage business before the automobile ruins you," he told them.

From where Willie and Dallas were sitting, the extinction of carriage manufacturing was less than apparent. Of Flint's 13,000 population, 1,500 men worked for Durant and Dort. The city fathers put up a wrought-iron arch over Saginaw Street proclaiming Flint to be "The Vehicle City." Cincinnati claimed it was home to carriage makers turning out 160,000 units in 1900, but no single company matched D & D. Its catalog included the Eclipse, the Standard, the Victoria, the Moline, and the Diamond models, and, for the California market, the Poppy. Besides wagons, buggies, carts, and sleighs sold under their own name, they made vehicles for farm equipment companies and mail order houses. D & D not only made its own wheels, axles, paints, varnishes, and buggy tops and controlled its own lumber supplies, it had interests in Blount Carriage and Buggy in Atlanta; Atlanta Wheel and Axle; Dominion Carriage, in Toronto; Pine Bluff Spoke, in Pine Bluff, Arkansas; Hughes-Purcell Paint, in Kansas City, Missouri; and hickory forests and mills in Tennessee and Arkansas. The peak year was 1895, when fourteen D & D plants in the United States and Canada turned out 75,000 carriages and wagons.

William Paterson's son-in-law Arthur Pound was a historian who, in 1922, published the first study of the social significance of carmaking. He lived for a time in Flint, and in his book offered an incisive assessment of Durant and his impact on Flint:

He was a mighty seller of goods, not primarily a financier; and, in order to have goods to sell, he built, it seems, somewhat too fast and furiously. In building factories he also built a city from 13,000 to 100,000 in twenty years. . . . Even in absentia he remained our leading citizen. We leaned upon him in ways that must have tried his patience. We could get no highly important public enterprise under way until he had given it his sanction by telegraph or messenger. Ever and anon we held him up for money. His name was on our lips oftener than that of any president except [Theodore] Roosevelt. So he was our hero, actual at the start, mythical toward the end—almost our god. In fact, I fancy some of our real estate men prayed to him o'nights, since he was clearly possessed of the power to make or break them. Our local autocrat was Billy, yet he graciously kept the velvet glove over the iron hand, and preferred to stand among us rather as the first among equals. . . . In return we gave him loyalty. . . . Labor troubles were rare. His old workmen knew him and talked about him to the new ones. All were aware that he played baseball as a kid, sold fire insurance as a youth, and battled through to the top by himself. All agreed he was generous and democratic, called folks by their first names, and was not above darting into a quick lunch for a sandwich.

As the new century dawned, Billy was a millionaire of thirty-nine—not ready for retirement, yet not quite sure where to look for new horizons.

5

Madison Square Garden

In the fall of 1900, more than 50,000 people paid admission to enter New York City's Madison Square Garden for the first automobile show in the United States. It was an elegant affair with rows of self-propelled road machines. Half of the American firms making motorcars exhibited 300 horseless carriages, ranging in price from $280 to $4,000. The Europeans were there, too, with, as most people agreed, better looking and more comfortable cars.

Although the first motorcar was made in Germany, the practical pioneering had taken place in France. In 1860, Jean Joseph Lenoir built and marketed a gas-burning 2-stroke engine. Two years later, Alphonse Beau de Rochas devised the 4-stroke principle. Although he never built an engine, Rochas established the conditions for optimum 4-stroke performance as intake, compression, ignition (power), and exhaust. Since his work was entirely theoretical, the credit for originating the 4-stroke engine usually goes to Nikolaus Otto, who built an engine in Deutz, Germany, and exhibited it in Paris in 1867.

Adolf Daimler at the tiller of an 1893 Daimler, with his father, Gottlieb Daimler, in the back

The first practical application of the Otto engine was the feat of German gunsmith Gottlieb Daimler. After working four years with Otto on stationary engines, Daimler installed an air-cooled motor between the front and rear seats of a lightweight, four-wheeled cart and, in 1886, drove the contraption around Bad Cannstatt. In neighboring Mannheim, Karl Benz was convinced self-propelled carts would supersede the horse and revolutionize transportation. Despite objections by associates who thought him unbalanced, Benz built a 2-cycle engine and circled a cinder track with his workers and wife running beside him. The car made four turns before a broken chain stopped it. Remarkably, Benz and Daimler never met.

Daimler believed the future lay in converting carriages to engine drive and that the motorcar would be a separate device. He licensed the French firm of Panhard & Levassor to build his engine. Emile Levassor placed the Daimler Phénix in front and covered it with a hood, thereby introducing the modern engineering layout. In 1895, Levassor won a Paris-Bordeaux-Paris race, covering the distance of 732 miles in 48 hours and 48 minutes, driving both legs of the event himself at an average speed of 15 mph. During these early days for automobiles, road racing, often sponsored by enthusiastic newspapers, spurred advancement and innovation.

The dawn of the automobile saw colorful men and a few daring ladies scorch new records into the record books by hurtling around dirt tracks and thundering down country lanes in death-defying town-to-town road races. Open road, intercity races had started in France in 1894 with the seventy-nine-mile Paris-Rouen Reliability Trial, the brainchild of the popular newspaper *Le Petit Journal*. Machines fielded by Levassor and his partner René Panhard and by bicycle builder Armand Peugeot were the joint winners of the first race, but a steam car pulling a semitrailer, driven by Count Albert de Dion, clocked the fastest performance. The judges awarded Dion's machine third prize on the technicality that it couldn't be driven by one man but needed a riding mechanic.

In 1898, driving a Panhard, Fernand Charron became the first to win a race crossing national borders. He raced against his business partner Léonce Girardot (known as "the eternal second") from Paris to Amsterdam and back at nearly 27 mph.

British enthusiasts were hampered in the new craze by a new Locomotives on Highways Act that forbade vehicles weighing less than three tons to travel more than 12 mph. Still, one of Charron's students, an Englishman named S. F. Edge, won a Paris-to-Innsbruck race in a British-built Napier, all other entrants having retired.

Americans were not far behind. In Springfield, Massachusetts, the brothers Charles and Frank Duryea constructed a gas-powered buggy in 1893. Apparently assembled out of existing components, the machine was a 1-cylinder gasoline engine with electric ignition installed in a secondhand cart the brothers bought for $70. The lightweight Duryea, built at various locations, and even assembled in Belgium and England for a time, appeared regularly from 1895, when Frank entered the first American road competition, sponsored by the *Chicago Herald-Tribune.*

The race was run on November 2 from Chicago to Evanston, Illinois, and back. The 54.36-mile race was something of an embarrassment for *Herald-Tribune* publisher Henry Kohlsaat, as only two competitors showed up: Frank Duryea and Oscar Mueller, the latter driving a Benz belonging to his father, owner of the Decatur Machine Shop. The Duryea quickly pulled ahead of the heavier Benz. Mueller had tire trouble, but the drive chain broke on the Duryea, forcing Frank to stop and do repairs. A farmer led his team and wagon across the Evanston-Chicago road just as Duryea, with his drive train repaired, reached the intersection. To avoid a collision, he veered off the road and ended in a ditch with his car's differential housing smashed. The problem notwithstanding, Mueller managed to drive to Chicago, averaging 10 miles an hour.

Kohlsaat considered this by-default win a nonevent and offered a $2,000 purse for the winner of a Thanksgiving Day race from Chicago to Milwaukee. Seventy-nine drivers showed up the day before, but by Thanksgiving morning four to six inches of snow had blanketed the city and the lakeshore, and a storm was blowing in from Lake Michigan. The weather forced Kohlsaat to shorten the race to Chicago to Evanston and back. Six contestants were willing to risk their machines and lined up at the start—and finish line—at the Midway Amphitheater on the World's Fair grounds. Everybody agreed that the pair of electric cars there was for show, as their batteries would run down fighting the snow. The four gasoline machine competitors were Frank in his repaired Duryea, Mueller in his Benz, and two brand-new Benzes, one entered by New York's R. H. Macy department store, which hoped to start selling Benzes in Chicago. To prevent cheating, Kohlsaat assigned an umpire to each entrant and forbade anyone else to ride with the driver. At the umpire draw, Charles Brady King, who would soon demonstrate the first motorcar to be built in Detroit, was named Mueller's man. Duryea thought himself less lucky, drawing Arthur White, a newspaperman from Toronto who weighed a third more than him.

The Macy Benz pulled ahead of Duryea and White before they were out of Chicago, but on the open road White's bulk gave the Duryea traction. After the turnaround in Evanston, Duryea and White met Mueller and King in the second Benz. The Macy Benz never finished the race. The Duryea motor quit on Chicago's Diversity Avenue near Clark Street. Frank lost 55 minutes repairing the "sparker" that supplied electricity to the two cylinders. White watched for the other cars, but nobody passed them during the repair. It was dark by the time Duryea and White reached the Midway Amphitheater. Duryea was proclaimed the winner, establishing a world record for a 55-mile course, averaging a little more than 7 mph. An hour and a half later, the Mueller Benz arrived, driven by King as Mueller had fainted in the afternoon and had been unable to drive.

By their performance, the Duryea and the Benz established that motor-driven cars could best any horse team. No horse and buggy, not even a stagecoach using horses in relays, could move passengers 55 miles in ten and a half hours through heavy snow, mud, and winter weather.

∽◦∾

Early automobiles were so notoriously unreliable that most models came with tool kits. Manufacturers told buyers not to fear being stranded in a stalled machine because there was nothing under the hood that a village blacksmith couldn't fix. Yet the simplest motorcar was a costly assortment of complex and touchy systems—power plant, transmission, ignition, and cooling. In the early years, only the Locomobile reached some kind of volume production, with sales building from 750 in 1900 to a peak of 2,780 two years later. The little Locomobile runabout, built by the Stanley twins, Francis and Freelan, offered a 20-mph cruising speed. The brothers had built the first Stanley Steamer in 1897. Despite the disadvantages of steam power plants—low thermal efficiency, great weight, and inconvenience of operation—the Stanley brothers continued to make Steamers until 1926 (at 126.66 mph, their 1906 Steamer set a world speed record).

Long-distance records were set in France, where *Le Petit Journal* continued to sponsor races. A month before the 1900 Madison Square Garden exhibit, a new Panhard & Levassor model won the 1,428 mile Tour de France race, and the Paris-based *New York Herald* upped the *Petit Journal* ante. Following the lead of its founder, James Gordon Bennett (he masterminded Henry Stanley's 1871 African search for explorer David Livingstone), the paper offered a new Coupe Internationale, quickly known as the Gordon Bennett Cup, an annual race among teams chosen by national motor clubs and run under the rules of the Automobile Club de France.

Wealthy Americans were quick to pick up the sport. In September 1900, William K. Vanderbilt drove a Daimler to victory on the Quidneck Park track at Newport, Rhode Island, covering the 5 miles in 8 minutes and 53.05 seconds. The fashionable attire for male speed demons covered them from head to toe to protect them from the dust that their machines kicked up on the country's unpaved roads. The auto accessories pages in the 1905 Sears & Roebuck catalog featured a linen duster buttoned up high around the throat and a linen or leather automobile cap with "flaps that can be turned down and fastened underneath the chin with elastic connecting band, thus protecting sides of face and neck from dust."

∽०∾

Willie Durant made it to the fourth Madison Square Garden show in 1904, but he caught the motor bug at home. Not that he was much impressed the first two times he climbed into a horseless carriage. In 1889, his cousin W. C. Orrell had persuaded him to come for a ride in his steam-powered motorcar. The noise was just too much for Willie, who told friends, "I was mighty provoked with anyone who would drive around annoying people that way."

The next time he climbed aboard a horseless carriage was in 1902. Judge Charles H. Wisner, an amateur photographer, architect, landscape painter, woodsman, and machinist, took Durant for a spin in a contraption he had built himself. To the diversion of churchgoers, the two men had to restart the machine several times, and although the motorized cart negotiated the streets well enough, it died at main intersections, where it had to climb over the slightly raised wooden crosswalks. The ride didn't impress Willie. When fifteen-year-old Margery went for a ride in a Panhard the same year, he criticized his daughter for taking such a foolish risk.

It was one of Durant's own men who assembled the first car made in Flint. Since nobody at D & D seemed to pay attention to A. B. C. Hardy's warning to get into the automobile business or face ruin, he put his money where his mouth was, scraped together $5,000, and rented shop space in a former cart shed. Eighteen months later, he rolled out fifty-two automobiles. The Flint Roadster was fire-engine red with brass trim, leather seats, and sold for $850. Instead of a tiller it had a steering wheel. Unfortunately, the little runabout was underpowered. Its 1-cylinder engine developed a mere 8.5 horsepower. Hardy's downfall was the Association of Licensed Automobile Manufacturers cartel.

In 1895, George Selden, a Rochester, New York, lawyer and inventor who never built a car himself, applied for and received U.S. patent No. 549,160 for an internal combustion engine. Two years later, a group led by former Secretary of the Navy William C. Whitney bought Selden's patent for $10,000. The Selden Patent Group fancied itself a kind of consumer watchdog, establishing standards of quality and protecting investors from "piratical hordes who desire to take advantage of the good work done by the pioneers to flood the market with trashy machines, made only to sell and not intended to go—at least for any great length of time." But the Selden group was a trust, similar to the Edison and Eastman cartels trying to regulate the newborn cinema. It not only used the patent to collect royalties but to decide who could build cars and, in some cases, how many. It established a minimum investment of $200,000 as one of the requirements to obtain a license to make cars. The Association of Licensed Automobile Manufacturers (ALAM) was the Selden group's enforcement arm. Shortly after a stranger visited A. B. C.'s shop, pretended to be interested in buying a Flint Roadster and asked for a list of "satisfied users," Hardy was served with fifty-two injunctions, one for each car sold. The ALAM ordered him to cease his carmaking until he paid $50 royalties on each car, and made acceptable arrangements with the Selden group, holder of the basic patent on the gasoline engine.

For Hardy, it was back to work for D & D. For Durant, the fight with the Selden group was a few years away. For Henry Ford, who became a serious carmaker the year the ALAM wrecked Hardy, a momentous and drawn-out struggle with the Selden group was just beginning.

Just before the Flint Roadster Company went out of

business, Jim Whiting of the Flint Wagon Works inspected A. B. C.'s idle shop and asked a lot of questions. The now white-haired, sixty-year-old wagon builder was intrigued by self-propelled vehicles. When he went to carriage conventions in New York, he dropped in at auto shows, and, as Hardy had done in Paris, talked manufacturers into offering him a demonstration ride. He also visited workshops in Detroit. The more he saw and learned, the more he became convinced the automobile would make the horse and buggy obsolete.

Cars were coming to Flint. The first person in town to *buy* a car was Herbert H. Hills, a young physician. The model Dr. Hills chose was the seventh Model B Buick, a two-speed, 2-cylinder tonneau model with a dark-blue wooden body that sold for $950. Like most cars of its time, the Model B had no windshield, no top, and no brakes—the driver used its planetary transmission for braking and, in an emergency, the back pedal. Hugh Dolnar, a reporter for *Cycle and Automobile Trade Journal,* was in town for the delivery and tryout. He wrote, "Dr. Hills has driven this car almost the whole time, day and night, over the very hilly and sandy country about Flint, and has had no repairs, except a split gasoline pipe, this day, Sept. 16, and believes he has the best car in the World."

The doctor invited Durant to tour the town with him. The machine wasn't too noisy. It didn't stall or refuse to negotiate the wooden crosswalks. This time Willie was impressed not only by the ride but by the little car's appearance, which he thought elegant. We do not know whether Durant bought Dr. Hills's Buick or the good doctor lent it to him, but for the rest of September and most of October, Willie climbed into the car almost every day and, come rain or shine, drove it out of town.

6

⌘

David Buick

"Fame beckoned to David Buick," said one of his contemporaries. "He sipped from the cup of greatness then spilled what it held." In less than five years, the Scottish-born machinist and plumber went from shop hand to businessman to eccentric self-destruction.

We know when and where David Dunbar Buick was born, but little else about his early life. His birthplace was 26 Green Street in Arbroth, a coastal village halfway between Glasgow and Aberdeen. The family name was originally spelled Buik. Much later Durant worried that people might pronounce it "Booick," but he liked unusual names for his cars. David Buick was born September 17, 1854, which made him seven years older than Durant. He was two when his father, Alexander Buick, a joiner by trade, moved the family to America, eventually to settle in Detroit. Alexander died when David was five. His mother remarried and for years ran a candy store. David delivered newspapers and worked on a farm. At fifteen he went to work for the Alexander Manufacturing Company, and worked himself

David Buick

up to foreman for the Detroit plumbing fixture manufacturer. At one point he seemed to have been an apprentice
machinist at James Flower & Brothers Manufacturing, a
company that also apprenticed Henry Ford.

The diminutive Buick (he stood all of 5 feet 5 inches)
married twice. His first wife, with whom he moved to Flint
in 1905, was Caroline. His second wife and mother of their
only son, Thomas, was named Margaret. David was both
something of a dreamer, witty and quick-tempered, and a
tobacco-chewing crank, with whom it was hard to do business. By all accounts, however, he was a gifted tinker. In
his late twenties, he invented different valves, water clos-
ets, a lawn sprinkler, and a flushing device. Twentieth-
century bathtubs and kitchen fixtures owe much to his
most important invention—cementing enamel to cast iron.

When Alexander Manufacturing failed in 1882, Buick
and William Sherwood, a former classmate, took over the
company and renamed it Buick & Sherwood Company,
"manufacturers and dealers in sanitary specialties." The

company was a success. Had the two school chums stuck to the toilets they proudly depicted on the Buick & Sherwood stationery, they would have become wealthy. David, however, got distracted by the internal combustion engine, which by 1895 was beginning to make noises around Detroit shops. "I had one horsedrawn dray to take my goods to town, but I needed another," he would say in 1928. "I couldn't afford a new team, although I got my second dray on credit; and I got to thinking about making an engine that would move the dray without horses."

Sherwood was not amused. The two partners were increasingly at odds as Buick fiddled with gasoline engines and neglected their bathroom business. In 1899, they sold their company to the Standard Sanitary Manufacturing Company of Pittsburgh for the hefty sum of $100,000. Sherwood stayed in plumbing and founded Sherwood Brass, a Detroit establishment that stayed independent until absorbed by Lear-Signer in 1970. David invested his share in the Buick Auto-Vim and Power Company, manufacturers of gasoline engines for farm and marine use. Buick was forty-seven in 1901 when he met a thirty-six-year-old bicycle shop owner who also couldn't leave gasoline engines alone.

Walter Lorenzo Marr was born in Lexington, Michigan. An orphan at six, he served an apprenticeship in an engineering firm, worked for the Wickes Brothers, a Saginaw sawmill and steamboat-engineering company for nine years, and in 1888 built a 1-cylinder engine designed by his plant superintendent. He set out on his own in 1896, opening a bicycle shop close to Henry Ford's backyard atelier on Detroit's Grand River Street. Much of Marr's machinery for building bikes was driven by various gasoline engines, and in 1898 he perfected a 4-cylinder engine and mounted it on a wagon. He had lots of trouble with it, but finally put a spark advance device on the car that almost solved the problem. Ford saw Marr drive up the street in his motor wagon and come to an exceptionally smooth stop.

In discussing the improvement he had already made, Marr realized he needed faster ignition. He spent more than a year experimenting with a chamber for feeding gasoline and air into the engine in a precise but variable mixture— a device soon to be called a carburetor. He built three motor wagons (a 4-cylinder car, a motor-powered tricycle, and a 1-cylinder car with a tiller to steer the vehicle, suspension, a special chassis, and tall, 44-inch buggy wheels. He had himself and his wife Abbie photographed in the 1-cylinder machine.

Buick and Marr met at the Detroit Yacht Club, where Marr was working with some friends on a marine motor. Buick watched the young mechanic work, and hired him on the spot. Marr, who wore a derby hat in the shop, was soon foreman and, three months later, manager of Buick Auto-Vim. Unfortunately, the period is sparsely recorded. Once Durant and General Motors made the Buick famous (the millionth Buick was built in 1923), Buick and Marr both claimed paternity of the first Buick and remembered things differently. David would recall how he and his son Thomas designed and manufactured a conventional, so-called L-head engine. But Marr would tell Flint historian Charles E. Hulse that *he* built the first Buick Auto-Vim marine engines, including one that beat everything in a 24-foot class on the Detroit River, but that he couldn't get Buick interested in automobiles.

Both men were temperamental. One of their quarrels is documented in a March 25, 1901, letter in which Buick fired Marr. Also documented is David's offer eleven days later to sell Walter "the Automobile, known as the Buick Automobile, for the sum of $300." For an additional $1,500, he would also hand over prototype engines and their designs, a delivery wagon body, two new carriage bodies, and one runabout body. Four months later a deal was signed: "In consideration of the sum of Two Hundred and twenty-five Dollars ($225.-) cash paid me this day, I hereby transfer and assign to Walter L. Marr all my right [*sic*], title and interest in the Automobile known as the Buick automobile." The letter was signed August 16, 1901.

Nothing much happened over the next year and a half. Marr worked part-time in the workshop behind the Buicks' Meldrum Street house. For a businessman in his forties, Buick was singularly inept with money. Much of his half of the $100,000 William Sherwood and he had received for selling their toilet and bathtub business was gone, and the Buick carmaking effort remained woefully underfinanced. Until 1902 nothing that could be described as the first Buick was assembled and tested. Steamers were still outpacing gas-powered cars and electric vehicles were not far behind. Marr built a single-cylinder engine that, in basic design, resembled the marine and stationary farm gasoline engines with which he and Buick were familiar. Overenthusiastic Buick historians would claim six Buicks were built in 1903, but only two are documented— one sold to Marr, the other to Benjamin Briscoe, a longtime friend of the Buicks and, with his brother Frank, a Detroit sheet metal manufacturer of garbage cans and radiators.

Marr continued to tinker and experiment. A talented engineer joined him. Eugene C. Richard was a Frenchman from the Alpine *département* of Savoie, who, before moving to Detroit, had learned about engines in Philadelphia and worked on the uncomplicated, lightweight machine that Ransom Eli Olds called the Oldsmobile. David Buick got along better with Richard (who insisted his name be pronounced *à la française,* "Ree-shar") than he did with Marr, but the two young men got along famously. By the summer of 1903, they built a new 2-cylinder engine with the valves designed into the head. On October 6, the U.S. Patent Office issued patent No. 740,924 to the Buick Manufacturing Company and inventor Eugene C. Richard for the "overhead valve" principle. Unlike the L-head engine in general use, the "valve-in-head" engine was built with the valves directly on the pistons. With this narrower and lower cylinder head, a more compact combustion chamber, and a faster fuel-burn rate, the valve-in-head engine added efficiency. The principle was quickly adopted by the entire automotive industry, only to be superseded by the V-type engine, in which the cylinders form an angle of 60 or 90 degrees that, in a crosscut, looks like a V.

Meanwhile, Buick's plumbing business exhausted his corporate assets, and bankers refused to finance his horseless carriage venture. No wonder. The first years of the new decade saw hundreds of start-ups work on self-propelled vehicles. Only five enterprises, however, managed to assemble and sell 100 cars: Alexander Winton's factory in Cleveland; "Ranny" Olds's motor works, moving from Detroit to Lansing; the Thomas B. Jeffery Company in Kenosha, Wisconsin; the Pope Manufacturing Company of Hartford, Connecticut, maker of the Columbia; and the Apperson Brothers Machine Shop in Kokomo, Indiana, making the Haynes-Apperson. Buick's only chance was to find private investors. Because he owed a couple of hundred dollars to Benjamin and Frank Briscoe, the brothers and their extended family in Flint eventually saved Buick.

Frank Briscoe was twenty-eight, Benjamin thirty-four, and for a pair of young businessmen they had done very well in sheet metals. Ben was especially eager to get into carmaking, and on May 19, 1903, he and Frank took over David Buick's business, incorporating it as the Buick Motor Car Company. Of the $100,000 in capital stock, the Briscoes got $99,700 and David $300. In a curious addendum, it was agreed that David could buy back the entire company if, within six months, he was able to reimburse the Briscoes the $3,500 he owed them. After November 20, 1903, however, Buick Motor Car Company belonged 99 percent to the Briscoe brothers and 1 percent to David.

The company was yet to market its first car and the

brothers soon realized their new enterprise was too rich for their blood. They knew nothing about automobiles, but when Frank visited his cousin Martha Stone in Flint, she and her real estate husband, Dwight Stone, arranged a meeting with Jim Whiting.

Whiting went to Detroit, and met David Buick. Making automobiles would fit Flint like a glove, Whiting explained. Besides a roll-up-the-sleeves civic pride, a skilled labor force, and a progressive frame of mind, Flint was the junction for two railroads—the Grand Trunk and the Pere Marquette. Shipping finished machines would be easy. Buick agreed to sell. On September 10, Whiting returned to Detroit with a cashier's check for $10,000, binding the sale of the Buick Motor Company to the Flint Wagon Works. Buick agreed that the reorganized company would keep his stock interest until dividends had paid back his debts.

∽o∾

Marr was not the only bike manufacturer puttering with gasoline engines. In thousands of barns, sheds, and shops, eager would-be carmakers experimented with horseless carriages. In Kenosha, Wisconsin, Thomas B. Jeffery switched from Rambler bicycles to Rambler motor runabouts with twin-cylinder engines, which were shown at the first Madison Square Garden motor show. In Des Moines, Iowa, Fred and August Duesenberg fastened a clip-on motor to one of their bikes. Better than Marr, Jeffery, and the Duesenberg brothers, Alexander Winton tended to his own publicity when his first feat went unnoticed.

Like Buick and Jeffery, Winton was a British immigrant, energetic, resourceful, and touchy, who had established a thriving bicycle business in Cleveland. In 1896, he mounted a gasoline engine on a buggy and drove it 5 miles from the Winton Cycle Company factory to Cleveland

Square. The power plant was a 2-cylinder internal combustion engine with a 5-inch bore and electrical ignition, similar to, but larger than, the Duryea motor. The increased power meant the vehicle could carry five passengers—six, if the driver didn't mind being squeezed a bit. The three passengers seated in the rear faced backwards. Two years before A. B. C. Hardy mounted a wheel to steer the Flint Roadster, Winton went from a tiller to a wheel. He was also the first to develop a practical storage battery.

The next summer, Winton drove an improved machine 700-some miles from Cleveland to New York City. Gasoline was a common cleaning fluid and stove fuel, so he had no trouble filling his tank on the way. Finding oil was more difficult. After eleven days of driving through dirt and mud—the actual travel time was 78 hours and 43 minutes—he chugged into New York City amid gawking pedestrians and frightened horses. "As I came down Broadway, I regretted the daylight," he would recall, "for I was literally clad in dust and sadly in need of a bath."

The feat was underreported, as the press didn't believe he did it. "The friendlessness of New York sank into my spirit and left no place for elation." After a hotel and a bath, he drove to the freight yard and, on the next available train, took his vehicle and himself back to Cleveland.

Still, he had demonstrated the strength and durability of his machine, and began building powerful and attractive cars selling for a hefty $1,000 each. Winton could be rigid with workers and customers. When Henry Ford applied for a job, Winton booted him out, convinced the young Detroit Edison Illuminating Company engineer lacked mechanical skills. When an irate customer pulled a Winton through the streets of Detroit behind a team of horses and a wagon with a sign saying, "This is the only way to drive a Winton," the Scotsman arranged to drive the same route in his Winton car, pulling a farm wagon with a jackass aboard. His sign read, "This is the only living creature

A Miss Nell Doyle and her 1904 Winton

unable to drive a Winton." He lost his temper when James W. Packard, a young manufacturer of electrical supplies from Warren, Ohio, came to the office with a laundry list of suggested improvements. Yelled Winton, "If you don't like the car, and you know so much, why don't you make a car of your own?" Packard went home and built the first Packard.

In 1899, Winton repeated the Cleveland–New York trip. This time, however, he brought along Cleveland reporter Charles Shanks, who filed dispatches on every leg and helped popularize the French word *automobile* (*chauffeur* and *garage* followed). Shanks turned each day's progress into a media event, especially after Winton and he were sent flying when the car hit a boulder near Fairport, New York. Wrote Shanks: "After shooting through space for twenty-five or thirty feet, we were permitted, by the law of gravity, to bump the ground with a force sufficient to jar the healthiest of nervous systems." A cheering throng greeted the pair when they arrived in New York City after less than 48 hours on the road.

Four years later, H. Nelson Jackson, a doctor from Burlington, Vermont, bought a used Winton and hired a mechanic and driver, Sewall K. Crocker. By train, Jackson, Crocker, and the Winton traveled to San Francisco. On May 23, 1903, the two men headed east in the car. Sixty-four days later, they drove up in front of the Waldorf Astoria Hotel in New York, touching off a celebration for the first coast-to-coast run.

᭐᭐᭐

In a front-page article headlined NEW INDUSTRY FOR FLINT, the September 11, 1903, edition of the *Flint Daily Journal* reported on groundbreaking on Kearsley Street near the Flint Wagon Works of a building to house the Buick Motor Company of Detroit. The new company would make "stationary and marine engines, automobile engines, transmissions, carburetors, spark plugs, etc." There was no mention of building motorcars.

Pressure on Whiting to get Flint into carmaking began immediately. The *Flint Daily Journal* echoed civic leaders in its September 12 editorial:

> Flint is the most natural center for the manufacture of autos in the whole country. It is the Vehicle City of the United States and in order to maintain this name, by which it is known from ocean to ocean, there must be developed factories here for the manufacture of automobiles.

The demand for Buick stationary engines kept the new plant going. But Marr, who came to Flint with the company, kept pleading for permission to build a pilot car with

Walter Marr *(at wheel)* and Thomas Buick in a 1903 Buick

the new powerful engine with overhead valves. Marr knew they had the most powerful engine in existence. In June 1904, Whiting relented. With the understanding that a complete Buick would have to prove it could match the Curved Dash Oldsmobile and the newest version of the Cadillac, he gave the go-ahead to build one machine. Marr called it the Model B. Whiting himself decided how to test it.

The first try was a circuitous, 230-mile run to Detroit and back. Whiting wanted the first trip to be a demonstration and publicity run, not a race, so Marr and David Buick's son Thomas stopped in Davison, Lapeer, Oxford, and Pontiac so people could have a look at the new Buick. The return trip followed the same route, and the two men drove the 115 miles in 217 minutes, a record for open-country driving. Near Pontiac, they became involved in a race with an electric car and ended up, as Marr put it, "showing the way" to the competitor. The *Flint Daily Journal* was there to take a photograph and report on the finish: "Tom Buick and W. L. Marr of the Buick Motor Company who left for Detroit on Saturday to give the first automobile turned out by the concern a trial on the road, returned late yesterday afternoon. The test of the machine was eminently satisfactory, and in fact exceeded expectations."

The first orders came in, but so did the bills. Like Dave Buick, A. B. C. Hardy, and the Briscoe brothers, Whiting was in over his head. The car business demanded financial resources of a magnitude that the Flint Wagon Works could not come up with. In less than six months, the venture swallowed nearly $40,000. And the Association of Licensed Automobile Manufacturers, which had closed down Hardy's shop, was waiting to pounce. Whiting thought of Durant, not only as a possible investor but also as the man who could save the day. When Whiting ran into Fred Aldrich, the secretary-treasurer of the Durant-Dort Carriage Company, at the 1904 Chicago carriage manufacturers' convention, he talked at length about the new business. Because Durant was in New York for an extended stay, Aldrich suggested that Whiting talk to Dallas Dort. Dort, in turn, gave Whiting Durant's address in New York. Whiting, however, decided to wait until David Buick, Marr, and Richard finished the new Model B so they would have something to show before inviting Durant into any partnership.

7

಼ೲ೦ೲ಼

Private Lives

Imperceptibly at first, Clara, the children, Flint, and the comforting reassurance of being the big fish in a small pond slipped away. Like his father, Willie was intrigued by capital, and his extended visits to New York City allowed him to delve into finance and commerce. Big ideas always sent his adrenaline throbbing, and New York was stimulating and expansive, and, for a midwesterner who had made his pile, challenging and permeable. Whether he fully realized it or not, he was outgrowing his early success, his marriage, and the hometown that had nourished his ascent and fulfilled his ambitions.

From what we know, Clara was still the dutiful wife. The marriage had begun to erode a few years earlier, but it was only when divorce became inevitable that she allowed herself to blame her husband. His absences were ever more frequent, and when he was gone he did not write, nor did he answer her letters. He was indifferent to her worry, and refused to tell her where he was.

Where was he? His mother had no difficulty finding him. Rebecca addressed her letters to Durant-Dort Securities Company, 52 Broadway, Room 1235, New York, N.Y. On his fortieth birthday, December 8, 1901, she poured her heart out:

My dear, dear boy

How are you today? Wish I might take you by the hand—give you a kiss—and a mother's blessing. These two are eventful dates—and come but once in our lifetime—and to me mean so much. . . . You have been a good boy, thoughtful, kind and patient, doing always for my comfort. It is a joy to have a thankful son. I more than appreciate the blessing though the expressions are so few. But you do understand it all, I know—and feel the strong tie of affection that binds our love. May it continue to the end—more perfect as the years go on.

He answered in kind:

My Dearest Mother:

How proud I am of you. How glad to be your son. You dear, good, kind, generous soul.

May God bless you and spare you to us many many years, each Christmas brighter and happier, made so by your own sweetness and charity, of which I know and for which I love and honor you.

Your "birthday letter" I prize beyond any gift I ever received. It is among my treasures. It is a pleasure to write such a letter—a comfort and satisfaction to receive it. I trust my feeble effort to serve the same purpose. I think we understand each other and will grow closer and dearer to each other as the years roll on.

To be always worthy of your affection and esteem and to return "a little" for "the much" you have done for me is the hope and prayer of

Your affectionate Son,
Willie

P.S. I'm very sorry the little gift was broken in transit. It was a great disappointment. I will try again after my return to N.Y.

If he could be said to be settled anywhere, it was in New York City. Shortly after his fortieth birthday, he moved to New York, and lived there for the rest of his life. Margery was nearby, attending girls' school in Tarrytown, New York. Thirteen-year-old Clifford was with Clara in Flint.

Letters from the now sixty-nine-year-old Rebecca included details that showed how removed her son was from his family. Clara was taking violin lessons "on Clifford's account," and both were enjoying their music, Rebecca reported. Cliff had a hard time concentrating on school. A letter dated November 4, 1902, tells of Flint's preparations for the Christmas season, of Clara's harvest of cornhusks and pumpkins, and ends with ardent wishes for Willie to come home.

❧

There was a darker chapter in the family history—Willie's sister had gone astray. Rosy had grown up in her brother's shadow. She had married at nineteen. The marriage to Wallace Willett had yielded a son and two daughters and ended in divorce. Since then, Rosy had drifted, and ended up in a rooming house on New York's West Twenty-second Street. Illness accompanied a downward slide.

The Crapo and Durant archives contain no documents on the relationship between the wealthy brother and the sister depending on welfare. However, in a May 3, 1903, letter that Rebecca wrote to her daughter, she praised Willie for doing what he could for Rosy and, apparently, for her children:

Dear Rosie:

Have received a letter from your friend telling how you are situated. I am very sorrow [*sic*] to know you are so ill, and suffering as I am sure you must. Wish I might write some word to comfort you—a true mother's heart goes out to her child no matter what the conditions when sickness like this strikes. Your brother, good boy, telephones me that every thing is being done for your comfort, and for you to know that your children are cared for and protected by love must take away some anxiety. I would like to do something for you—to soothe if possible the pains of heart and body—so long denied me. The kind and loving Father will not forsake his children. You have my sympathy and love with pity that you are away from a home. Wallace [Rosy's son] will leave for New York tonight and Willie will arrive in New York tomorrow night. Goodbye with love,

Mother.

Who was the friend? A lover?

Rosy never read her mother's letter. She died the day after it was written. The doctor who attended Rosy lived a few doors down Twenty-second Street and was summoned at the last minute. On the death certificate, he wrote that she died of cerebral hemorrhage due to "exhaustion" at the age of forty-five years, six months, and fifteen days.

So, like William Clark Durant, his daughter died under obscure and perhaps shameful circumstances while his successful son began dabbling in Wall Street. There were rumors back in Flint that Durant-Dort Securities had a seat on the New York Exchange. The rumors were wrong, but between 1901 and 1904, Durant was playing the market and learning the ropes of high finance. The handmaiden of progress was commerce, and New York City was the headquarters of the rail, the oil, the steel, and the manufacturing industries of the confident new century. Life and opportunities coursed richly along the avenues of Manhattan with their confident architecture, celebrated fashions, cosmopolitan denizens, and elegant women. Rosy's destiny belonged to the flip side of that great city's triumphant capitalism. A letter from Rebecca to Willie, written two weeks after Rosy's death, hinted at evil too dark for a grief-stricken elderly lady to spell out.

> My dear, dear boy
>
> Could I take your hand in mine, feel your loving touch, your helpfulness and sympathy, it would express more than I can write. For even today my heart is full, my eyes overflowing with tears. These last sad duties are always hard [even] with your brother love and deep pity for the unfortunate sister and the mother far away. . . .
>
> But with all the sadness there is comfort in the thought that you could do it, and that she has never wanted for things she would accept. I try to feel no regrets, think only of the numerous blessings. Yet the mother love will grieve and the mother hearts ache . . . She is free from all harm, and the kind, loving Father, knowing the good that was in her—for she had many lovable traits of character—will help her on to something better with him.
>
> I did feel anxious those few days of waiting . . . that something worse was to come—and that fear hanging over the mind, helpless to make it any different, has been taken away. . . . Glad to be away from the criticism of the natural[ly] curious. The report was generally known, and Anna [Rosy's daughter?] was questioned as to the truth. To be away from it all is much better, although to be free from it, never. . . . I should not and will not let it blind me to the many things that are comforting. . . . Write soon, if only a little note, and tell me of your own dear self.

Rebecca lived to be ninety. For another twenty-one years, she faithfully wrote to Willie, who replied in his fashion, but from 1903 Rosy disappeared from their correspondence.

෴

Willie was forty, rich, and at a loss as to what he would do with the rest of his life. So long as he didn't risk his entire wad on outguessing the market, he could play the student of serious money, the Wall Street gentleman amateur, who on occasion took a flier on an attractive stock. We do not know whether he had in mind to continue on the fringe of Wall Street or whether he contemplated other horizons. What we do know is that in early 1904 Fred Aldrich came to see him. Jim Whiting had asked Fred to sound out Willie on the idea of coming home and helping Whiting and a group of Flint associates rescue a promising start in automobiles.

8

‿∽∽

Carmaking

Durant was back in Flint in late August 1904. He stayed at home with Clara, Margery, and Cliff, and seemed to have reintegrated his role as husband. In her divorce petition four years later, Clara would swear that until 1906 Willie and she had shared the conjugal bed.

News quickly spread that something important was in the air. There were suppers when Clara surreptitiously paid Cliff five cents to behave at the dinner table. Margery would remember evenings when Jim Whiting, Fred Aldrich, Dallas Dort, her father's lawyer John Carton, David Buick, and others sat with her father until all hours, "emitting an unending stream of facts, figures, suggestions, protests."

Willie kept testing the Model B. He also noticed the Buick attracted crowds—as any car did in 1904. The valve-in-head engine gave the Buick more power for its size than any other car, but there were days when the car came limping back. When that happened, he took the vehicle directly to David Buick and Walter Marr, who would drop whatever they were doing and repair the machine. Tooling

An executive ride in 1904: *(backseat)* Charles Cummings and James Whiting, *(front)* Walter Marr at the wheel and Thomas Buick

around in the Model B convinced Willie that a motorcar agent, or dealer, would have to be prepared to provide continual service to each customer.

Billy took Jim Whiting on spins. Once they sat parked in front of Whiting's house, talking for more than an hour. There was no question Durant told Whiting that he would be in total control. Whiting accordingly offered him the presidency. Willie declined. Raising money would be a full-time job. He couldn't be distracted by executive duties, and suggested Charles Begole be named CEO. Begole was the son of former Michigan governor Josiah Begole, and a partner in Begole, Fox and Company, operator of one of Flint's larger lumber mills.

On November 1, everybody signed on the bottom line. Begole replaced Whiting as president. With 1,505 shares,

Whiting remained the majority stockholder, followed by David Buick with his 1,500 shares and Begole with 1,000 shares.

Willie was quick to realize that he had to show investors something worth investing in, that only increased production justified increased capitalization. Moving on both fronts, he persuaded stockholders of a Flint utility company to invest $275,000 in Buick, and bought a 220-acre farm on Flint's north side for a new factory. Jackson might be a hundred miles away, but while the new plant was being built on Flint's north side, Durant moved part of the operations to Jackson, where the D & D Carriage Company occupied a large wheelwright. Here, five to eight Model Bs were assembled every week from bodies, engines, and transmissions turned out in the Kearsley Street plant in Flint. To complete the new factory and boost production in Jackson, Willie raised $100,000. Next, he had a Buick loaded on a railway car and dispatched to New York City. The car was exhibited at the Automobile Show. Billy was there to show and sell. Wrote Clara to a friend a few weeks after the show ended: "William has just returned from the auto show in New York, where he sold 1,108 machines. The Buick is certainly a success."

Using a trick captains of industry would employ again and again to make civic leaders invest in businesses that would bring them wealth and jobs, Durant played Jackson against Flint during the summer of 1905. It was not practical to have operations in two places a hundred miles apart, he told the city fathers in both towns. The Buick Motor Company would have to centralize in one place. Where it consolidated depended on where it found financing. If Jackson could raise $500,000 so that Buick could be capitalized at the $1 million it needed, then, he told the city leaders, Jackson would become the home of Buick.

There is no doubt that the play was little more than a ruse to concentrate the minds of Flint's establishment.

Durant was the fair-haired boy who, with Dallas Dort, had brought the town wealth and riches. By midsummer Flint outbid Jackson by half a million dollars. On Monday, September 11, 1905, Flint's four banks, its four major carriage and wagon companies, and hundreds of Flint organizations and individuals bought stock that increased the Buick Motor Company's capitalization to $1.5 million. In reporting the news the next day, the *Flint Journal* spelled out the stay-in-Flint stipulation:

> Yesterday afternoon Buick stockholders voted to increase the capital stock from $500,000 to $1,500,000, divided $900,000 stock and $600,000 preferred shares. A large amount of the additional stock has already been taken by local interests, and the balance has takers in sight. The directors of all four Flint banks personally pledged $90,000, in cash, for which they received $100,000 in Buick stock. So there could be no misunderstanding, the directors of the Genesee Bank included in their pledge agreement the following provision: "This subscription is made with the understanding that the Buick Motor Company will discontinue its Jackson plant and locate its entire business at Flint, commencing construction work upon its new buildings as soon as plans can be prepared and weather will permit."

For another three months, Buicks continued to be assembled in Jackson and to be shipped from there by rail. The Jackson plant was closed at the end of 1905 and final assembly shifted to the new Flint factory, which featured 14 acres under its roof and was by far the biggest car-making facility.

New recruits joined Marr and David Buick. Enos de Waters came from the Janney Motor Company of Jackson, another component supplier brought into existence by Durant. Also from the Jackson plant came William Little. This former maker of buckboards was a big, colorful man nicknamed Big Billy. He nearly caused Durant's death when they tried out new brakes in 1906. After complaints of faulty brakes from new Buick owners, Willie had asked Little to try to improve the brakes. The next day, Little swung by the downtown Dresden Hotel after Durant had lunched with businesspeople and invited the boss for a test run of a car equipped with the new brakes. Durant climbed into the back seat and Little took off. When he hit the new brakes, they locked, sending Willie head first into the front seat and onto the ground. Little and a couple of bystanders came to Durant's rescue. But Willie picked himself up and said:

"Well you certainly got some brakes, Bill."

"Get in, Mr. Durant, and I'll drive you back to the plant."

"No thanks. I'll walk."

Big Billy was a show-off. To park downtown, he liked to skid to the curb in a U-turn.

∽o∾

Arthur C. Mason, another new recruit, came from Cadillac. Mason knew engines and had a sense of humor that pleased Billy. Mason's most important contribution was working on a high-compression engine. The average engine functioned at 1,800 revolutions per minute. Mason, however, was experimenting with an engine running at 4,000 rpm. Although a consultant condemned their high-compression motor, Mason worked day and night on it. When he was ready for a demonstration, he called Durant, urged him not to reject the new idea, then bent down and hugged the engine, his head resting on the cylinder block. "Start it up," he pleaded. "If it goes, I may as well go with it."

The new engine performed beautifully and allowed Buick to sell cars with top performance ratings. Late in life, Durant would recall how at least one prominent citizen was afraid of Mason's high-revolution engine:

> After a short visit [the man] made no effort to conceal his apprehension and put himself on record against the whole automobile venture and against the high-speed motor in particular. He stated that I was gambling my whole established carriage business for a visionary and passing fancy. As I had great respect for his opinion, I began to feel that there might be something in his warning.

A specialist Willie hired to check out the new engine called it unsound, dangerous, and likely to explode. Mason was furious. Durant stuck with Mason, and in notes for his autobiography would write:

> Needless to say Mason's work was crowned by a great success, as he was largely responsible for Buick's quick recognition as a leading motorcar. And his theory was adopted by automobile manufacturers the world over. Power, the achievement of Mason's long experiments and hard work, became synonymous with Buick. We played on that one item: Power! Power to outclimb, power to outspeed anything on wheels in our class. With Buick we sold the assurance that the power to perform was there.

By 1906, the Buick Motor Company occupied the largest and most modern plant facilities in the world. With its success, the population of Flint doubled, from 15,000 to 30,000. The north side took on the look of a boomtown. Tent villages sprang up on the banks of the Flint River. Buick added night shifts. Hotels and boardinghouses rented the same rooms "for the day or for the night." Recruiters combed the East Coast for craftsmen and the Deep South for laborers, paying railway fares to Flint and giving out meals until new hires received their first pay envelope. The Flint payroll jumped to the third largest in Michigan, exceeded only by Detroit and Lansing. From 1907, a thousand new homes were built every year.

Writing with the hindsight of twenty-four and sixty-two years respectively, the industry's two historians would give all the credit to Durant. In 1933, Arthur Pound would attribute Buick's surge to market leadership to the "courage" of Durant: "Buick dared to produce in large quantities when most of its competitors were proceeding cautiously on restricted schedules. It pioneered in the development of attractive retail stores in larger centers, and drew able, ambitious men into both wholesale and retail selling. There, perhaps, was Mr. Durant's greatest contribution to the technique of automobile administration."

"The record growth that began in 1905 stemmed directly from the economic explosion led by the town's little giant, Billy Durant," Richard Crabb would note in 1969. "He was in the process of accomplishing again, in the age of horsepower what he had done in the horse-drawn era."

The 1905 capitalization to $1.5 million secured the Buick Motor Company a license from the Selden Patent Group, and membership in the Association of Licensed Automobile Manufacturers.

9

⌇⌇⌇

The Selden Cartel

Durant hated the Selden cartel, withheld royalty payments, and sued the Association of Licensed Automobile Manufacturers (ALAM). But it was his future associate and rival Henry Ford who wagered the life of his young company to finally overthrow the monopoly.

Henry Ford threw down the gauntlet in 1903 after James Couzens, the punctilious Canadian who from the beginning was Ford's confidant and financial taskmaster, tried to reach an accommodation with the cartel, only to be told by Frederick L. Smith, treasurer of Olds and acting president of the ALAM, that "the Selden crowd can put you out of business—and will." Almost ten years younger than Ford, Couzens was indefatigable, ambitious, and so humorless it was said that when he cracked his annual smile, the ice on the Great Lakes started to break.

When the ALAM declared war, Ford and Couzens were ready. In an ad published in the July 28, 1903, edition of the *Detroit News* and addressed "To Dealers, Importers, Agents and Users of Our Gasoline Automobiles," it said:

"We will protect you against any prosecution for alleged infringement of patents. The Selden patent does not cover any practicable machine; no practicable machine can be made from it, and never was so far as we can ascertain." The announcement ended defiantly: "Mr. Ford, driving his own machine, beat Mr. Winton at Grosse Pointe track in 1901. We have always been winners."

The Selden group saw no alternative but to sue. Filed in a New York City court at the end of 1903, the suit prompted Couzens to say, "It may take years to thresh the matter out in the courts . . . we have no apprehensions as to the result of this suit." Years indeed. It was not until 1909—a year after Ford had launched the Model T—that the trial got under way.

Henry Ford was, like Durant, a latecomer to the business. Ford was a plant engineer at the Detroit Edison Illuminating Company who in his spare time bought parts on credit, piece by piece, and tinkered both at work and in his backyard. He liked to tell how in 1895 he had built a little engine and a month after the running of the *Chicago Times-Herald*'s snowy Thanksgiving Day Chicago–Evanston race had brought it home to show it to his wife. Clara Bryant Ford was expecting her parents for Christmas and was in the middle of cooking when Henry said he needed her to help him start it. He plugged a crude spark plug into the household electrical supply, then asked Clara to drip gasoline into the fuel intake and turn a valve while he spun the flywheel. The kitchen light flickered, and the engine coughed. After an adjustment and another spin, it suddenly belched into life, shooting flames and smoke from its exhaust.

Since then, Henry had built a demonstration quadricycle, and convinced several friends to bankroll the Detroit Automobile Company. He had quit his job at the Edison Company, which, like Buick's start-up attempt, collapsed in debt. In an odd twist, the family man decided to go into motor racing. In 1901 he built a 2-cylinder machine of massive dimensions and lined it up at a dirt track in Detroit, and beat a Winton to the punch. He was forty when he tried again in June 1903, and managed to organize the Ford Motor Company with $28,500 in capital. Chauncey Depew, former president of the New York Central Railroad, talked his nephew out of a fortune by advising him against investing $5,000 in Ford's business, observing that "the horseless carriage will never supplant the horse."

On Detroit's Mack Street, the underfinanced Ford Motor Company put together Model As. Like the early Buicks, the Fords were assembled from off-the-shelf parts. The wooden body shells and upholstery came from the C. R. Wilson Carriage Company, and the basic machinery was built by two red-haired brothers, John F. and Horace E. Dodge, who already supplied power plants for Ransom E. Olds's Oldsmobile.

Sales, fortunately, took off. By March 1904, the Ford Motor Company had sold 658 cars. By the end of the year, twenty-five Model As left a new factory on the northern edge of Detroit every day.

∾○∾

Durant, meanwhile, was a member in good standing of the Association of Licensed Automobile Manufacturers. He never bought a Selden patent for Buick, but picked up one at a fire sale of the failed Pope-Robinson Company of Hartford, Connecticut. Albert Pope was another bicycle manufacturer who had joined forces with financier William C. Whitney and his Electric Vehicle Company to make a line of gasoline-driven automobiles with hyphenated names such as the Pope-Tribune and the Pope-Toledo. Pope bought a Selden license and opened factories in Hagerstown, Maryland, and Indianapolis, but his company collapsed into receivership.

The ALAM welcomed Durant into the fold, especially after he recapitalized Buick to $1.5 million in 1905. Three years later when he founded General Motors and folded Buick and Cadillac into the new entity, his lawyer, John J. Carton, told him the Selden patent was meaningless. Durant stopped paying royalties. The ALAM sued. Billy countersued, claiming conspiracy in restraint of trade. Next, he let everybody know how many—or, more precisely, how *few*—cars his ALAM competitors were making.

He published the confidential production figures of all ALAM member companies. The ranking was published anonymously, but the trade group decided Durant was the instigator not only because Buick and Cadillac topped the list, but also because "the names of all General Motors concerns were printed . . . in heavy type." The ALAM censured Durant. Not that he cared. Buick and Cadillac were indeed the leaders and the Buick Motor Company's net worth was the highest in the industry.

Durant was in Ford's corner throughout the latter's two-month trial. "At times," automotive historian Richard Crabb would write, "the courtroom proceedings took on the elements of an industry witch hunt." The Selden lawyers attempted to make Ford's success appear as a social evil. "I came in from Oyster Bay by car," said one of the Selden lawyers. "We didn't kill anyone, but everybody on the road hated us, and it was probably sheer luck that we didn't have a collision. I think you are creating a social problem with your car."

"No, my friend, you're mistaken," said Ford. "I'm not creating a social problem at all. I am going to democratize the automobile. When I'm through everybody will be able to afford one, and about everybody will have one. The horse will have disappeared from our highways, the automobile will be taken for granted and there won't be any problem."

The details were technical and over a million words were entered into the record. Tempers flared on occasion, but Ford kept his under control. He shrewdly used the trial to portray himself as the David facing a Goliath out to strangle free enterprise. He was the champion of the working man, the farmer, and small professional people. The public loved it. The press box was standing room only.

Midway through the trial, the forty-six-year-old Ford joined Mayor George B. McClellan at the starting line of a 3,100-mile New York–Seattle race. The lineup sported two Model Ts, and Ford's team leader Frederic Coudert turned to McClellan and, with mock innocence, said, "Your Honor, there is something that puzzles me. I don't see a Selden car. I see a Ford car, two Ford cars, but I see no Selden car!"

President William Howard Taft was in on the send-off, pressing a golden telegraph key in Washington that signaled McClellan, the son of the famed Civil War general, to fire the starting pistol. Two weeks later, Ford loaded himself and a gaggle of reporters aboard a train to Snoqualmie Pass, Washington, so they could report on him helping shovel snow on the Continental Divide to enable his Ford and the other drivers to get through.

Henry Ford won the transcontinental road race, but lost the trial.

On September 15, Judge Charles Merrill Hough ruled against Ford's contention that his internal combustion engine was not based on the plans for which Selden had received his patent fourteen years earlier. No matter what frills Ford added, Judge Hough reasoned, an internal combustion engine was still an internal combustion engine.

While Ford appealed, Durant threw in the towel. He paid the Selden Patent Group $1 million in back dues. He hoped Ford would win on appeal, but was himself a believer in patents. Throughout his career, he bought patents on devices he thought might provide important improvements. A few months after Ford's court defeat, Durant sent Herb Lewis to Fargo, North Dakota, to investigate a patent for sale. Lewis returned to report the patent could be had for $10,000, but recommended against buying it. Durant thought $10,000 a bargain and purchased it.

The Selden trust dug its own grave by threatening to sue dealers who sold, and consumers who bought, non-licensed cars. Disastrously overreaching, the cartel tried to enforce production ceilings and was sued by the Velie Motor Company of Moline, Illinois. The suit disclosed that this small manufacturer of light, inexpensive cars had been directed to pay $14,000 as an entrance fee to the ALAM, to limit its 1910 output to 2,500 vehicles, and its 1911 production to the still lower figure of 2,000 cars.

The public cheered when the Court of Appeals of New York held that all internal combustion engines were not alike, that the engine used by the Ford Motor Company was the Otto type, and that Selden himself had "appreciated the superiority" of the Otto engine. "We cannot," added one of the judges, "make another choice for him [Selden] at the expense of these defendants, who neither legally or morally owe him anything."

Ford was an unknown when he first resisted the Selden monopoly in 1903. The trial—and his adversaries—gave him public relations advantages that he and his company never dreamed of. He became a folk hero because he stuck close to the script of the American dream. Although he was soon to join John D. Rockefeller and Andrew Mellon as a billionaire, he had nothing of the aura of nouveau riche (in 1914 he was still not listed in *Who's Who in America*). His mechanical skills were legendary, and he loved nothing better than rolling up his sleeves and fiddling with gears and engine parts. He solved a problem of weight distribution by sheer inspiration and often left scientific minds baffled. Defending a decision, he once said, "Well, I can't prove it, but I can smell it."

The Selden group could no longer intimidate would-be dealers by telling them they might be held liable for infringement damages, and the Selden win gave the Ford Motor Company vast new markets. A year after the court victory, Ford produced 70,000 cars. Ford took himself, Clara, and their son, Edsel, on a trip to Europe. It was one of the happiest times the family had ever known.

10

Competition

The Buick had been little more than an engine in an improvised body when Durant capitalized the company to the tune of $100,000, went to the 1904 New York Automobile Show, and came back with orders for 1,108 roadsters. The year before Henry Leland and his production wizard Horace Dodge had shown off their elegant Cadillac at the Madison Square Garden show, and delivered 1,895 orders.

The sixty-year-old Leland and his thirty-six-year-old son, Wilfred, were Detroit's first carmakers, having opened a factory on Trombly Avenue in 1893. They named their car after the man who had founded the city nearly two hundred years earlier—Antoine Laumet de la Mothe Cadillac. Like the Three Musketeers, Antoine was a Gascon. He traced his ancestors to the eleventh century, and although the family was poor by the time he entered the army of Louis XIV, he did possess a coat of arms. The Lelands affixed the Cadillac *écusson* to the radiator cap of their machines. A hundred years later, it is the only coat of arms of authentic origin in use on any American car.

Leland *père* was a Vermonter who, after marrying schoolteacher Ellen Hull, spent eighteen years at the Brown & Sharpe Company of Providence, Rhode Island, the country's foremost machine toolmaker. It was here that he grasped the significance of interchangeable parts and systematic assembly of complicated machinery. This knowledge carried over into carmaking. He introduced changeable parts, perfected the V-8 engine, and helped invent the self-starter and the electrical system in cars. Wilfred was a twenty-one-year-old medical student when his father persuaded him to drop out of school and join him in the shop. Wilfred developed the new industry's business management and finance.

Henry Leland's machine shop was the first capable of producing a continuous supply of parts machined to 1/10,000th of an inch. Inventors of many new mechanisms came to Trombly Avenue to work out manufacturing problems. From its beginning in 1903, the Cadillac was the standard every other car was measured by. Instead of a tiller, the driver maneuvered it with a steering wheel. The small, air-cooled engine, mounted in the middle of the chassis for balance, was located under the front seat with a hand crank on the side. Only six bolts fastened the engine to the chassis, and the motor housing was designed so that worn bearings could be exchanged without removing the crankshaft. The Cadillac had two patent leather guards, or fenders. There was no running board and no top, but for an extra charge heavy brass kerosene lamps were included. It became the first American motorcar to win the Royal Automobile Club of London's Dewar's Trophy in 1908 for the standardization of its parts.

But the Lelands were not Detroit's first builders of a horseless carriage. Before them, and before Henry Ford, there was Charles Brady King, the army officer's son who in 1895 provided weight and traction for Oscar Mueller in the Chicago-Evanston race and actually drove the Benz across the finish line. King liked machinery and was clever with his hands. At the Chicago's World's Fair in 1893, he was taken with the display of a small 2-cycle gasoline engine, intended primarily for marine use. He went home to Detroit convinced he would mount such an engine on a land vehicle. He hired a German immigrant named John Lauer to help him. Together, they mounted an engine King had built on a wagon ordered from a firm that made circus vehicles, and on March 6, 1896, King climbed on board and clattered down the street with Henry Ford bicycling beside him. The *Detroit Free Press* was there to report the feat in its March 7, 1896, edition: "The first horseless carriage seen in this city was out on the streets last night." The *Detroit Journal* interviewed King, who told the newspaper that the Prince of Wales had recently ordered a similar vehicle, adding, "They are much in vogue among the English aristocracy." King managed to sell five of his "motor wagons" before he ran out of money, and learned that mastering the economic realities of his invention was harder than mechanical problems. He ended up selling his engine works to the Olds Motor Works.

❧

When Billy wanted to know more about carmaking, he didn't take the train southeast to Detroit but the train southwest to Lansing, because it was in the state capital that Ransom Eli Olds's motor works were humming.

From an early age in his father's shop Ransom was determined to invent an alternative to the horse, whose smell he could not abide. His father, Pliny, was an Ohio blacksmith who scraped enough money together to move to Lansing and open a shop on River Street that made and repaired steam engines. As a boy, Ransom's household duties included getting up at five o'clock. Before breakfast, his job was to light two household fires, and in the workshop fire up the boiler that provided the power for the steam engine. After his school day, he was back in the machine shop in the afternoon. He was an expert machinist by the time he finished high school and started building engines in a lean-to beside the Olds's barn. Neighbors warned the parents that "Ranse" would blow his head off experimenting with gasoline, but his father helped him, and together they built a crude internal combustion engine based on the Otto principle. At twenty-one, Ranse bought a half-share in his father's business for $3,000 in savings and an $800 promissory note.

By the time Durant and Dort were expanding their horseless carriage building in 1892, Olds had perfected a gasoline engine and bought out his father. He was selling engines from coast to coast, and exporting them to Great Britain. During D & D's pinnacle year, Ranse road tested a gasoline buggy that, a year later, was such a regular feature on Lansing's unpaved streets that a local capitalist named E. W. Sparrow persuaded two friends to join him in raising $50,000 to bankroll the Olds Motor Vehicle Company.

The company made few automobiles to begin with, but, like David Buick and Walter Marr, built and sold stationary gas engines, with marine power units a profitable sideline. It was after a disastrous foray into $1,250 luxury cars that Ranse had the proverbial blinding flash of intuition: "After a long, sleepless night, I decided to discard all my former plans and build a little one-cylinder runabout, for I was convinced that if success came it must be through a more simple machine. The plans, which had formulated in my mind, were very clear. It was my idea to build a machine which would weigh around 500 pounds and would sell for around $500."

The result of his brainstorm was the curved-dash

Oldsmobile. The vehicle was mounted on bicycle wheels and featured a single-cylinder engine under the body, simple enough so that "anyone could run it, and the construction such that it could be repaired at any local shop." To make his point he had a photographer snap a picture of his ten-year-old daughter Gladys driving it.

The curved-dash Olds weighed 700 pounds and sold for $650. By 1902 some 4,000 of the little Oldsmobiles were sold. At the 1903 New York Automobile Show, Ransom talked A. G. Spalding & Company into ordering 100 cars to start a New York Olds agency. The order was canceled, however, after a directors' meeting decided no one could sell that many cars in New York City. R. M. Owen, the Olds agent in Cleveland, and his financier Roy Rainey told Ranse that sales in Cleveland had been so good they wouldn't mind opening a New York dealership. To their proposal of ordering 500 cars, Ransom suggested, "Why not make it a thousand cars, boys, and get some notice." The same night Owen and Rainey signed a 1,000-car contract.

౪౦౬

What Durant learned in Lansing was that carmaking stood wagon manufacturing on its head, and for financial reasons. Whereas D & D owned most of the means of production and didn't rely on outside suppliers, neither Olds nor any of his competitors had the financial resources to *make* parts. Like Henry Ford and the Lelands, Ranny Olds ordered engines from the Dodge brothers, who had machine shops in Detroit and across the river in Windsor, Ontario, Canada. He bought roller bearings from a New Jersey firm recently taken over by a young graduate engineer, Alfred P. Sloan. For radiators, he turned to the Briscoe brothers' sheet-metal works.

Making automobiles proved more demanding than even

precision toolmaker Henry Leland realized. The large-scale replication of power plant, transmission, ignition, and cooling parts demanded new definitions of precision and planning, and therefore discouraged seed money. The mortality rate for new auto companies between 1900 and 1908 was 60 percent.

The Buick Motor Company did not possess the Lelands' sophistication nor, as yet, Olds's hefty turnover, but it had something the others didn't: Durant, Walter Marr, and Eugene Richard. Willie worked hard on the marketing, and with Charles Van Horne, a sales manager promoted from the Jackson plant, crisscrossed the country while, back in Flint, Marr and Richard perfected the valve-in-head engine.

The new Model C Buick was a 2-cylinder, 22-horse-power car living up to Durant's new sales pitch: "We do with two cylinders what others try with four." (His next slogan proclaimed, "We build nothing but high grade automobiles, and when better automobiles are made, Buick will build them.")

Durant wanted dealers who could provide both smart showrooms and—a novelty—after-sale services. Legends of his prowess as a salesman grew like campfire stories. On a layover in Detroit, waiting for a New York train, Willie got a list of hard prospects from his dealer on Jefferson Avenue. Half an hour later, he slapped orders and deposits for cars on the dealer's desk and grabbed a cab for the station. Harry Noyes, his New England dealer, and Harry Pence of Minneapolis bested him. Both set out with caravans of Buicks and gathered crowds in hamlets, showing off cars, taking partial payments in produce, dropping sold cars off a freight train that followed them, and making their way back by rail, counting their receipts.

As families who had never owned a horse decided they needed an automobile, and thousands of clerks and small businessmen began driving to and from work in their new machines, Durant had no trouble imagining a car in every garage. "Durant sees—actually sees—90 million people just aching to roll along the roads of this country in automobiles," a Detroit reporter wrote after interviewing him. "And he wishes to fill that void." One evening when Dallas Dort and Charley Nash were over for dinner, they would remember, Billy fingered the keyboard of a player piano while talking ecstatically about the future. One company might sell ten, twenty, fifty—yes, a hundred thousand and more automobiles a year.

"Dallas," said Nash, "Billy's crazy."

These were W. C. Durant's pinnacle years, the years when his faith in himself was absolute and he hoisted himself and a lot of other men to fame and fortune. These were the years when he effortlessly drew gifted people to him. And he kept hiring them.

Harry Shiland, a Massachusetts dealer who personally overhauled every machine he delivered, was not impressed with the early Buicks, and told Durant, "You aren't selling cars to mechanics. Cars have to be foolproof for the average doctor or lawyer or businessman to want them." Durant invited Shiland to Flint, and after he heard more criticism, convinced him to join Buick as service director. Yet to come was Walter Chrysler, a Kansan with a passion for engineering. The Union Pacific Railroad repaired its locomotives in Ellis, Kansas, Chrysler's hometown, and young Walter started as an engine cleaner. He rose to master mechanic when the internal combustion engine displaced his interest in steam. At the 1908 Chicago Automobile Show, he saw a Locomobile touring car, painted ivory white with red cushions and trims. The top was khaki, supported by wood bows, and on the running board was a handsome toolbox. He spent four days at the auto show. The last day he ordered the $5,000 Locomobile, borrowed part of the payment from a banker friend, and went home to tell his wife, Della Forker, what he had done. "She said nothing," he would recall, "but it seemed as though

the kitchen door banged shut a little harder than usual."
When the Locomobile arrived in a freight car, Della couldn't
wait for Walter to learn how to drive the machine. Before
taking her for a spin, however, he took the Locomobile
apart.

Locomobile was another company Durant would one
day take over.

∾o∾

The Durant era at Buick was barely three months old when
delivery of axles taught Willie, Charles Begole, Walter Marr,
Eugene Richard, Charles Nash, and the rest of the brain
trust that building cars was ten times more complicated
than manufacturing carriages, and demanded accuracy
and discipline unknown in buggy making. Work stopped if
any one of hundreds of components was a millimeter off or
not there on time. Buick, Oldsmobile, and Cadillac bought
axles from the Weston-Mott Company, in Utica, New York,
and roller bearings from the Hyatt Roller Bearing Company of Harrison, New Jersey. John Wesley Hyatt had invented celluloid as a substitute for ivory so that billiard
balls could be made more cheaply, and had turned his attention to the design of tapered roller bearings. Alfred P.
Sloan had joined the company on graduating from the
Massachusetts Institute of Technology. Hyatt was a better
inventor than businessman, and Sloan's father stepped in
with a $5,000 loan, which saved the company and made
young Sloan the president.

Sloan *père et fils* acquired control of Hyatt just as the
motor industry's appetite for roller bearings skyrocketed.
Carmakers couldn't get the bearings fast enough and discovered they were at the mercy of railway dispatchers. To
help his new clients, Sloan hired agents to ride the caboose
of freight trains and "cajole, bribe, or fight, as the occasion

90

Harry Bassett at Flint Buick headquarters, circa 1910

demanded," to keep bearings moving. When it came to axles, Durant had the mountain moved to Muhammad. He had Charles Stewart Mott relocate his Utica factory to Flint.

In mid-July 1905, Mott, Durant, Whiting, Carton, and their wives toured the construction site on the old Hamilton farm. The walls were up and streetcar tracks were being laid. Mott was sufficiently impressed by the site—and by Durant's promise to invest $100,000 in a new half-million-dollar Weston-Mott of Michigan plant to be built next to the new Buick factory—to sign a contract. With machinery moved from Utica, the Weston-Mott plant was up and running the following February. Mott moved his family to Flint and later became the city's mayor. With Mott came Harry Bassett, who would one day be the president of Buick. Bassett was often the butt of practical jokes conjured up by Bob Burman and Lewis Strang, drivers for Buick's racing team.

They all lived within walking distance of each other.

Bassett and Big Bill Little were neighbors. Doors were never locked. Charles Nash would remember how Bassett arrived one evening with the next day's Weston-Mott payroll, and calmly left two valises containing $60,000 in cash at home overnight.

∽∽∽

Durant kept buying companies. The Reliance Motor Truck Company of Owosso, Michigan, gave him trucks, and the Welch Motor Car Company of Pontiac oversized passenger cars. These and other purchases stripped Buick of cash, but Willie believed assets were there to be used, not hoarded.

Sloan came to visit Mott's new factory and would remember Flint in 1906—without Durant (and anticipating by a year and a half the creation of General Motors):

> I recall that both sides of Saginaw Street, the main street of Flint, were lined with hitching posts, and on Saturday night the street was crowded with the horses, wagon, and carriages that brought the farmers into town for their weekly shopping and night out. In that setting a small society of automobile and parts producers met socially and on business for several years: Mr. Mott, Charles Nash, Walter Chrysler, Harry Bassett, myself, and others, all of whom, except myself, were then in General Motors. I must have seen Mr. Durant there, too, but I can only recall seeing him on the train between New York and Detroit, and our saying "Good evening" and "Good morning."

Sloan got a dressing down from old Henry Leland for the tolerances the Hyatt Company allowed in their roller bearings. With calipers in hand, Leland showed the young MIT graduate the discrepancies in diameters. "You must grind your bearings," the white-haired Leland said; "even though you make thousands, the first and the last should be precisely alike." Leland walked Sloan over to the window, showed him a heap of rejected Weston-Mott axles in the yard, and told Sloan that unless he would guarantee bearings ground to within a thousandth of an inch in accuracy, the Hyatt products would also end up on the scrap pile. Only precision to within a thousandth of an inch made parts interchangeable. The rebuke taught Sloan the first lesson in mass production.

The 1906 output reached 2,295 cars, and 4,600 Buicks were built in 1907, which was nearly half the entire vehicle registration in the United States two years earlier. The 1906 Model F, a 2-cylinder touring car that sold for about $1,200, won wide acceptance when it ran from New York to San Francisco in 24 days, 8 hours, and 45 minutes. In a

On the road in a Buick, 1908

well-publicized race in Illinois, a lighter Buick Model G runabout swept to the finish ahead of a Cadillac, a Ford, and two Maxwells (made by the Briscoe brothers).

Less than three years after switching from carts to automobiles, Durant had discovered that no matter how fast the supply of new Buicks grew, demand outstripped production. A backlog persisted even with day, evening, and overnight shifts. The company's net worth by the end of 1908 was $3.4 million, and almost all the growth was attributable to reinvested earnings.

The man whose name emblazoned ever more cars drifted into oblivion. In his mid-fifties, Buick felt alienated from the fever pitch of the new order and in 1906 resigned. Unable to hang on to money, he owed $92.58 to Durant's personal lawyer John Carton. In the end Billy paid it, sending a covering note to Carton: "Mr. Buick wishes me to say that until a few moments ago this was more money than he had in the world. He disliked very much to make this admission and possibly this is the reason why you have not heard from him before."

The dividends had not paid back the debt Buick owed the Briscoe brothers. To be totally free, he surrendered his stock to Buick Motor Company, which paid off the Briscoes. A decade later, Ben Briscoe calculated that David Buick's stock would have been worth nearly $10 million. Durant gave David an undisclosed sum, reportedly $100,000. Buick invested badly and died in obscurity in 1929.

11

Affair of the Heart

Margery's April 18, 1906, wedding was an event. The groom was Dr. Edwin Campbell, a man closer to his father-in-law's age than to the nineteen-year-old bride, but he was a catch. He was the physician to the town's best families, and, it was said, no one was anybody in Flint if Dr. Campbell hadn't delivered him or her. Margery was radiant, and as her father led her up the aisle of St. Paul's Episcopal Church in short, hurried steps, she whispered, "Don't go so fast, dear."

Flint knew Billy and Clara's marriage was terminal when, upon the newlyweds' return from their honeymoon, Durant moved into his daughter and son-in-law's new house at 415 Stevens Street. "Pops," as Margery called him, was traveling a lot, but she and Ed catered to him when he was in town. A downstairs room in their new home was his, ready with clean linen at all times, and a suitcase packed for the next trip. Dr. Campbell continued his practice, and his young wife helped him by keeping the books and sending out his bills. After a while, Margery and Ed were drawn

Margery Durant

into her father's vortex. Ed abandoned medicine, became his father-in-law's full-time assistant, and later a board member of various Durant ventures.

The separation took its toll on Clara, who rightfully suspected there was another woman in her husband's life. Ed arranged for his mother-in-law to spend the winter of 1906–1907 at a rest home in Pinehurst, North Carolina, in the company of a nurse he recommended. He was later helpful in negotiating his in-laws' divorce settlement.

The woman in Billy's life was nineteen. Catherine Lederer was a pretty, doe-eyed, and demure girl from Jackson, Michigan. The traditional story is that Margery met Catherine when she and her brother visited their father in Jackson, where he always stayed at the Hotel Otsego. The two girls became friends, and Margery introduced Catherine to her father. Catherine made enough of an impression on the forty-five-year-old Billy for him to offer the two young women tickets to the theater. After the performance, he drove them home, and managed a moment alone with Miss Lederer.

Catherine Lederer Durant

The less edifying truth is that Catherine was barely
nineteen and working as a summer replacement at the
post office when Billy met her and offered her a job as his
secretary. What lends credence to this version of events
is a letter from Billy to Charles Mott, dated June 3, 1905,
with the typist's initials CL at the bottom. We do not know
the fullness of their relationship, but, given the Victorian
strictures that ruled much of his conduct, it seems impudent
to conjecture too libidinously on Billy's comportment. Besides, Catherine's mother did not approve of the match. She
changed her mind, however, when she met her daughter's
commanding, if mature, suitor.

With the birth of William Campbell in 1907, Margery made Billy a grandfather. In due time, Rebecca was in on this affair of the heart, which, she and her son agreed, first of all demanded a clean break with Clara. Herself a divorcée, Rebecca assigned no blame to the woman who had been her daughter-in-law for thirty years, nor did she reproach her "dear boy." On March 30, 1908, she wrote Billy a comforting letter saying she wished he could have been spared the disappointment of a broken home, and that she understood his struggle "both in body and mind":

> It's hard to see what good can come from so much trouble, but one sure thing—we have to meet it and accept it with good grace—do the best we can, keeping a courage that will take us to the end. So, my dear boy, keep up a good heart. It might be something worse. Take good care of your health. When one is good and strong they can endure trouble and hard work better . . . Goodbye. We shall be glad to see you back again. It is so different when you are here.
>
> With a great deal of love,
Mother

As was the custom, the wronged woman got the satisfaction, if that is the word, of asking for a divorce. Michigan law permitted divorce only by reason of one party's insanity, desertion, or extreme cruelty. Before Circuit Judge William Gage for the County of Genesee, Clara accused her husband of "the usual [sic] wanton and extreme cruelty." Decorous comportment demanded that Willie not respond, thereby acknowledging misconduct. Whether Clara followed counsel's instructions or meant what she said, she told the court she had tried to persuade her husband to change his behavior. His response, however, had been cruel indifference. He had repulsed any and all her advances, and "used profane language to her, and informed her that he would do and act as he pleased." She swore that they had "cohabited together" until September 1906, and after that had occupied different rooms in the house.

Judge Gage granted the decree of divorce on May 27, 1908, and, no doubt as a courtesy toward Flint's premier citizen, ordered the record "suppressed" so that no accounts reached the newspapers. Clara received $150,000 in cash and securities and turned back to Willie some Durant-Dort stock he had registered in her name. Nineteen-year-old Clifford stayed with his mother, who, a short time later, moved to California.

The next day, Billy married Catherine in New York City, far from the eyes and ears of Flint and Jackson journalists.

♠

Marriage did not change his lifestyle. For the first years as man and wife, Billy and Catherine—he called her Muddy—lived in hotels, the Murray Hill Hotel in New York, the Dresden in Flint. He kept up his hectic pace and there were weeks at a time when his new wife didn't see him. They eventually rented an apartment at 565 Park Avenue. Rebecca, now approaching her eightieth birthday, came to live with them part of the year.

Billy and Catherine remained childless.

♠

As much as Margery was the dutiful daughter who, when she could find her Pops, called him every day, Cliff drifted out of his father's orbit. He attended the Pennsylvania Military College, and in the 1910 yearbook was described as a musical genius. After graduation, he went to California to live with his mother.

Billy heaped affection and wealth on Margery. "To be near my father," as Margery put it, the Campbells moved to New York City and settled just a few blocks away at 635 Park Avenue. She expressed her feelings for her father in an effusive letter thanking him for an unspecified gift on the occasion of her twenty-fifth birthday:

Dearest Pops:

There are some things, which come to us in our lives, even in twenty-five years, that we feel so deeply, we cannot talk of them, and *this* is one of them.

I just can't find words to tell you how much I thank you and how much I appreciate your doing such a great big wonderful thing for me. You have always been so good to me and mine, and so generous with us, but this is so much, Pops. I just can't believe it, but still it is just like you. Surely no one ever had such a father before.

I wish that I might do something for you, in return, but I have no opportunity. If one ever comes, I hope I may show in some way how much I appreciate all you have done for me. In the meantime, I shall try all the harder to make myself worthy of such a trust, and to be as unselfish as you. Surely it will be a great pleasure in being able to do for those who are unfortunate.

The day has been so happy, just as my whole life has been, and the dear children had dinner with us tonight. William had a big cake, which was a great surprise, and we had a beautiful time. I wish you might have been here.

There is one thing, Pops, which is sure. I haven't learned in this [sic] twenty-five years how to express my thoughts on paper. Let us hope for better luck in the next twenty-five. However, you *know* that your little girl is very grateful in her heart, don't you Pops dear.

With a great deal of love
Margery

P.S. I am not going to have any more birthdays.

Shortly after Margery gave birth to a daughter, Edwina, Billy appointed Dr. Campbell to the Buick board of directors.

12

⌒⌒⌒

Checkered Flags

During the summer of 1906, Durant was at a car race in Detroit when Loren Hodge, a Buick mechanic who worked under Marr and Richard, introduced him to a driver with a walrus mustache and a thick French accent. Louis Chevrolet had a cigarette glued to his lips, which irritated Billy. But Chevrolet had just won the day's three races for Buick, and a handshake was in order. The way Hodge explained it, Chevrolet was not connected with any official team. So Hodge had asked him if he'd like to take the Buick for a spin. Louis loved the feel of the racer, and, with Hodge as his partner-mechanic, had won the day's triple crown.

The meeting in Detroit changed both men's lives, but Durant never got used to Chevrolet's *mégot*. A cigarette or, more often, a burned-out stub was always in his mouth. Photos usually have him in helmet and goggles, hands on the wheel in a Buick racer, the cigarette dangling in the left corner of his mouth. There is a picture of him at the wheel during the road testing of a stripped-down Buick Model 16.

Louis Chevrolet

Another photo shows him, his brother Arthur, and their seven-man racing team leaning on a picket fence with a sign saying "Good Morning Buick Roadsters, Drivers and Mechanicians [*sic*]." When Chevrolet and Durant were photographed in a group picture at the 1912 launch of the Chevrolet Classic Six, Louis sported no cigarette, but three other men still separated him from Billy.

Chevrolet was a big man, powerfully built. Until the invention of the self-starter, gasoline engines were hand-cranked, a nuisance that not only left women stuck with slow electric cars, but resulted in thousands of dollars of insurance claims for broken arms every year. Louis was an ox of a man. Once after he cranked a car and it back-fired on him, he held on and bent the crank in his hands. Before and after races, the 210-pound Louis loved to thrust his hands into the oily guts of an engine and tear it apart with the precision of an open-heart surgeon.

He was Swiss-French, born on Christmas Day, 1879,

the son of a watchmaker. By the time he was ten, the family had moved across the border to Beaune, a small town in the Burgundy region of France where his younger brothers, Gaston and Arthur, were born. The Chevrolet boys got little formal education. While still a child, Louis was the guide to a blind wine merchant. In his teens, he invented and built a wine pump. It was as an apprentice to the automobile company of Mors, Darracq, Hotchkiss & de Dion-Bouton that he experienced the allure of powerful machinery and speed—building and racing motorcars. He especially liked Count Albert de Dion and the count's brother-in-law, Georges Bouton. The Dion-Bouton partnership started making steam engines, switched to gasoline machines, and until World War I would remain a thriving enterprise. De Dion sent his young mechanic to America in 1900 to work in the Dion-Bouton atelier in Brooklyn. Three years later, Louis took advantage of an opportunity to drive a 90-horsepower Fiat at the Hippodrome in Morris Park, New York, and was soon barnstorming with a Fiat racing group.

Besides the handshake at the Detroit racetrack, there are at least two other stories on how he and Durant met. One retelling has Chevrolet and his brothers showing up in Flint in 1907 and applying for jobs at the Buick factory. According to this version, Louis drove faster and more daringly than Arthur, so Billy hired Louis to race cars and Arthur to be his chauffeur. By another account Durant inherited the Chevrolet brothers when he purchased the Marquette Motor Company, a little-known carmaker in Saginaw, Michigan, specializing in high-quality racing cars.

∽o∾

A New York–New Jersey dealer invented car racing Buick style with a flair for publicity. On Thanksgiving Day, 1904, the bespectacled H. J. Koehler gunned a 2-cylinder Buick engine mounted on a stripped-down chassis up Eagle Rock near Newark, New Jersey, in 2 minutes and 18.24 seconds, thereby slashing a previous record in half. Walter Marr was there, and explained to baffled journalists and spectators surrounding Koehler and the winning machine that the victory was due to the valve-in-head motor. A month later, Koehler sold two Buicks with the amazing new engine.

Koehler raced again the following Fourth of July, and won the 2-cylinder class category in a 100-mile, four-state race. In October 1906, he entered a 100-mile race for stripped touring cars at the Empire Track in Yonkers, New York. The competing cars were a Mercedes, a Packard, two Cadillacs, a Matheson, and an Oldsmobile. A driver named Keeler was in the Oldsmobile and more or less dominated the race for the first 17 miles, with the Matheson and the Buick in second and third place. Down the straightaway on the 18th mile, the Matheson lost a rear wheel, and Keeler was out front until mile 58, when he was forced into the pit for a tire change. That put Koehler ahead, pursued by Keeler who, on new tires, overtook the Buick, only to develop tire trouble again at mile 90. Koehler took the checkered flag for Buick a mere 15.24 seconds ahead of Keeler. In two years, Koehler won thirty-six racing cups and medals, and translated his winnings into booming sales. On October 1, 1906, he placed an order for 500 Buicks—350 2-cylinder cars and 150 4-cylinder vehicles. The $700,000 order represented one-tenth of the annual Flint output.

Durant was quick to see the publicity value of sending a Buick from New York to San Francisco for the 24-day coast-to-coast record in 1906. Two years later he invented a race between a Buick and an airplane. The Buick won. More important, he let Marr, Richard, and their favorite mechanic, Loren Hodge, set up a Buick racing crew, which soon grew into a twelve-man team. Their star driver until

Chevrolet joined was "Wild" Bob Burman. A farm boy from Imlay City, Michigan, Burman had started as one of the Buick works' first employees, and was an engine inspector with a taste for racing cars when Durant picked him for the Buick team in 1907. Burman believed in luck. "It either holds together and I win running wide open, or it breaks and I lose," he said. He was killed driving a Peugeot in a 1916 California race he helped to organize.

The Buick team traveled from race to race in special railway cars. A rolling machine shop, complete with blacksmith's forge, was built in a leased baggage car, and a second freight car housed eight racers. The team took advantage of their competitor's misfortunes and knew how to work fast. In qualifying heats for the November 1908 Savannah, Georgia, Grand Prix, a Mercedes Benz with an underslung suspension impressed everybody. The car wrecked in front of the Buick team's encampment. In the dead of night, team members with lanterns went over the Benz wreck until they understood its suspension, and wired instructions to Flint. New parts were built in hours, loaded into the freight car, and once the train had arrived in Savannah, Burman's new 50-horsepower machine was transformed from standard suspension to underslung. Not that it worked. Burman was eighteenth for the first two laps, and dropped out in the third.

A month earlier, Durant was with the team in a 250-mile race in Lowell, Massachusetts. Burman, in a 40-horsepower Buick Model G, was running second to veteran Lewis Strang in an Isotta Fraschini, when he suddenly pulled off the track and into the Buick repair shop. When he came back out and gunned after Strang, officials spotted a new radiator and front axle, and disqualified him. Willie wired Harry Shiland, the Massachusetts dealer, that the Model 5 and Burman both behaved beautifully, and that "our disqualification was perfectly just, due to our repair force not understanding the rules." Two weeks later in Montreal,

Burman drove the Model 5 to eleven of fourteen event victories, tied once, and lost twice. Impressed, Strang joined the Buick team.

Chevrolet, Burman, Strang, and George DeWitt drove Buick machines to victories in the Mardi Gras Speed Contest in New Orleans, the Pasadena-Altadena Hill Climb in Los Angeles, a 100-mile event in Daytona, Florida, the Lookout Mountain Climb in Chattanooga, Tennessee, and a free-for-all contest in Nashville. On occasion, they lost. Burman, Chevrolet, and Strang were in the 1909 Indiana Trophy Race, a 232-mile, 10-lap event at Crown Point. The Buick team was favored to win, but Strang's car lost a gear at 25 miles, Chevrolet's failed at 30. Burman was leading when he broke a valve. He limped around the track until he found Strang's abandoned car off the edge of the course and helped himself to spare parts. Officials caught him in the act and disqualified him.

The following day, Burman and Chevrolet were in Marquette-Buick machines for the distinguished Cobe Toby competition, a 396.6-mile race during which cars were sent off at one-minute intervals.

At Durant's suggestion, Chevrolet had gone to Saginaw to oversee the assembling of the Marquette-Buicks, which were anything but "stock" Buicks. Durant and Chevrolet both wanted faster cars, and the so-called Marquette-Buicks that Chevrolet and the Marquette mechanics assembled were, like the racing machines Ettore Bugatti was constructing in Molsheim, Alsace, virtually hand-built. Durant agreed to the hyphened Marquette-Buick name after subordinates suggested they might be in trouble if word got out that, except for the engines, these cars weren't Buicks at all. Chevrolet had two Marquette-Buicks built for the Cobe Trophy endurance contest, one for Burman and one for himself. The race was considered so important in Flint that a telegraph station was set up at the track so progress reports could be wired back to the factory. David

Buick, the forgotten founding father, was among the men watching the results clatter in.

The race began at 8 A.M. Burman was in the lead for the first two laps, but on lap three lost control and went off course. By lap five he was out of competition. Chevrolet gained on a Knox that broke a valve, but remained 22 minutes behind a Locomobile until it headed for a pit stop with ignition problems. Louis lost a cylinder—back in Flint, Buick and the guys groaned—but continued on three rods. Behind him, the Locomobile was back in the race and gaining on him. Ahead of him was the repaired Knox.

The telegraph was silent for a while. When it burst into action and announced the news of Louis's 3-cylinder winning by 65 seconds, the room went wild.

A youthful and envious admirer of the Buick racing team was eighteen-year-old Clifford. Still living with his mother in California, he managed to meet Burman, Strang, and Chevrolet. We do not know whether Willie vetoed his son's desire to join the team—Cliff would not race at Indianapolis until he was thirty—but the family no doubt sighed in relief when, on a trip back East, he fell in love with Adelaide Frost, a pretty young woman from Grand Rapids who looked a lot like his mother. They married in 1909 and settled in Los Angeles.

The Indianapolis Motor Speedway opened in August 1909 and the Buick Motor Company fielded fifteen cars and its star drivers Lewis Strang, Bob Burman, and Gaston Chevrolet. It was Louis Chevrolet, Burman, and Strang for the Prest-O-Lite Trophy. However remarkable the Buick team was in class events based on cubic centimeter size and sprint racing, it lacked the control and integration to enter the big time. Wisely no doubt, Durant kept the team out of the major events of the day—the Vanderbilts, the Grand Prizes, and 24-hour marathon races, where Buicks would be pitted against the best European machines. To beat the best cars the Europeans had to offer, Terry B.

Dunham and Lawrence R. Gustin would write in *The Buick: A Complete History,* "would require a rigid discipline within the team if a respectable showing was to be expected—and Buick managers had long since thrown up their hands regarding that." In too many races, the boys—Burman was twenty-four, Chevrolet thirty-six, in 1908—were competing against each other as much as against drivers and machines not built in Flint or Saginaw.

∽

Durant pulled Buick ahead of the competition by continuing to build and hoard cars during the Panic of 1907. It all began with legislation to tighten the Interstate Commerce Commission's jurisdiction over railways. Although President Theodore Roosevelt made concessions to the railways, large business interests were rattled. Stocks became volatile. The panic started in October when a merger of a chain of banks fell through and the Knickerbocker Trust Company of New York collapsed. Banks refused new loans and called in existing ones, and the credit crunch hit the automobile industry from both ends. Consumers could not finance purchases and carmakers had no cash reserves. Durant's continuous buying spree and nonchalant attitude toward cash flow made the Buick Motor Company especially vulnerable. Willie paid suppliers with promissory notes, and the suppliers in turn used "Durant script" to pay their debt. Some banks accepted the script at a discount. Customers also paid with I.O.U. certificates, which he endorsed and passed on, but the payroll could not be met with promissory notes and securities.

On the national level, the government intervened by offering $150 million in bonds yielding 2 and 3 percent. On Buick's level, Willie managed to keep bill collectors at bay and his factories running. Where the Lelands and Olds cut back and laid off workers, Durant piled up inventory, storing Buicks in barns and empty warehouses. The crisis was brought to an end by vigorous government action in the credit market and by large financial interests under the leadership of J. Pierpont Morgan, who entered the market to stop the decline. Morgan's intervention dampened the financial anxiety, but the financier's enemies charged him with manipulating the market for his own ends. Even Teddy Roosevelt blamed the "malefactors of great wealth" for the panic—a line Durant would soon adopt.

By the spring of 1908, when would-be buyers of Cadillacs and Olds were told deliveries would be a few months off, Buick dealers had cars to sell. "He was one hell of a gambler," Charles Mott would recall years later. "To this day, I don't know how he was able to handle it financially, but he did."

Durant sensed the exploding business was marching toward consolidation. What he needed was access to big money.

13

⁓୦⁓

Thinking Big

Durant spent a good part of the winter of 1907–1908 talking to J. P. Morgan & Company about underwriting one-third of a $1.5 million issue for a group to be called United Motors Corporation. His introduction came through J. Pierpont Morgan's son-in-law Herbert L. Satterlee, the scion of an old New York family and two years Willie's junior. Satterlee had married Louisa Morgan in 1900; Pierpont's more notorious daughter, Anne, was a lesbian who, to her father's greater chagrin, dabbled in socialism.

The House of Morgan had organized the International Harvester Corporation out of five separate, quarrelsome companies, and at their first meeting, Satterlee, a partner in the law offices of Ward, Hayden and Satterlee, listened attentively to Durant's idea of bringing together several automotive manufacturers. Durant and his old friend Ben Briscoe had already discussed a merger. Between them, the Buick and Maxwell-Briscoe factories could produce 13,000 cars a year. If the Ford Motor Company and Ransom E. Olds's Reo auto works were added, the conglomerate would be unbeatable.

Ranny Olds had walked out of the Olds Motor Works in 1904 in a dispute with his associate Samuel L. Smith and the latter's son, Frederick. As Fred Smith took over Olds, Ranny found new backers and, using his own initials for the corporate name, created Reo. "The world moves," the advertisement for the new car said. "You need no longer pay fabulous prices for intricate mistakes and doubtful experiments. Mr. R. E. Olds has built the Reo Car." To the Smiths' embarrassment, the new Reo outsold the curved-dash Olds, which was fast becoming a museum piece. Smith tied the Olds Motor Works' fortunes to a large, 4-cylinder touring car selling at almost four times the price of the old runabout.

The merger talks were pretty advanced. After spending one Sunday with James Couzens going over the Ford plant and discussing ways to structure a deal, Durant had met Frank Briscoe several times in Detroit and New York City, and Briscoe followed up with meetings with Ranny Olds and Henry Ford. In his autobiographical notes, Durant would remember recommending they give star billing to the blunt and impulsive Ford. "I suggested he [Briscoe] first see Henry Ford, who was in the limelight, liked publicity and unless he could lead the procession would not play." Ford said he was willing to discuss the idea. Olds was also open.

All four had gotten together at the old Penobscot Building in Detroit to discuss the delicate matter of how much each company was worth. When Briscoe said they had to come up with figures they could take to Morgan, his suggestion was greeted with self-conscious silence. Finally, Billy plunged in. "If we put the value of $10 million on Ford, would Henry consider $6 million a reasonable figure for Reo?"

Ford said he had no idea what Reo was worth.

Willie pushed on. If we agree that Ford is worth $10 million and Reo $6 million, would $5 million seem reasonable for Maxwell-Briscoe? The question seemed to irritate Briscoe, who asked, "What about Buick?" Willie parried by saying appraisers and auditors should answer that one.

After money, they discussed management. Briscoe suggested they set up a central steering committee and fuse their purchasing, engineering, advertising, and sales departments. Billy thought that was too complicated. All he wanted was a holding company with no interference in each carmaker's internal operations.

"Ho, ho," Briscoe smiled. "Durant is for states' rights. I am for a union."

Their next meeting took place in Satterlee's New York law office on January 24–25, 1908. Ford had wanted to use another attorney, Job Hedges. Had they used Hedges, Briscoe would later write, the Ford Motor Company might have been a founding member of General Motors.

The two days of talk clarified issues to the point where the deal unraveled. Ford was ready to launch his Model T and Durant readily agreed with him that consolidations tended to increase prices. Ford favored keeping prices under a thousand dollars so that people could buy his cars and enjoy "the benefit of cheap transportation." Things fell apart the second day when Ford met privately with Satterlee and refused to take shares in the proposed four-party cartel. By some accounts, Ford wanted $3 million in cash, although Durant would claim no actual figure was put on the table. By other accounts, the indispensable Jim Couzens did the negotiations with Durant while Ford was sick with lumbago and, to soothe his back, was lying on the cool bathroom floor in his hotel.

Satterlee was baffled. Nobody had told him any of the partners wanted money to unload their companies. Olds now followed suit. Ford was depressed by losing the Selden trial. He and Olds met on their own and decided they preferred to sell out and retire rather than buy into a stock deal. Satterlee took Durant into an adjoining room and asked what was going on. Billy said it was all news to him, too, and pulled Briscoe into the huddle. Briscoe could only guess that Ford had changed his mind. Satterlee went back to Ford and Olds and told them it was up to the bankers to decide whether to finance their buyout. In the meantime, he suggested the parties meet again and perfect their plan. Discussions did drag on through the spring and into the summer. The *Flint Journal* got wind of the talks and in its July 3 edition reported that Buick and Maxwell-Briscoe were set to merge and that Durant would be the general manager of the new consolidation. Buick officials refused to comment.

The first J. P. Morgan partner Billy met with was George W. Perkins. This former New York Life Insurance vice president was an exception to the Morgan upper-crust mold. He had started out as a grocery clerk and liked to say, "I began life sorting lemons and I have been doing it ever since." Like Billy, he traveled incessantly and their first parley took place in Perkins's private railway car coupled to a Chicago–New York express. Billy joined Perkins in his rolling drawing room in Chicago. Six hours later, when he detrained in Albany for a return trip to Detroit and Flint, Perkins's encouragement was still ringing in his ears. The Morgan partner had sneered at Durant's forecast of selling 500,000 cars a year. The arithmetic was fatally flawed, Perkins later told Briscoe, because a car cost the average worker a year's wages. He nevertheless declared himself sympathetic to the merger idea.

Next, Billy was invited to 23 Wall Street to meet with J. P. Morgan's "Attorney-General," Francis L. Stetson. The starchy lawyer and dean of the New York bar resented reading details of the negotiations—and the tentative commitment of J. P. Morgan & Company—in the July 31, 1908, *New York Times*. Stetson was sure Durant had leaked the story, and called him "the greatest living promoter outside of prison bars." By that he no doubt meant that Durant's merger talk might be nothing more than an attempt to boost the Buick stock after the 1907 panic. Neither the Buick stock nor any of the other carmakers' securities were as yet listed on the New York Stock Exchange, but they were on the Detroit stock exchange, and Stetson suspected Durant's headlong expansion had been fueled by issuing stock that was probably overvalued. In their face-to-face meeting, however, Stetson was affable. He had heard fine things about Buick, he told Durant, and merely wanted confirmation that Durant was in control of the Buick stock. Billy replied that that was indeed the case. Stockholders had signed over proxies to him, and their shares were deposited in a Flint bank.

Pierpont himself no longer got involved in deals worth less than $10 million. He did agree, however, to see the industrialist from Michigan. We do not know whether Satterlee forewarned his father-in-law that Ford and Olds had pulled out, but it is more than reasonable to believe he did. What we do know is that Billy was preceded by less than flattering word of mouth from Stetson.

Everything about J. P. spelled breeding. At sixty-eight, the banker was getting beefy and bald, but his well-tended mustache remained thick and trimmed in the walrus style. A skin disease had scarred the handsome features of his youth and left him with a bulbous red nose (which was much caricatured in the press). Yet dressed in suit and waistcoat and sporting wing collar, ascot cravat, and starched cuffs, he radiated to-the-manor-born self-confidence. The imperial glance of his hazel eyes added to his formidable and, to many, forbidding personality.

The Morgans of Llandaff in Glamorgan had five centuries of lineage and history behind them when Miles Morgan arrived in America in 1636, sixteen years after the *Mayflower* had beached on the coast of Massachusetts. Pierpont was Miles's great-great-great-great-grandson, and, due to the remarkable money he made, he was the first in his line of prudent, respectable folk to influence the history of America. When the U.S. government was 24 hours from default in 1895, Pierpont talked enough horse sense into President Grover Cleveland to let J. P. Morgan & Company organize the private placement abroad of $62 million in Treasury notes. Morgan's action saved the creditworthiness of the United States. When a senator later asked why, to prevent another panic, other bankers shouldn't do the same, Pierpont replied, "They *could* not do it."

J. P. could not believe the horse was going to be replaced by self-propelled road vehicles. He owned an electric motor car, but much preferred his carriage. He was convinced the automobile was another bicycle fad, and the midwestern mechanical wizards and entrepreneurs like W. C. Durant sitting across from him were fly-by-night upstarts. The possession of a glittering limousine was, like the ownership of the yachts the Vanderbilts, Rockefellers, and Astors sailed *en saison,* either a mark of distinction or evidence of extravagance. Imported roadsters were playthings for sporting millionaires, and even Made in USA cars, being handmade, were expensive. Over 142,000 motor vehicles might be registered in the United States, but that still only added up to one car for every fifty families. And the *Detroit Saturday Night* still advised its readers that chauffeurs were best recruited from the ranks of former coachmen because, as dutiful members of the servant class, they could be counted on to know "exactly what is expected of them by their masters."

After a few minutes with Durant, he dismissed Billy, later calling him "an unstable visionary."

᠀

There are deep ironies in the patrician banker's attitude. One merciful explanation is that he was a man of the nineteenth century (he was born in 1837) and that his views on transportation were arrested with the railways. A less charitable excuse is his shortsightedness. Had he, Stetson, Perkins, or their underlings dug a little deeper they would have discovered that carmaking was on the cusp of critical mass. Ford was on the eve of dramatic output figures for his $950 Model T, built, he proclaimed, "for the average man." By year's end, Buick built 8,820 cars; Ford's output reached 6,181, and Cadillac's 2,380 automobiles, for a total of 17,381.

Durant's reaction to being turned down by J. Pierpont himself is contained in a letter to *his* lawyer. On July 2, he wrote to Carton from Buick's Boston sales branch:

> Had a long, hot session with our friends in New York yesterday and was pretty nearly used up at the finish. If you think it is an easy matter to get money from New York capitalists to finance a motor car proposition in Michigan, you have another guess coming. Notwithstanding the fact that quoted rates are very low, money is hard to get owing to a somewhat unaccountable feeling of uneasiness and a general distrust of the automobile proposition.

To Billy's surprise, Perkins hinted that the deal wasn't dead, that the merger idea had merit. Perkins suggested that instead of United Motors, Durant call the consolidation International Motor Car Company (to remind Pierpont of the International Harvester merger?). Willie had no problem with that. A few days later, he was in for a bigger surprise when Ben Briscoe said, "Let's go it alone. We two."

But Durant no longer needed J. P. Morgan and not even Briscoe. During the negotiations, he had jumped on an express train to Detroit and talked to Samuel Smith and his two sons, Fred and Angus. To keep Olds Motor Works solvent the Smiths had pumped $1 million into the company, and were ready to meet Durant at any ungodly hour. Fred Smith would recall how Durant arrived after midnight, roused everybody, and, after a 3 A.M. gallop through the Olds plant, discussed a possible merger until sunup.

Willie returned to New York and met with Satterlee. Here is how he remembers it:

> Mr. Satterlee said, "Mr. Durant, you only have Buick, how can you have a consolidation?" I replied that I would have no difficulty in securing another company, as a matter of fact I had one in mind at the moment— the Olds Motor Works in Lansing, Michigan. The company—one of the oldest in the business—was controlled by Mr. S. L. Smith of Detroit, and was being operated by his sons, Fred and Angus Smith, whom I knew intimately. While the company was not a success, I believed it had possibilities. Mr. Henry Russell, vice-president of the Michigan Central Railroad, a great friend of Mr. Smith, was president of the Olds Motor Works. I was acquainted with Mr. Russell and said I would wire him immediately asking if he would meet me in Lansing the following Saturday, mentioning the fact that I would like to discuss a possible merger of Olds and Buick, which I did.
>
> Satterlee asked about the capitalization and how the common stock was to be issued. I told him I had in the Buick organization a competent engineer, by the name of Walter Marr, with whom I had worked closely for several years, that the engineering success of the Buick was due largely to his efforts, that he was a crank on carburetors and had taken numerous patents; that he was very fond of me, had named his only son after me, and I

was quite sure he would set aside for my use a sufficient number of patents and applications against which the common stock could be issued.

Satterlee suggested incorporating in New Jersey. Unlike Michigan, the Garden State placed almost no restrictions on the activities of a firm incorporated in the state. When, on September 10, Durant received a letter from Ward, Hayden and Satterlee, the mystery of why Perkins had suggested calling the new company International Motor Company became apparent. Billy had given the Morgan partner ideas. Perkins wanted the name for possible automotive empire building of his own.

"We find it impractical to use the 'International Motor Company,'" the letter said. "We might use the 'United Motor Car Company' were it not for the fact that there is already a 'United Motors Car Company' in that state [New Jersey]. We suggest the name 'General Motors Company,' which we have ascertained can be used." Curtis R. Hatheway, a young Ward, Hayden and Satterlee attorney, filed articles of incorporation in Trenton with the office of the New Jersey secretary of state.

General Motors was born September 16, 1908. The articles of incorporation named it General Motors Company of New Jersey with a capital stock of $2,000. William M. Eaton, a onetime manager of a Michigan utility and currently an officer with a Wall Street investment firm, was named president. Durant was appointed vice president, and Hatheway secretary. Twelve days later, Durant gave the newborn firm a healthy $12.5 million infusion of capital, and suggested it buy the Buick Motor Company. The price was modest—$3.75 million—but since Durant was selling the company to himself it didn't matter. Buick Motor had been the fastest growing company in the industry. Whatever gems might be appended, Buick was the jewel in the crown.

Briscoe was not so lucky. After parting ways with Durant, Ben Briscoe organized the United States Motor Company, then merged it with the Columbia Motor Car Company of Hartford, Connecticut. The company went into receivership in 1912.

‿o‿

Billy moved with dazzling speed. For $240,000, GM immediately bought the W. F. Stewart body plant next to the Buick factory in Flint and leased it to Buick. Next, GM purchased all of the common stock of the Olds Motor Works in a $3 million stock swap (only $17,279 was paid in cash), and named Fred Smith and Henry Russell to the GM board. To make Olds instantly profitable, Durant allowed the new division to sell a slightly larger version of the hot-selling Buick Model 10.

Billy was at the Oldsmobile plant in Lansing with his engineer and production manager when the Model 10 body arrived by truck from Flint. "I asked to have the body cut lengthwise from front to rear and crosswise in the center from side to side, giving me an opportunity to widen and lengthen the body, changing the size and appearance completely," he would write. "When finished it was a handsome creation, painted and trimmed to meet the Oldsmobile standard and priced to the trade at $1200. This gave to Oldsmobile dealers a very handsome small car without interfering in any way with the Buick Model 10."

Next, Durant snatched up the Oakland Company, a carmaker located in Pontiac, Michigan, just north of Detroit. Making automobiles was a belated and desperate endeavor for Edward M. Murphy, who had made buggies and wagons, since 1893, and was an old friend of Billy's. Sensing the demise of horse-drawn vehicles, Murphy found a retired timber baron who helped him raise

$300,000 to convert to automobile production. A 4-cylinder machine called the Oakland Model K was built in 1908. Only 278 Model Ks were sold, and Durant's bid was welcome by Murphy's partners, but not by Murphy himself. The acquisition cost General Motors $201,000. A less pliant board of directors than Durant's might have questioned paying ten times the amount spent on Buick and Oldsmobile on the unproven Oakland. But Billy's next deal was a perfect score.

With factories in Flint, Lansing, and now Pontiac, Billy wanted a facility in Detroit, increasingly the industry's center of gravity. He set his sights on the Cadillac Motor Company, which was marketing the most highly regarded high-priced car in the country. After the 1907 panic and dip in sales, Cadillac was on its way back up to a 6,000-a-year production. The new Cadillac "30" was breaking sales records.

Old Henry Leland drove a hard bargain: Durant had ten days to pay $4.125 million in cash, not stock. After that the price might go up. Willie had Arnold Goss, a Buick executive, commute between Flint and Detroit. Each time Goss showed up in Leland's office, the price went up. At $4.5 million, the parties agreed. Durant had ten days to come up with the money.

Durant called it a bargain and, in retrospect, Leland came to the same conclusion. Willie came to Detroit for the sale—to date the largest financial transaction at the Detroit stock exchange. After the bank formalities, he summoned Henry and Wilfred to his hotel room at the Russell House and made them offers to stay on as managers. The Lelands told him they had established certain principles and would not be interested in continuing unless these standards were maintained.

"That's exactly what I want," Willie answered. "I want you to continue to run Cadillac exactly as though it were still your own. You will receive no directions from anyone."

☙

The buying spree continued. Durant had a hard time finding spark plugs for the high-compression, valve-in-head Buick engine, but on a business trip to Boston, he met a Frenchman who had devised a superior porcelain spark plug. The thirty-year-old Albert Champion was another builder of bicycles; he had come to America as a bike racer, won American and world championships, and returned to France to study automobiles. He was back in the United States in 1900, tried auto racing, and almost lost a leg in a racing accident. Durant wasn't looking for a racecar driver, but Champion's spark plugs were innovative enough for Billy to convince the Frenchman to move to Flint. The Buick works were so hard up for room that the new spark plug company was given office space in a corner of the Hamilton farm headquarters. After a building was erected to house the A. C. Spark Plug Company, Champion turned out thousands of units every week. He was a multimillionaire when he died in 1927 while visiting Paris, the city of his birth.

Durant loved to bend over architects' blueprints and to play with scale models of new plants. Oakland's general manager, Lee Dunlap, would remember how, in 1910, the boss came to Pontiac for what Dunlap expected to be several days of expansion discussions. After a few hours, however, Durant announced that he was off to Flint. Dunlap managed to give Durant a quick inspection tour of the building site before Billy told him to bring an expansion plan to Flint the next day. Recalled Dunlap:

Albert Champion

There wasn't any plan, and none could be drawn on such short notice, but his will being law and our need great, something had to be done. So I called in a couple of our draftsmen to help me and that night we made a toy factory layout—existing buildings in one color, desired buildings in another. We drew a map of the whole property, showing streets and railway sidings, and then glued the existing buildings to it in their exact locations. Feeling like a small boy with a new toy, I took this layout to Flint and rather fearfully placed it before the chief. I needn't have been alarmed at our amateur layout. He was pleased pink. We had a grand time fitting our new buildings into the picture as it was spread on his desk. We placed those new buildings first here, then there, debating the situation. When we agreed as to where they should go, he said, "Glue them down and call W. E. Wood."

Mr. Wood came in after a few minutes and received an order for their construction. In the whole history of America up to that time, buildings had never risen as swiftly as those did. Contractor Wood had men, materials and machines moving toward Pontiac within twenty-four hours, and we were installing machinery in part of the structures within three weeks. But, of course, we could not be equally swift in paying for them. That was something else. But for the time being none of us worried too much over that; we figured the "Little Fellow" would find the money somewhere. Which he did, in the end, though we know there was plenty of trouble before the bills were receipted. These early years in the automobile business were marked by tremendous personal activity and a very grave shortage of capital. Anyone going direct from the carriage manufacture to automobile manufacture could have little conception of the large use of capital required in the new field.

Twenty years later, Fred Smith of the Olds division would credit Durant with divining the advantages of fused manufacturing before anyone else.

Durant saw the possibilities of a strong combination earlier and more clearly than anyone else in or out of the industry and he put it over, a feat more staggering at the time than can be easily appreciated today. In spite of frequent and earnest scraps with W. C., I had at least the intelligence to see in him the strongest and most courageous individual then in the business and the master salesman of all time. No man ever lived who could sell such a variety of commodities in so short a space of time, cigars, buggies, automobiles, ideas and himself, believing wholeheartedly in his wares and in the last item especially.

GM's corporate center of gravity was wherever Durant happened to be, and he was in constant motion, rushing from factory to factory, though the main axis was New York–to–Flint return trips. To go after new targets made for boldness and kept Billy ahead of his own brainstorms. Bankers, however, were skittish about lending to General Motors for fear the whole unwieldy construct would collapse. For its master, the financial education was just beginning.

14

⌒⊙⌒

Darwinian Lessons

During the darkest hours of the Selden litigation, Jim Couzens, Ford's pince-nez'ed, stone-faced treasurer, had not only convinced his boss and partner to expand, but found the money to build a new facility in the Highland Park section of Detroit. The new plant gave the Ford Motor Company the muscle to outproduce and perhaps outsell General Motors. "Henceforth," wrote the *Detroit Saturday Night* in 1910, "the history of this industry will be the story of a conflict between giants." Two years later, Ford built 170,000 Model Ts—over three times the combined 50,000 Buick, Oldsmobile, Cadillac, and Oakland output. Durant decided the way to regain the lead was to come up with a new car. He asked Louis Chevrolet if he was interested in designing and building one.

First, however, there was a matter of money.

It was a little late for investment bankers to repeat J. Pierpont Morgan's jibe that automobiles were a rerun of the bicycle craze. Durant's youthful empire accounted for 22 percent of the North American output, employed

14,000 people, and in fixed plant investment was worth $14 million. If inventories on hand were included, the total value was $40 million. Durant and his directors had willed GM into existence by laying out $6.2 million in cash and $26 million in stock. In less than two years, he had bought $54 million of properties that were earning annual profits in the range of $10 million. Analyzing the figures in 1928, Lawrence A. Seltzer would write in his *Financial History of the American Automobile Industry* that the GM assets had cost Durant under $33 million, and less than a fifth of that had been in cash. He suspected Durant had paid too much for the Maxwell-Briscoe Company, but in his twenty-year hindsight, approved the birth of the GM prodigy.

Yet the unease of financial institutions persisted. A bank's refusal to lend GM $2 million in 1909 reflected the persistent nervousness of financial institutions over the Promethean carnage that called itself the automobile industry. Durant wanted the $2 million to buy the Ford Motor Company. Judge Charles Hough's October 1909 ruling upholding the Selden patent took its toll on Henry Ford. "We thought we were in great jeopardy," his lawyer John Anderson would remember. "We were feeling very blue indeed."

Ford was torn between selling out to Durant and challenging the Selden cartel. Willie came to Detroit and offered to buy out Ford for $8 million. Ford agreed, but insisted on "gold on the table." GM's board of directors authorized the purchase, but Henry regained his feisty mood. He put up bonds totaling $12 million to indemnify any Ford dealer or customer who might be sued by the ALAM. "We will fight on to a finish," he telegraphed his dealers.

❦

Nearly 300 different cars were being made and marketed, and the number of new entrants almost matched the number of carmakers going out of business. The attrition was brutal. In 1909, eighteen new firms began building cars. In 1910, eighteen went belly up, and only one entered the fray.

Bankers worried about exposure. The automobile business was in the hands of folksy tinkers in over their heads (Ford, Olds), glib four-flushers (Durant), and 300 lesser entrepreneurs, all basically making the same product, all with little follow-through for customer service. A speaker at a bankers' convention warned that the finances of many car manufacturers were shaky and their spending reckless. If bankers were not prudent, he added balefully, a financial panic was a distinct possibility. After all, what was General Motors if not a holding; that is, a company created to hold the shares of an increasingly bewildering number of companies but not itself making anything.

And it was a one-man show. If bankers didn't realize it, a glance at the November 1910 *Motor World* would enlighten them. The magazine summed up GM's first two years:

> It was quickly made plain that General Motors was a "one-man" institution. Durant was its general and he was his own colonel, his own major and his own lieutenant. He dominated it from top to bottom and brooked no interference. He is a prodigious worker and the wonder is how he attended to so many details, great and small, and lived through it all. He kept one eye on his factories and another on the stock ticker, and the while he dreamed of world conquests.

The companies in the GM fold could not build cars fast enough. The top-of-the-line Cadillacs sold like hotcakes, and night shifts were added at Buick. In February 1908, the Buick factory on West Kearsley had started building engines seven days a week, and supplied car assemblies to the new Hamilton plant, where workers also worked overtime. By March, 2,100 employees turned out fifty cars a day. To increase the output to eighty cars a day, Durant hired 350 more workers. In November, Buick announced that it needed a thousand more workers, and even then could not fill back orders until the following July. And GM expanded overseas. Buick chassis were shipped to Bedford Motors in London, where coachwork was added and the cars were sold under the name Bedford Buick. In 1912 the name was changed to General Motors (Europe).

܍

But, like Ford, Durant needed to expand. A year after Ford launched his beloved Model T in 1908, production reached 78,000, only to double again the following year.

In March 1910, GM floated a million-dollar stock issue to build a new engine plant. Durant took the opportunity to tell stockholders that "General Motors securities are valuable to hold as a permanent investment." Buick employees certainly believed their boss because they signed up for $122,000 themselves. Flint's four banks subscribed $380,000, and the remaining half million was raised from banks in Detroit, Cincinnati, and New York City. The appraised value of Buick alone, Durant wrote in a GM publication, was $17 million. In a letter to holders of GM preferred stock, however, he said the stock was undervalued because brokers traded "for their own personal gain." The letter was ill advised. It was impolitic to accuse the people who were going to raise capital for him of speculating against him. In April, the ground began shifting under his feet. The cause was a market correction, but it shook the overleveraged auto business to its roots.

Nervous banks cut off credit needed to buy supplies and pay workers, and the Buick, Cadillac, and Oldsmobile divisions were forced to close. Durant joggled while creditors assessed Buick's debt alone to be between $6.7 and $7.7

A 1910 Buick

million. Meeting in New York City, the creditors named a committee to reorganize management and to apply "a restriction of enthusiasm."

A restriction of enthusiasm? Billy was livid. "By May 1st, our bank loans were all called and we were deprived of every dollar of working capital—the lifeblood of our institutions—which brought about the complete stoppage of our business with a loss to us of more than $60,000 a day."

Two Detroit banks loaned GM half a million so it could meet a Cadillac payroll while loyal dealers slipped suitcases of cash to Flint—money could not be transferred through bank accounts since it would be seized to cover overdrafts. Loans were floated. Next, Durant hit the road, and managed to borrow $8 million in $100,000 and $200,000 installments from a number of country banks which had once financed his buggy and wagon dealers. A. B. C. Hardy, who traveled with him and Arnold Goss, told how, in a drenching rainstorm, their train stopped in Elkhart, Indiana. "Far down the dark and dismal street shone one electric sign—

BANK," Hardy would remember. "Durant shook Goss, who was dozing dejectedly in a corner. 'Wake up, Goss,' said Durant. 'There's one we missed.'"

Willie also summoned Wilfred Leland to visit banks with him. In his memoirs, the younger Leland would recall these trips:

> In each instance he would introduce me to the president of the bank or to the officer with whom he was in the habit of carrying on business relations. He would explain with evident satisfaction that General Motors had acquired Cadillac, and that he wanted the bank official to become acquainted with me and wanted me to tell him a little about the financial condition of Cadillac. I would then give a résumé of Cadillac affairs and would make needed explanations and answer questions that might be asked.
>
> We made trips to many different banks and in every instance, the substance of the statement made by the bank official was, "Well, Mr. Leland, if the Cadillac stood alone, we would be glad to loan up to the limit. But the Cadillac is now a part of General Motors and is involved in all the complications and entanglements of that organization and we cannot loan a dollar."

GM was now a collection of some twenty-five firms, some partly and most wholly owned, making automobiles, taxicabs, parts, and accessories, and straddling the Canadian border. One of Billy's better moves was to buy a 40 percent interest in the McLaughlin Motor Car Company of Oshawa, Ontario. Durant knew Samuel McLaughlin from their carriage days, and in 1905 convinced McLaughlin to make Buicks under license. The McLaughlin Company became the foundation of General Motors of Canada. Sam McLaughlin was still its chairman when, in 1972, he died at age 100.

If Cadillac, Oakland (Pontiac), Olds, A.C. spark plugs,

and McLaughlin were solid gold, a couple of the acquisitions were little more than long odds bets on innovations. The Cartercar Company of Pontiac owned a patent on a friction drive that Byron T. Carter hoped would eliminate gearshifting, and the Elmore Company of Clyde, Ohio, made a 2-cylinder engine used in motorboats. Durant's worst buy was the Heany Lamp Company in York, Pennsylvania. John Albert Heany claimed he was the inventor of the tungsten filament in electric lightbulbs, but his patent rights were cloudy and eventually voided. Moreover, the company was losing money. Within four months of the purchase, GM had to pump money into Heany.

The list of firms and plants Durant had folded into GM over an extraordinary year and a half included:

Buick Motor Company, Flint
W. F. Stewart Company plant number 4, Flint
Olds Motor Works, Lansing
Seagar Engine Works, Lansing
Oakland Motor Car Company, Pontiac
Marquette Motor Company, Saginaw
Cadillac Motor Company, Detroit
Michigan Motor Casting Company, Flint
Randolph Truck Company, Flint
Champion Ignition Company, Flint
Reliance Motor Truck Company, Owosso, Michigan
Rainier Motor Company, Saginaw
Welch Motor Car Company, Pontiac
Welch-Detroit Company, Detroit
Jackson-Church-Wilcox Company, Jackson, Michigan
Michigan Auto Parts Company, Detroit
Rapid Motor Vehicle Company, Pontiac
Cartercar Company, Pontiac
Ewing Automobile, Geneva, Ohio
Elmore Manufacturing Company, Clyde, Ohio
Dow Rim Company, New York City
Northway Motor & Manufacturing Company, Detroit
Bedford Motors Company, London, England

National Motor Cab Company
Novelty Incandescent Lamp Company
Heany Lamp Company, York, Pennsylvania
Brown-Lipe-Chapin Company, Syracuse, New York
Oak Park Power Company, Flint

Durant also bought Weston-Mott stock until GM owned 49 percent, and contracted for a ten-year supply of Buick axles. Charles Mott was mayor of Flint in 1913, when GM acquired the rest of Weston-Mott and made him the wealthiest man in Michigan.

General Motors was an exercise in monetary acrobatics. John Carton, Durant's old friend and lawyer, warned Billy that buying dubious assets like Heany Lamp in order to issue more stock bordered on investor fraud. Decades later, Carton would say, "Billy never thought that General Motors would become the big manufacturer that it did, what [he] desired, most of all, were large stock issues in which he, from an inside position, could dicker and trade."

Echoes of Billy's father?

∽०∾

By 1910 there was not enough money to finance expansions and purchase supplies, and a sudden dip in economic confidence brought General Motors to the brink of collapse. Willie thought of a five-for-one stock split to throw more shares on the market, then decided against it as too slow and too late. While a GM director approached the Boston investment house of Lee, Higginson and Company, Willie got the board to authorize the sale of Welch-Detroit and the component supplier, the Michigan Auto Parts Company. Marquette Motor, the racing car specialist in Saginaw, was also put up for sale.

In New York City, Kuhn, Loeb and Company turned

down Durant. In Chicago, Continental Savings and Trust Company was ready to lend $7.5 million, and later $9.5 million, but backed away because GM lacked a central bookkeeping system. This was an eye-opener to the GM board of directors as well. To their discomfort, they discovered they couldn't determine how much money was owed or needed. On September 19, the board admitted there was no reliable record of GM's debt. It was agreed that in the absence of a $12 million loan to "muddle through," bankruptcy was days, perhaps only hours, away.

Lights burned late at Durant's Buick office. Hoping for a scoop or at least a hint of the drama, Art Sarvis, a *Flint Journal* reporter, made it a habit to linger in a downtown restaurant until the wee hours when, on his way home, "the Man" usually stopped for one more cup of coffee. On an occasion when Sarvis was interviewing Durant in his office, they were interrupted by a phone call. Sarvis realized the voice at the other end was that of a banker because the conversation was about a multimillion-dollar loan. The banker obviously feared a market glut, because Durant suddenly interrupted him, saying, "No sir, there is no such thing as a saturation point—not until every man, woman, and eligible child in the country has an automobile!" To keep up the value of GM shares, Willie issued appeals to stockholders not to sell, telling them big things were in the wind. He issued flyers from what was called the General Motors Securities Company in New York City, pointing out that while the shares of U.S. Steel, International Harvester, General Electric, American Car and Foundry, and other major industrials had dropped six to ten points in June, General Motors common stock had advanced five points.

Cadillac was the most profitable division, and Wilfred Leland joined Durant at a decisive September 25 meeting with investment bankers at the Chase National Bank in New York City. J. C. Van Cleaf, vice president of the

National Park Bank, presided. Leland would have a vivid
memory of the seating arrangement and the opening salvos:

> The directors' table was lined with the representatives
> of the various banks. Mr. Durant and the heads of the
> active units of General Motors were seated a little dis-
> tance to the side ready to answer the questions. . . . The
> bankers maintained a very critical attitude toward Mr.
> Durant, their sharpest criticism directed toward the af-
> fairs of the Buick Motor Company and its indebtedness
> of $8,000,000. As the discussions proceeded, the bankers
> voiced their disapproval one by one; a banker would say,
> "I cannot lend any more," or "I will not extend my loan
> another day." General Motors was a sinking ship to which
> no one offered sympathy or a helping hand.

To weather the crisis, Durant told the bankers, GM
needed $15 million in fresh loans. He turned over the pre-
sentation of the Buick finances to Arnold Goss. Buick could
report high sales. Unfortunately, Goss admitted under
questioning, low earnings and mounting debt would offset
the sales. It didn't look good.

The day dragged on. By four in the afternoon, Van
Cleaf turned to Leland, saying they had not heard from
the Cadillac division. In 40 minutes, Leland turned everything around. The bankers liked his report on Cadillac's
operations and profits. Cadillac, he said, had been in operation longer than any of the others, and had always made
money. The meeting adjourned at 6 P.M. until ten the next
morning. As Leland was about to leave, Van Cleaf asked
him to wait while some of the bankers met in executive
session. Half an hour later, Van Cleaf came out and told
Leland that the Cadillac presentation had convinced them
the collapse of GM was perhaps not inevitable. "The operations you have explained to us have deeply interested us."

Leland—not Durant—was invited to meet at the Belmont Hotel with a committee of five bankers. Instead of

thinking of how to liquidate General Motors, they should all concentrate on how it could be saved. "After all, Cadillac alone was earning almost two million a year and General Motors had made ten million," he would remember saying. "Surely fifteen million is not such a great sum to loan to a business earning at that rate." By midnight, everybody was for a rescue. At 2:30 A.M., a $15 million package was put together by the New York investment houses of J. and W. Seligman and Boston's Lee, Higginson. The meeting broke up with Leland being instructed not to talk to Durant until everybody reconvened again at 10 A.M.

We do not know whether in the middle of the night Leland made a quiet phone call to his chairman. What we do know is that when everybody reconvened, Durant showed the strain of a night of anxiety. He had feared the worst and would later say that the bankers' proposal to save GM was "the surprise of my life."

The terms were stiff. Control of GM was put in the hands of a board of five trustees, three of whom were representatives of the bankers. They were James Wallace, president of the Central Trust of New York, Frederick Strauss of J. W. Seligman and Company, and Anthony N. Brady, owner of gas and electric companies and trolley lines in New York City, Philadelphia, Washington, Utica, New York, and Albany. The trustees elected Boston banker James Jackson Storrow interim president with final word on policy and administration. Durant remained vice president. To make room for Wallace, Strauss, and Brady, who, for the length of the loan, would handle day-to-day operations, they demanded the resignation not only of Durant's son-in-law Ed and three other board members, but also of Wilfred Leland, who had made them think rescue instead of liquidation.

Storrow of Lee, Higginson and Company was an old-line Boston Yankee. His mother's ancestors included Oliver H. Perry, one of the heroes of the War of 1812. On his paternal side, his grandfather was a civil engineer, and his father a lawyer who had won a major patent case for Alexander Graham Bell. Young James had followed his father's footsteps and, after graduating from Harvard Law School, passed all the expected milestones—marriage, a child, a town house on Beacon Hill, and a country home near Waltham. Lee, Higginson was an old-line investment firm, founded in 1848 by John Clarke Lee and George Higginson. From 1865 to 1900, the partnership's principal business had been securities for western railroads and the first public offering of American Telegraph and Telephone. As interim president of the bundled Michigan car manufacturers, Storrow was in over his head. He had enough sense, however, to realize he needed an insider to run the Flint operations. His choice for president of Buick was, at Willie's recommendation, Charles Nash. Since Charlie had started as a blacksmith at the Flint Road Cart Company twenty years earlier, he had worked himself up to superintendent of Durant-Dort operations, then moved to Buick to fill the vacuum that Billy's empire building left behind in Flint. People wondered what the Beacon Hill Brahmin and the Illinois orphan who still kept the first nickel he had earned had in common. The match was fortuitous. Nash felt comfortable with Storrow's conservative perspective, and the banker soon relished Nash's economizing talent and distaste for waste. Together, they immediately agreed to cut executive salaries in half, including Charlie's own.

Durant was dismayed at the bankers' lack of appreciation of what he had wrought. What was especially galling was that from a production standpoint, 1910 turned out to be a banner year. The *Wall Street Journal* echoed his sentiment in its October 6, 1910, edition, quoting a member of the voting trust: "We have been looking into the company's affairs for sometime, and have found it a paying proposition, its only trouble having been overenthusiasm on the part of its managers. . . . We believe the future of the company is all that could be desired."

There were lessons to go around for both sides. The bankers realized the strength and potential of the young industry. When Seligman and Lee, Higginson floated the $15 million loan in five-year notes yielding 6 percent, the institutions represented at the Chase Bank conference snapped them up before a public offering could be made. The capitalization of GM by the country's leading banks showed the financial markets there were investment opportunities in the automobile industry. Within months, investment bankers were willing to underwrite loans extending over a period of years.

Willie was still the vice president of General Motors, and although he was powerless to stop the board from selling off unprofitable subsidiaries, only he knew his "baby" and its complexity. In notes written for his autobiography thirty years later, he deplored the fact that the bankers had taken from him his gift for "quick decision and leadership":

Many of the new men, friends of the parties in control (splendid men, no doubt, in lines in which they were familiar), never having had experience in, or with, automobile design and production, with ideas of their own as to how business should be run, training in banking rather than practical lines, made my position a difficult one, and I realized that I was up against a real problem.

I discovered also that some of my own organization "weak sisters," so to speak, men who felt that they could lift themselves up by catering to the "powers that be," were not quite 100 percent (Have you ever found a large organization where you could absolutely count on every man in it?). Although I wished to please and be cooperative, I felt that I could not adapt myself to the situation, which I alone had created, and that I was wasting my time. I had been given a title and a position, but the support, the cooperation, the spirit, the unselfishness that is needed in every successful undertaking, was not there. In a way, it was the same old story, "too many cooks"; a board of directors comprised of bankers, action by committees, and the lack of knowledge that comes only with experience. I saw some of my cherished ideas laid aside for future action, never to be revived. Opportunities that should have been taken care of with quickness and decision were not considered. The things that counted so much in the past, which gave General Motors its unique and powerful position, were subordinated to "liquidate and pay." Pay whom and for what? The people who took control of the business and received $9.5 million in cash and securities as a commission for a five-year loan of $12,250,000.

The lessons for the industry and for Durant were Darwinian. Market forces ruthlessly weeded out the weak. There were 300 carmakers in 1910. By the outbreak of World War I four years later, there were 50. The lesson for Billy was that the sources of capital available to him diminished in proportion to the success of his consolidation. He depended on a shrinking reservoir of big money and had pitted himself against forces whose powers to undo him he had refused to see.

15

⌒⊙⌒

A "New Baby"

It was nothing new for father to begin again. I think it is only fair to say that he had already started off with a clean slate at least a dozen times in the thirty years since he had left school. The average man measures the size and importance of "beginning again" by the amount of money involved or the distance of the goal to be attained. He is influenced by doubts that he may be overwhelmed by debt or exhausted by the distance he has to travel.

Not so my father. His philosophy took little heed of either money or distance in the sense of obstacles to his ideal. When in his early days he ceased to sell real estate and traveled for a cigar manufacturer he was moving in a definite direction. So again, in 1910, when he found himself free from the burden of General Motors he shifted to a new line of endeavor with quiet assurance that it was the next step in the direction he wished his life to go.

Willie didn't care much for *My Father,* the book Margery wrote and G. P. Putnam published in 1929. He thought it too gushing, too saccharine.

139

In her introduction to the formation of the Chevrolet Motor Company, she described Pops as the man who had sat at the head of the table: "To his desk came men from all over the country, asking favors, begging him to buy, wanting his advice. A thousand things conspired to make him arrogant."

A sharper assessment of Durant appeared in the November 1910 issue of *Motor World:*

> To say that every thinking person identified with the automobile industry is breathing more freely now that the banking interests have stepped in on W.C. Durant, the prime mover and directing genius of the General Motors Co., is but to describe mildly the feeling that exists. The feeling is . . . that an element of real peril to the entire industry has been circumvented and chastened. To have a bit and checkrein placed between his teeth must saw sorely on the mouth of Durant himself. He now is in the toils of Wall Street, so to speak, and must do its bidding.

All James Storrow and the banks wanted was to have GM pay back the $15 million so they could retire from the company. They demanded that Durant, in addition to his vice presidency, accept the chairmanship of a new finance committee. His buying spree and his financial sleight of hand were the areas where he was most heavily criticized. Giving him the chairmanship was an admission that they needed him. He was uncomfortable sitting in on finance committee meetings whose sole function was to liquidate his acquisitions. The bankers wanted to ax everything but the two most profitable companies, Buick and Cadillac, but old Henry Leland persuaded them to keep the group alive. Nevertheless, the Cartercar, Elmore, Ewing, and Rainier divisions were written off and sold for scrap metal. "They say I shouldn't have bought the Cartercar," Durant told A. B. C. Hardy. "Well, how was anyone to know the Carter wasn't the thing? It had friction drive and no other car had it. How could I tell what these engineers would say next? And then there's Elmore, with its 2-cycle engine. That's the kind they were using on motorboats; maybe 2-cycles was going to be the thing for automobiles. I was for getting every car in sight, playing safe all along the line."

Not all the bankers saw Durant as the villain of the play. Twenty years later, Storrow's biographer would quote a New York banker as remembering Durant as a "genius," very unlike ordinary businessmen:

> In many respects he is a child in emotions, in temperament and in mental balance, yet possessed of wonderful energy and ability along with certain other well-defined lines. He is sensitive and proud, and successful leadership, I think, really counts more with him than financial success.

Storrow saw the dangers in splintering the Durant GM into factions. Cracks happened anyway with the new management's decision to discontinue the Buick Model 10. Abandoning the Model 10, Willie realized, meant giving up the under-$1,000 market to Henry Ford's Model T.

Instead of getting mad, he decided to get even. He'd make his own small, inexpensive Model 10s. For $200,000 on 5 percent promissory notes, he picked up the old Front Wagon Works factory where the first Flint Buicks had been built. The West Kearsley Street property came with buildings, land, assembly bays, equipment, axles, wheels, and an inventory of Buick stationary engines. On August 31, 1911, he incorporated the Mason Motor Company, installed Arthur C. Mason on West Kearsley, and had the onetime Buick manager and developer of the first high-compression engine go to work on an innovative engine design. A month later, Durant founded the Little Motor Car Company, and in the West Kearsley plant made space for Big Bill Little to start making Little runabouts. The power train for the Little cars would be Mason engines.

Storrow realized he was no match for the volatile automobile business, and after two months he and his bankers resigned in favor of a slate of Detroit businessmen. Thomas Neal, manager of Acme Lead and Color Works, became president; James Shaw, with an accounting background, was named treasurer. Durant continued in the office of vice president. At the bankers' insistence, GM applied for and received permission to list its stock on the New York Stock Exchange.

☙◦❧

Demand for automobiles continued to expand but the industry was roiled by conflicts during the winter of 1910–1911. Henry Ford and Ransom Olds had wanted out two years earlier when Durant had sparred with J. Pierpont Morgan. Now Ford was the industry leader—18,664 Model Ts were sold in 1909—and Oldsmobile was one of the weaker cards of the GM deck. For 1910, the division came out with a colossal 6-cylinder car, which carried its 12-foot wheelbase aloft on 42-inch wheels. To climb aboard, driver and passengers had to negotiate a double-stepped running board. One of the cars raced the Twentieth Century Limited express from New York to Albany—and won—after which the model took the name Limited. The behemoth was discontinued a year later.

Like the rising movie moguls out in Hollywood, what Billy needed was a hit.

☙◦❧

Racing had taught Louis Chevrolet a lot about what made a car reliable. "Since dependability was the major problem with cars at this time," Richard Crabb would write, "Chevrolet believed he could develop a better car." In October 1910, Durant went to see Chevrolet and asked him if he was interested in becoming an automobile designer. Billy explained that what he was after was a vehicle along the French light car lines. Louis nodded, and Billy set him up in a small garage at 3939 Grand River Avenue in Detroit. The way Billy saw it, Louis had never designed a car before, but he had plunged his hands in enough engines and solved enough automobile problems to qualify.

Louis hired Etienne Planche, a Frenchman he had worked with in a Brooklyn car shop ten years earlier. Planche had designed the Roebling-Planche, the forerunner of the Spartan American Mercer, and during the winter of 1910–1911, the pair designed and built a 6-cylinder prototype that Billy okayed.

On May 30, 1911, a press release spelled out the news:

W. C. Durant of the General Motors company and racer Louis Chevrolet, one of the speed wonders of the day and a co-worker with Mr. Durant in the manufacture and exploitation of fast cars, will establish a factory in Detroit for the manufacture of a new high-priced car.

Omitted from the press release was the understanding that while Billy would finance the new company, Louie's payment would be 100 shares of its stock. Since it was increasingly important to be present in Detroit, a large garage was rented on West Grand Boulevard for the Chevrolet Motor Car Company, which was to assemble 6-cylinder cars from purchased components. While Louis and Etienne perfected the prototype, Durant sent Big Bill Little to Detroit to help out.

Durant raised money in Flint. The town had kept its affection for its favorite son and this time bankrolled him to the tune of $825,000 to start up not only for Chevrolet Motor Car, but also for a brand new engine plant. The

Mason Motor Company would make the power plants for the Chevrolet cars and upgrade the Little engine.

With the Buick workforce cut back, Little and Mason had no trouble hiring experienced workers. Priced at $650, 2,500 of the 4-cylinder Little roadsters were sold in the first year.

∽०∾

An accident on Detroit's Isle Park Bridge on a December day in 1910 got Henry Leland in such a funk that he regretted he had ever built a car. On reflection, he decided to find the solution. A woman driver stalled on the ramp to the bridge. A passing motorist stopped to help. He was Byron T. Carter, of the late GM Cartercar division. He cranked the motor for the woman, but did not realize that the spark had not been delayed. The engine backfired and the crank broke his arm and smashed his face and jaw. Two Cadillac engineers out driving with their wives stopped to assist. They started the woman's car, sent her home, and took the injured Carter to the hospital. Although Carter's jaw and arm did not seem to be serious injuries, he died a few weeks later of gangrene and pneumonia.

Durant—and the rest of the industry—realized that if cars were to have a future, a self-starter had to be invented. Not that engineers hadn't tried, some with springs, others with acetylene gas, still others with compressed air and tire pumps. But most agreed the answer probably was electrical. The question was who would be first.

Henry Leland called his engineers together and told them they had a big job to do. "The Cadillac car will kill no more men if we can help it," he told the morning get-together. "Lay all the other projects aside. We are going to develop a fool-proof device for starting Cadillac motors."

Wilfred Leland told Earl Howard, his assistant sales

manager, of the project. Howard remembered that when he worked at the National Cash Register Company in Dayton, Ohio, an engineer named Charles Kettering had invented a very small electric motor for operating cash registers. Perhaps Kettering's experience, he suggested, was the answer. Wilfred got on the phone and called Kettering in Dayton. The next day, Kettering came to Detroit.

Young Kettering had been destined for the ministry and was already in divinity school when he convinced his parents he could perhaps better serve God by devoting himself to engineering. He went to work for the National Cash Register Company, and made profitable improvements in its products. With Edward A. Deeds, who had built a car from a kit in his backyard, Kettering set up the Dayton Engineering Laboratories Company, or Delco, in 1908 to develop, test and market innovations. The Delco team worked in Deeds's barn-turned-machine shop until all hours. Olive Kettering supplied the coffee and sandwiches to keep husband and "barn gang" going.

On January 6, 1911, Howard shipped a Cadillac to Dayton for Kettering to work on. Cars already had electrical components for lighting and ignition, and Kettering realized *how* these systems worked together was the key. By trial and error the Delco engineers came up with a gearing mechanism that allowed the generator to run on a 1:1 ratio with the engine when the car was driving, but which could be geared up for more torque during the starting process. The barn gang finished a miniaturized starting-generating system on January 14 that ran perfectly over 100 trials. On February 8, they installed the unit in the Cadillac, worked out several bugs, and, a week later, sent the car back to Detroit for the Lelands' testing and approval. Four months later, Cadillac committed to the self-starter, and by November, Leland ordered 12,000 starting, lighting, and ignition systems from Delco.

Five years later, for $5 million in cash and $3 million in stock, Durant brought Delco into the GM fold.

∽o∾

The Little and Mason companies were moving forward in Flint, and on November 28, 1911, the city gave Billy a bash that became known as the Wizard's Banquet. One hundred fifty people came together at the Masonic Temple for the tribute to the town hero. While community notables sang Durant's praise, male guests were offered Flint-made cigars of the kind Billy had once sold 22,000 of on one trip to Port Huron, Michigan. The Havanas came in boxes with Durant's portrait and the mock label "El Capital de Industria." In gratitude, Billy declared with some poetic license, "Do not think that I have left Flint and am coming back. I never have been away from this city."

∽o∾

Louis Chevrolet and his team had their first prototype ready in late 1911. He tested it secretly at four in the morning on a road outside Detroit, hitting 110 mph. On his way back, he was stopped by a roadblock, hauled off to jail, and, before the local magistrate, fined $30—$5 for speeding and $25 for impersonating himself as a famous race driver.

Billy was less than overwhelmed. He found the prototype too big and too expensive, but he was so anxious to get it on the market for the spring sales period that he ordered it into production. He asked Bill Little to come down to Detroit and help out while A. B. C. Hardy came on board to assume management of Little and Mason Motors.

Built largely with credit from firms supplying materials

and parts, the car was called the Chevrolet Classic 6. It was a luxurious 6-cylinder touring car big enough to carry five passengers. Its size and power played on Louis Chevrolet's celebrity as the beefy racecar driver who had set records with some of the most powerful machines ever built. The Classic 6 sold at the factory gate for a steep $2,150. In a tribute to Louis' fame and Billy's salesmanship, the small shop built and sold 3,000 of these cars in 1912. Louis joined the sales campaign. He placed a pencil on the motor and asked a reporter to watch while he revved up to 2,000 rpm. The pencil didn't move. This was possible, he explained, because of a crankshaft design that kept the weight of the reciprocating parts to a minimum and featured integral counterweights, which acted as supplemental flywheels.

To give him cash, Dallas Dort overcame earlier qualms and became a backer of his old partner. It was now 25 years ago that Billy and Dallas had started out with one finished cart and a lot of enthusiasm, but for makers of horse-drawn buggies the end was nigh. Between 1910 and 1911 stockholders in the Durant-Dort Carriage Company had seen their profits drop by $100,000, and everyone was eager to convert their remaining assets into the stock of Durant's new companies. The stockholders approved a subscription to Chevrolet Motor stock for $1,225,000. Dallas became a vice president.

Willie had one more card up his sleeve. Taking the automotive world by storm one more time, he launched the Republic Motor Company, first in Delaware, the favored home of holding companies, then in New York, and finally in Michigan. Republic would be the umbrella of the Mason, Little, and Chevrolet companies and, in Willie's mind, soon rival General Motors. His allies included his son-in-law Ed Campbell, Dort, Little, and Curtis Hatheway, the young Ward, Hayden and Satterlee attorney who four years earlier had filed the GM articles of incorporation. Announcing the formation of Republic in its July 11, 1912, issue, *Motor World* reported:

> W. C. Durant is again on the road to complete happiness. It is no secret that since control of $40,000,000 General Motors Company passed out of his hands, Durant has been restless—so restless that he has placed irons of his own in the fire, among them Chevrolet Motor Company in Detroit and Little Motor Company in Flint; and these are to form the basis of a $65,000,000 corporation which, to all practical purposes, will be Durant's own.

A plant to assemble Little cars was soon opened in New York City. Other factories were planned for Philadelphia, Boston, Cincinnati, Saint Louis, Minneapolis, Kansas City, Portland, San Francisco, and Los Angeles. To impress investors more than anything else, Billy bought a factory site on Woodward Avenue in Highland Park, Michigan, directly across from the Ford Motor Company. Here he erected a large billboard. On this site, it proclaimed, the Chevrolet Motor Company would build a "large, completely modern factory."

No such plant was ever built. In the excitement over the Chevrolet launch, the Mason and Little successes, and the recovery of Buick, Olds, and Cadillac (the Kettering self-starter brought women into the car market for the first time), Willie realized that although GM's renewed strength was more than enough to pay off the $15 million loan, the bankers had no intention of giving up control.

16

∽o∾

Back in the Saddle

When Walter Chrysler joined General Motors, Durant immediately charmed him. As Chrysler would write in his memoirs:

> I cannot hope to find words to express the charm of the man. He has the most winning personality of anyone I've ever known. He could coax a bird right down out of a tree, I think. I remember the first time my wife and I entered his home. . . . In five minutes he had me feeling as if I owned the place.

Chrysler was making $12,000 a year managing the American Locomotive Company works in Pittsburgh, and he was less than impressed when James J. Storrow asked him to become the works manager of Buick Motor Company for $6,000 a year. Charles Nash was the CEO of General Motors, hard working and compliant with orders from the bankers to whom he owed his rise. It was therefore Storrow, not Nash, who discovered Chrysler and asked the railroad manager to run Buick. Working for half his American

Locomotive salary was not exactly an enticement, but Chrysler wanted to get into the automobile business. He accepted Storrow's offer, and moved himself, his wife Della, and their four children to Flint.

Durant could afford to be charming. He was exactly where he wanted to be. He was his own man at Chevrolet, Mason, and Little, and, albeit the shunted-aside vice president of General Motors, he was very much on the inside of the big company he still considered his "baby." A daring idea occurred to him. Instead of turning Republic into a national organization the hard way by building plants and distributorships in New York, Philadelphia, Boston, Cincinnati, and a half dozen other cities, why not snatch back GM?

The dateline for paying off the banks was approaching, and in early 1913, he began quietly buying up GM stock. His plan depended on an expansion of motorcar ownership that he, better than the bankers, sensed was just around the corner. The way to do it was obvious. First, he would use his growing GM stock as security to meld the Little and Chevrolet companies into one. With national distribution of the Chevrolet, he would launch a "name" as muscular as Buick or Ford. With this new firm's earnings, he would trade Chevrolet stock for GM common stock. When he, his friends, and the Chevrolet Motor Car Company obtained 51 percent of GM's outstanding common stock, he would walk into the GM boardroom and stage a palace coup.

In August 1913, he began to put his plan in motion. While Louis Chevrolet was in France, Durant moved the Chevrolet Detroit plant to Flint, merged it with the Little company, and put A. B. C. Hardy in charge. The cold figures spelled out the reason for a merger: the Little Six was making money, the big Chevrolet Classic 6 was not. When Louis returned from his holiday in France, he was not pleased. Everything was different from the way it had been before he left. He was left out of the loop. He swallowed his pride, however, and stayed on, jealous of Hardy, who wanted to rename the car because Chevrolet was too hard on American tongues.

Durant told A. B. C. it was too late to rename the car. Billy tried to keep Louis happy by suggesting he work on a smaller 6-cylinder engine for the Little. Louis felt humiliated. His name was associated with achieving big and impossible things. In December, he blew up over a comment Billy made about his famous cigarettes. Louis should give up his cigarettes for cigars, Billy suggested, because cigars were more dignified for a corporate official. Furious, Louis snapped, "I sold you my car and I sold you my name, but I'm not going to sell myself to you. I'm going to smoke my cigarettes as much as I want. And I'm getting out."

In a huff that mirrored David Buick's departure, he quit the world of Billy Durant. By coincidence, Walter Marr left Buick at about the same time. Ill health forced Marr to resign as chief engineer and to retire to the Blue Ridge Mountain resort of Signal Mountain, Tennessee. He still kept his association with the company, however, and new Buick models were submitted for his approval at Signal Mountain.

Foolishly, Chevrolet sold his sizable stake to Durant for a modest sum, went back to the speedways, and built powerful new racecars. He founded the Frontenac Motor Company in 1914, and was sporadically successful—his Frontenac racer won the Indianapolis 500 in 1920. He later joined forces with Glenn Martin, a Baltimore Ford dealer, to build airplane engines. Louis designed and won a patent for a 10-cylinder radial Chevrolair aircraft engine in 1932, but the Great Depression sank the enterprise. His two wins at the Indy 500 were the source of his pride in later years, never the millions of cars that bore his name. He died at sixty-two in 1941, and was buried in Indianapolis, the city of his racing triumphs.

∽○∽

Durant sold the factory site in Highland Park, Michigan, on which he had planned to build the new Chevrolet factory, and bought the entire block between Fifty-sixth and Fifty-seventh Streets on Eleventh Avenue on Manhattan's West Side. To ship parts by railroad from Flint and Detroit to the assembly floor in New York City was not expensive, but the point of building cars in Manhattan was not economics but publicity or "stagecraft," as one of Durant's advertising directors put it, to impress Wall Street and opinion leaders. Advertisements invited people to visit the factory "in the heart of New York City, four blocks from Broadway." In his notes for his autobiography, Durant observed: "Grownup people are very much like children in many respects. They like to see the wheel go 'round."

In the merry-go-round of names, the Little metamorphosed into the Chevrolet—the last of the Little automobiles were built during the summer of 1913, a few months before the first valve-in-head Chevrolets were introduced—and the Republic Motor Company changed into the Chevrolet Motor Company.

The two Chevrolet models launched in 1914 started an extraordinary run for Billy. The Baby Grand was the last of the big Chevrolets, and the Royal Mail Roadster the first of the Little cars with the Chevrolet name. The Baby Grand sold for $875, a bit more than Henry Ford's Model T, which cost $850 (a teacher's annual salary). At $750, the Royal Mail cost $100 less than a Tin Lizzie. Durant liked to say he got the idea of the bow tie nameplate while he and Catherine were on a trip to France shortly after their marriage. He saw the bow tie motif on the wallpaper in a Paris hotel, and arranged to get a small sample. But Catherine remembered it differently: Billy spotted the bow tie in the rotogravure section of a Sunday newspaper while they vacationed in Hot Springs, Virginia.

Test driver Homer Hartwick at the wheel of a 6-cylinder Little Motor, 1914

Durant wanted the new car to have a distinct identity of its own, and to highlight the Chevy individuality, hired Jacob ("Jake") Newmark as his advertising chief. They had known each other since 1908, when Newmark became the advertising manager of the Oakland Motor Car Company. For the next 25 years, they would be in almost daily contact.

Thus bow ties emblazoned the radiators of the 1914 models, and Newmark's advertising hinted the new car would be a worthy competitor to Ralph de Palma's Grand Prix Mercedes. "The Chevrolet which finished second place was built in the New York factory in 29 hours at a cost of less than $1,250," one ad warbled. "It beat cars costing nearly ten times that amount."

Besides costs, building cars on the West Side of Manhattan was a mixed blessing. The area around Fifty-seventh Street and Eleventh Avenue was known as Murderers' Row, and after street thugs tried to shake down his workers at the end of night shifts, Billy had to buy protection from both the hoodlums and Tammany Hall politicians. On the

A 1914 Chevrolet touring car shown at the 1933 Chicago World's Fair

positive side, he had a place to show off to bankers. The Royal Mail was driven around Central Park for 27.9 miles on one measured gallon of gasoline.

Durant's need for capital to finance the Chevrolet's explosive growth was unremitting. In May 1914, he wrote to his old Flint banker friend Arthur Bishop suggesting that between $100,000 and $200,000 be raised to buy out Arthur Mason. Seeing his name on the hood of cars went to the head of Mason, who less than ten years before had put that same head on the engine block of his 4,000 rpm motor and told Billy, "Start it up. If it goes, I may as well go with it." Now Durant wrote to Bishop, "It occurred to me that if we could find a tactful and diplomatic party with capital, who would be willing to go in and help Mason, supplying capital for Mason under a contract which would amply protect both parties, that the desired result would be accomplished and everybody satisfied and happy." The money was found and the Chevy output soared to 63,000 cars in 1916, and nearly doubling again in 1917 to 111,500 cars. Much of the financing was short-term, tie-over loans extended by Louis Graveret Kaufman, president of the Chatham and Phoenix and Marquette National Bank of New York City.

Kaufman was another self-made man from Michigan. From shoveling ore in the iron-mining town of Marquette, he had become the mine's superintendent, and, at twenty-five, graduated to banking at the Marquette County Savings Bank. In New York, he had taken over the Chatham National Bank, merged it with the Phoenix National, and developed the novel concept of opening branches within the city. He gloried in the fact that antitrust regulators in Washington had allowed him to remain president of Chatham and Phoenix and Marquette National Bank, and liked to tell people that one of his directors was the brother of Mrs. Woodrow Wilson. When Durant and Kaufman met for the first time in the latter's Ritz-Carlton suite in early 1914, and the banker finally got around to asking the Chevrolet boss how much he needed to borrow, the answer was to the point. "Eventually, we can use many times the capital and surplus of your bank. But for the present, five million will do."

With a loan from Kaufman, the Chevrolet Motor Company bought the Maxwell Motor Company's factory in Tarrytown, New York, and opened regional sales headquarters in Atlanta, Saint Louis, Kansas City, and Oshawa, Ontario. Sam McLaughlin was assembling Buicks in Oshawa, and, at his father's insistence, still making horse-drawn farm wagons. Over dinner at Pabst's Restaurant on Columbus Circle in New York, McLaughlin said only two things prevented him from building Chevrolets—lack of space and his father's possible reluctance to admit the end of the horse-and-buggy era. Billy got "Governor" George McLaughlin on the phone long distance and persuaded him to end the carriage business and let his son build Chevrolets instead. Two months later, the first Canadian-made Chevrolet was ready for showing.

The Tin Lizzie that $850 bought in 1908 came without

a speedometer, windshield wipers, or even doors, and the gas gauge was a long thin stick that the owner had to find for himself and insert in the tank. Since then assembly lines had allowed Henry Ford to incorporate such features and still lower the price to $490. For the 1915 model year, Chevrolet unveiled the Chevrolet Four-Ninety, so named because the touring car sold at the factory for $490. There were few Americans who didn't know that "four-ninety" was exactly the price for a Model T. The Four-Ninety, designed by former Buick test driver and engineer Alfred Sturt, scored because, unlike the Model T, it came with the Cadillac self-starter and electrical system (Ford didn't cave in and license Charles Kettering's self-starter until the 1917 model year). The Four-Ninety was unveiled on New Year's Day, 1915, and put into production as soon as the Tarrytown factory was ready. At the close of business on June 19, the Chevrolet Motor Car Company had accepted orders from dealers and distributors for 46,611 cars, all secured by cash deposits. Wrote Billy to a friend: "Since June 19, we have orders for more than 1,000 cars per day." Henry Ford responded by lowering the price of Model Ts to $440.

What allowed Ford to cut prices while increasing the wages of his workers was the assembly line. Frederick "Speedy" Taylor, the father of the stopwatch-and-clipboard approach to factory life, showed Ford and his managers time-and-motion techniques. Isaac Singer, Cyrus McCormick, and Samuel Colt had mass-produced by passing their sewing machines, reapers, and firearms through factories in a series of jerks. Automobile manufacturers inherited the work methods of buggy makers. On stationary workbenches, mechanics built up engines, which were passed on to the next team of workers, who assembled chassis and attached axles and wheels before the chassis were rolled to the upholstery shop. The process involved progressive movement but no continuous flow. In Ford's new "Taylorized" Highland Park plant, workers lined up side by side along a moving conveyor belt. As the belt moved engines forward, workers fitted crankshafts and pistons. The result was stunning. One man could now do what three or four had done before. After the assembly systems produced so much they were threatening to flood the final chassis assembly, snags were worked out during the summer of 1913. Managers with stopwatches repositioned men and machines, leading to a drop in the number of man-hours needed to complete a chassis from 12 to 5 hours and 50 minutes. More tinkering led to new gains, and within months, Highland Park was a labyrinth of belts, assembly lines, and feeder lines on which parts were matched into subassemblies to deliver dashboards and body-and-top lines. "Every piece of work in the shops moves," Ford acclaimed. "Save ten steps a day for each of 12,000 employees, and you will have saved fifty miles of wasted motion and misspent energy."

Durant adapted the assembly line in less than ten months. The first assembly line was introduced in the old Imperial Wheel plant in Flint, with running gear and bodies added to the assembling of Chevrolet engines.

∽o∾

Chevrolet's growth was impressive. Willie announced a sales goal of 25,000 for 1914, only to have A. B. C. Hardy tell him, accurately, that all they could possibly produce that year was 5,000 cars. "So great was the demand," historian Arthur Pound would write, "that if a shipment was not taken off the railroad track promptly by the consignee, someone else in the community could be depended upon to lift it without delay." Branch offices were opened in Oakland, California, and Atlanta.

Impressed by the runaway success, old friends from the

buggy-making days wired and telephoned Billy. Russell Gardner said he would be delighted to build Chevrolets in Saint Louis. He put his money where his mouth was and organized a locally financed $1 million Chevrolet Motor Company of Saint Louis. R. S. McLaughlin assembled the Four-Ninety in Toronto. Norman de Vaux was equally ready to assemble Four-Nineties in Oakland, California, adding that he would be glad to have Billy's son as a sales executive. This was a welcome offer. Like his sister, Cliff had little to do but to live off his father's money and bask in his glory. His marriage to Adelaide Frost was in trouble. Approaching thirty, he spent his time on golf courses and racetracks, and was increasingly fascinated by racecar driving. He had shown up in Detroit for the launch of the first Chevy, sitting for the photographer in the driver's seat while his bowler-hatted father and cigarette-puffing Louis stood on the sidewalk. Soon thereafter Adelaide divorced Cliff, and after a whirlwind courtship married Eddie Rickenbacker, the soon-to-be World War I ace flyer.

Both of Adelaide's husbands dabbled in car racing. Rickenbacker raced for Duesenberg and Peugeot at the Indianapolis Speedway before the war; Cliff qualified for the 1919 Indianapolis 500, but dropped out with steering trouble after fifty-four laps. Cliff played golf when he wasn't posing for cameras in Detroit or racing cars in Indianapolis and Daytona. Like his father—and grandfather—he also dabbled in the stock market.

∞∽

The bankers' rule of General Motors, meanwhile, was less than bracing. Concerned only with protecting their $15 million loan and interests, they refused to pay dividends or to raise the salaries of the people who ran the moneymaking divisions. In 1910, the year they had demoted Durant, GM

Cliff Durant

produced 21 percent of the country's automobiles. In 1915, the output was down to 8.5 percent. Instead of seizing opportunities and catching Henry Ford's coattails (Ford's sales soared from 30,000 to 735,000 a year between 1910 and 1916), the bankers ordered Charles Nash, elected president after Storrow's departure, to close some plants and to concentrate work in others. Their refusal to pay dividends left the stock sluggish. Since the summer of 1911 it had bounced between $25 and $99 a share, and in January 1915 stood at $82. Durant moved forward with his planned coup d'état.

His success with Chevrolet worked wonders with disgruntled GM stockholders. He bought GM Voting Trust Certificates on the market between $25 and $40 until his purchases pushed stock prices to $55 at the outbreak of World War I in Europe. When he offered five shares of Chevrolet for one of General Motors, the result surprised even him. Hundreds of holders of the less-than-stellar GM stock brought so many suitcases of stock to the Chevrolet offices on Fifty-seventh Street that their certificates were stored in bushel baskets. He kept buying, even when the market price reached $220 in 1915. On August 22, Willie sent a message to his cousin George Willson in Flint, telling him not to sell any of his GM holdings. A week later, he wired Willson: HOLD EVERY SHARE YOU HAVE REGARDLESS OF PRICE CHANGES.

On September 23, 1915, Durant incorporated the Chevrolet Motor Company of Delaware at $20 million. Republic Motors was dropped and Chevrolet of Delaware assumed the role of a holding company for the other carmakers Willie had brought into existence. He was ready for the GM board meeting, which would authorize the last payment to the bank trustees and elect a new slate of directors. His allies included Arnold Goss, the former Buick executive with whom he had barnstormed banks in 1910, as well as Dallas Dort, McLaughlin, and Kaufman. Charles Mott—who, at Durant's urging, had relocated his axle factory from Utica, New York, to Flint and become the mayor of his adopted town—would probably come down on the side of the bankers. On the eve of the meeting, Durant spelled out his strategy to his son-in-law:

> . . . Everything coming fine. Proxies galore with some of the nicest letters you ever read. The opposition is out with their hammers and anvil chorus has already started. . . . Goss doing excellent work, and Kaufman— say, he's a beaut . . . I even saw Dallas come back quick and strong in answer to my telegram. His "sure" was worth a lot to me. McLaughlin with me yesterday, wants me to have a talk with Nash and explain my plan— thinks it will do a lot of good. I want to find out from Charlie [Nash] how he would feel with regard to Dallas on the board. Charlie is not very broad and might not like to "take orders" from his old boss. Nash is to be President if he will accept. Mott is to be offered a posi-

tion whether he is for or against me (I think the latter), but the rest of the bunch say, I shall go on the board— my time will be entirely devoted to Chevrolet. That is good enough and big enough for me.

We have orders for over 100,000 cars now on our books and not including Canada. Sam McLaughlin says at the Toronto fair, he never saw anything like it in his life. Chevrolet is the attraction, and orders and money is being forced upon them in "chunks."

To make absolutely sure he had a majority of GM stock for a decisive assault, Billy and three associates spent the night counting and recounting certificates.

Durant would leave no personal account of the September 16 meeting, which opened at 2 P.M. in room 282 of the Belmont Hotel. In a magazine article entitled "The Lively Life of the Gambling Giant," Booton Herndon would write how, when Durant arrived, Nash wanted a word with him.

"Now, er, Mr. Durant," he said, for he had trouble calling his former boss by the first name, "a majority of the board has agreed to renew the [trust] agreement. So let's not have any trouble."

"There won't be any trouble Charlie," said Durant. "We won't renew the agreement, but there won't be any trouble. It just so happens that I own General Motors."

In Lawrence Gustin's Durant biography, it is James Storrow who approached Durant before the meeting and asked that there be no quarrel, to which Willie answered, "I'm in control of General Motors today."

There were a few new faces in the room. Kaufman had invited as observers Pierre S. du Pont and E. I. Du Pont de Nemours treasurer John J. Raskob. Before the guns of August had thundered in Europe, Raskob had taken a flier on the GM stock, buying 500 common shares at $70 a share.

His boss Pierre Samuel, or P. S., du Pont* had followed suit.

Raskob was a brainy go-getter of Willie's ilk. The future millionaire and Democratic national chairman was the son of a cigar maker of Alsatian descent and an Irish mother who ran a boardinghouse near Niagara Falls, New York. Young John was a devout Catholic who put himself through school as a newspaper boy and worked as a railway steward. In 1900, Pierre S. du Pont hired him as a bookkeeper. Ten years later, Raskob was the company's one-man brain trust. It was said that Pierre S. was the one who breathed in and Raskob the one who breathed out. Durant had no objection to the presence of the balding, pince-nez'ed du Pont and his diminutive lieutenant.

The banker control was not renewed. On a motion by Nash seconded by Durant, the board declared a 50 percent dividend—$50 a share on stock which had sold for as little as $25 a share two years earlier and recently as high as $220—for the first time since the bankers had taken control. In his usual courteous manner, Billy asked to address the meeting. When he had everybody's attention, he announced that the Chevrolet Motor Company owned controlling interest in the General Motors Company, and offered to bring Chevrolet into GM. Stunned silence and disbelief greeted his words. One board member didn't believe Willie had the stock and proxies for a palace coup and threatened a court fight to determine whether Billy in fact held a majority.

The board was split on naming the new board. Both

---

*Until 1799, the family spelled its name the traditional way, Dupont. Pierre Samuel capitalized the preposition and separated it from the noun, thereby styling himself Pierre S. Du Pont. In deference, his son lowercased the preposition, and du Pont has been mostly used for family signatures. When referring to the family as a whole, the capitalized form, Du Pont, is used.

the Nash-Storrow faction and Durant-Kaufman camp nominated six men. As the factions stalemated, the "observers" du Pont and Raskob realized they could be kingmakers. At Raskob's shrewd advice, P. S. stayed neutral. By early evening, the deadlock was broken when during a recess Storrow told du Pont the bankers would like him to name three directors not connected with either faction. The idea was accepted and du Pont agreed to serve, and to name two others. "Twinkling his blue eyes with all due humility," du Pont biographer Gerard Colby would write, "Pierre accepted, named Raskob, Du Pont Vice-president J. Armory Haskell and cousin and brother-in-law Henry Berlin."

Both sides were accommodating. Nash said the agreement resulted from the "broad view" by Durant, and Billy replied that all sides had compromised.

Of the ten seats, seven were in Billy's corner—that is, if du Pont, Raskob, Haskell, and Berlin were counted as Durant allies. Nash was reelected president. The threat of a court challenge to count Durant's proxies became irrelevant a year later when the General Motors Corporation of Delaware was formed to take over the assets of GM. When the actual ownership of shares was resolved, the Chevrolet Motor Company owned exactly 450,000 of the 825,589 shares of GM common stock outstanding. Billy had not been bluffing.

He took Catherine to dinner that night and told her, "I took General Motors back from the bankers today."

"Oh, Willie," she replied. "At least we could have gone to the restaurant in the Plaza."

17

⤔⚬⤝

A Different Animal

There was something surreal in this tail-wagging-the-dog takeover of General Motors by Chevrolet. In the days that followed the coup, however, the newspapers concentrated on the human story, calling Billy Durant's comeback the return of a colorful personage. The *New York Evening Mail* wrote that because Billy did it with a smile, he was better than the late E. H. Harriman, the railroad tycoon who had been detested by rivals and denounced by President Theodore Roosevelt. The *New York Commerce and Finance* called Durant a genius: "No man has played a larger part in the progress of the motor car." Besides the composition of the new board, the newspapers seized on its agreement to pay out a $50 cash dividend. Brokers who had sold short were stunned and scrambled to cover their positions. Wall Street endorsed the consolidation by bidding up the GM stock during the first week after the merger. For weeks, Billy had telegraphed friends back in Flint to hang on to their GM stock. By September 22, the GM stock reached $340 and, it was said in Flint, "many fortunes have been made in the last few weeks." By December, the stock climbed to $558.*

Billy received approving letters and telegrams. Arthur Mason wrote: "You deserve it all and anything more you want. Please accept my last shirt." A. B. C. Hardy wired: PROUD TO SERVE UNDER A GENERAL WHO WINS OUT BY SUCH FAIR METHODS AND PATIENT PERSISTENCE AS YOURS. Delos Fall, Billy's former science teacher, now at Michigan's Albion College, wrote: "The world loves and applauds a winner and you have my sincere congratulations on your great success. However, I loved you before your successes came, ever since our High School experiences. May the dear Lord bless you, Will, is the earnest prayer of your onetime teacher." "More power to you," wrote Oldsmobile's Fred Smith, "your success pleases a lot of people who admire a well-scrapped scrap and an ability to bide the time till the other pup chewed himself tired." Harry Shiland wrote, "Congratulations, you did it! Permit me, the next time you are in Detroit, to buy chop suey at two-o'clock in the morning." Enclosing a newspaper clipping, Louis Kaufman added, "Long Live the King."

Yet, as Heraclitus had observed 2,500 years earlier, no one steps twice into the same river. The hodgepodge of carmakers and component manufacturers Durant brought together between 1908 and 1910 had, in the intervening years, mutated into a whole new animal. Willie, on the other hand, remained his unpredictable self, traveling, as in the old days, out of reach, and annoying his patrician chairman, Pierre S. du Pont, by his hunches, his mercurial style. Billy once cancelled a board meeting on the grounds he had no particular business to discuss.

Indeed, inherited wealth impressed neither Billy nor the rest of the shirtsleeve midwesterners who, in less than

---

*In 1999 money, $558.00 equals $9,000.54. Source: Federal Reserve Bank, Philadelphia.

twenty years, had built the automobile industry into a business colossus—the 1916 model year saw Oldsmobile produce the millionth General Motors car. "Powerful people without imagination like his own clearly bored him," Bernard Weisberger would write. "His behavior showed plainly that he preferred his own desk, his phone lines to brokers, his anonymous checkers partners or his old chums over their company." In du Pont, he met his corporate opposite.

Pierre S. was a shy, retiring man who was more comfortable with organizational charts than with people. His natural environment was the boardroom and executive office, not the E. I. Du Pont de Nemours laboratories and factories. To him, the corporation, not its product, was the vital ingredient of success. The organization, he believed, was greater than the sum of its individual parts. Only by making research, manufacturing, and selling subservient to the principle of return on investment could a corporation keep its assets in the constantly changing and unruly marketplace.

Pierre pressed Billy for more input from the board of

Pierre S. du Pont

directors. Billy winced, but agreed to set up a five-member finance committee. Besides himself and du Pont, the committee members were Raskob, Kaufman, and John Mc-Clement, the board member who, in 1910, had approached Lee, Higginson in Boston about a bailout.

The way Billy saw it, his job was to strengthen and unify. He felt he had his feet solidly planted in the economic and social truth of the times. General Motors was now North America's second biggest carmaker—Ford was still the competition to beat. Over a quarter of a million Ford Model Ts rolled off the Highland Park assembly lines every year and orders were perpetually ahead of production. The fact that there was no time to paint the cars in anything but black led Henry Ford to make his much quoted wisecrack that people could have any color so long as it was black.

Ford could do no wrong. The farm boy in him was so embarrassed by his riches that he took 20 percent off the retail price. When the result was even more sales, he announced that if 300,000 Americans bought Model Ts in 1914 he would return $50 to every person who bought a car. The gesture cost him $15 million, but 308,000 cars were sold. Next, he caused a storm by raising the pay of his 13,000 workforce from $2 to $5 a day. The raise was so steep—GM paid its workers around $2.35 a day—that it made headlines across the country. While the *New York Evening Post* called it "a magnificent act of generosity, the *New York Times* prophesied "serious disturbances" and the *Wall Street Journal* accused Ford of "economic blunders if not crimes" by injecting "spiritual principles into a field where they do not belong." Captains of industry said Ford was ruining the country. Again, he was a winner. In combination with the drop in cost that increased volume gave him, the wage increase boosted morale and productivity.

❧

There were changes this time around, personal changes as Billy and Catherine began a social life commensurate with his earnings. His declared income for 1916 was $3,419,000, the bulk of it ($2,769,000) in stock gains. His 1917 income tax returns have not survived, but the following year his gross income was $5,872,000 (a shade under $100 million in today's money).

The Durants moved into an apartment overlooking Central Park at 907 Fifth Avenue on the corner of Seventy-second Street. The rent was $16,500 a year. Catherine decorated the apartment stylishly with wall-to-wall carpeting, statues and carvings, silk and silver. In November 1917, they bought a seaside villa in Deal, New Jersey, from the heirs of Jacob Rothschild.

Raymere was a seventeen-room Florentine residence surrounded by hedges, gardens, a lawn, a fishpond and a fountain that in opulence almost matched Fair Lane, Henry Ford's Grosse Pointe, Michigan, estate on Lake St.-Clair. Located on Ocean Avenue north of Asbury Park, the $115,000 Raymere property was 25 miles south of the tip of Manhattan as the crow flies, but considerably longer via the New York and Long Branch Railroad. Except in winter, Billy began to commute from Raymere to his Fifty-seventh Street office. The interior decor Catherine chose with the help of designers and tradespeople included Louis XV benches, bishops' chairs, Ch'ien Lung vases, and a Knabe Ampico baby grand piano on which Catherine, Margery, and visiting friends played. Below Flemish tapestries and nineteenth-century oil landscapes, the reception hall contained Sèvres vases, Persian silk rugs, and hand-carved wing chairs. Here, the host might join his guests in a weak Scotch-and-water before dinner, served from Cauldron porcelain, set with flowers from the Durants' garden. The living room offered bronze lamps, Chippendale benches, gold cigarette boxes, and silver candy baskets. The billiard room featured satinwood and rosewood parquetry, and a gaming table primarily for cards, although it ingeniously concealed a roulette wheel. Said Walter Chrysler when he was invited down for a weekend: "I had never experienced luxury to compare with Billy Durant's house."

Willie would outdo himself when he invited various GM managers to be his guests. Besides rounds of dinners and entertainment, the highlights were golf tournaments in which all visitors would participate. He provided the prizes—and sometimes they ran into sums of sizable four figures. Catherine presided over the cocktail hour, during which her husband often limited himself to a glass of champagne. Catherine drank several stiff martinis. On occasion she needed a strong arm to escort her to the dinner table. She might have been an industrialist's pampered wife, but she had the knack for keeping her husband healthily in awe of her.

Rebecca kept up her one-way correspondence, urging Billy to write to her, but thankful that he ordered his secretary Winfred Murphy (Billy called him Winn) to carry out her modest requests and keep in touch. Perhaps confusing Winn with the abbreviated William, she wrote a "My dear boy" letter that apparently included less than pristine photos:

> Afternoon
> Received by morning mail, letter from Wm Murphy. The pictures quite good—not true to life. Yet I would not discourage the artists. It must have been the surroundings or poor sunlight. Try again. Practice makes perfect. The weather continues perfect, the trees green—everyone busy. Write me a note soon. George has a new auto. Everyone calls it a "beauty"—finest in city. I've not seen it. Write soon. Thanks to Mr. Murphy. With love
> > Mother

As the head of a huge and highly profitable corporation, Billy was back in his element. He tempered his impulse to expand, and also refrained from giving in to urges of sweet revenge. He asked Nash to remain president even though it soon became clear to both men that Charlie's days were numbered. His childhood and adolescence as an orphan struggling through grinding poverty had instilled in Nash a respect for money that had made him side with the bankers. He felt pained and humiliated at being squeezed between the blue-blooded rectitude of James Storrow, whom he admired, and Durant, who had hired him as a blacksmith back in 1890 and whose early support had led to the GM presidency.

After taking control, Billy immediately focused on an irritant that Nash and the bankers had let fester. They had never restored the Lelands' salaries, which they so diligently had cut in 1910. Nor had they given Walter Chrysler a raise. It was as if they were tone deaf to *who* brought in the profits that made it possible to write down $12 million in bad assets, retire the $15 million debt, and pay dividends.

Cadillac had made profits every year and had introduced a V-8 engine that was both a technical and commercial success. In three years, Walter Chrysler had whipped Buick into an efficient company while working on half salary. He had rebelled shortly before the Durant takeover, walking into Nash's office and saying, "Charley, I want $25,000 a year."

"Walter!"

Chrysler would tell what happened next in his autobiography, published when Nash and Durant were still alive:

> Chrysler: "Now Charley, we've gotten along fine. We are making good. Here in Buick, we've got the one company that has been making money."
>
> "Walter—"
>
> "Just a minute until I have finished. I've waited a long time before saying this. When I came here I was getting $12,000; I took this job for $6,000, and you haven't given me a raise. I want $25,000 a year, or I'm going to leave you."

"Walter, this is something I'll have to talk about with Mr. Storrow."

I walked out smoking one of my own panatelas.

In a couple of days I learned that Storrow had arrived in town. Nash and Storrow were in conference. Then word was brought that they would like to see me down in Charley's office.

"What's this all about, Walter?"

"Not much to it. You know how I came here. You know I was getting $12,000, and now I'm getting $6,000; after three years of the hardest work—I want $25,000 a year. By—"

"Don't get excited, Walter." Mr. Storrow did everything but pat me like a pet horse. "Don't get excited; you're going to get your $25,000."

"Yes? Well, thank you; and by the way, next year I want $50,000." I was forty years old. When I got home, I really started to enjoy the raise.

Chrysler was not alone in feeling used by Nash and the bankers. During a quick trip to Michigan, Durant learned of the Lelands' unhappiness. Few people had contributed more than Henry and Wilfred to improvements in engineering and manufacturing, yet no one had thought of restoring their earnings.

∽ơ∾

Chevrolet was so hot that Durant reduced the trade-in offer of five shares of Chevrolet for one GM share to four for one. This implied depreciation of GM did not sit well with the Storrow faction. Early in 1916, stockholders received circular letters, signed by eight of the directors, that deplored the idea of giving control of GM to upstart Chevrolet. If a significant number of stockholders agreed, a new voting trust would be created. Seven of the signers represented investment houses in Boston, New York City, and Detroit. The eighth, and not surprising, name was that of Charles Mott. That this longtime beneficiary of Durant's empire building (and mayor of Flint) joined the revolt added weight to the bankers' offensive. By March, two directors had left the anti-Durant coalition, but Charles Nash lent his name to the list of directors willing to become the new voting trustees. The momentum was with Durant. The chance to earn hundreds of dollars above the market price by swapping one GM share for four Chevrolet shares killed the revolt, and even some of his opponents sold or traded their securities.

Durant was not a vengeful man. He could forgive, even praise, Nash's tenure during the bankers' 5-year rule, but to have joined the revolt that, had it been successful, would have denied Billy his hard-fought comeback was treachery. Early in March, when Durant wired Nash to ask if he had lent his name to the supporters of the voting trust, Charlie replied evasively, eventually admitting ineptitude but not falsehoods. Much later, Nash would claim that Billy offered him a hefty salary to stay on, but that seemed to have been before Nash's name appeared on the March 1 circular letter. Durant's personal secretary Winfred Murphy would recall Durant telling Nash, "Well, Charley, you're through."

⌒⌒

Nash's resignation was accepted at a June meeting, where William C. Durant was nominated and duly elected president of General Motors, assuming for the first time that particular title. Albert Strauss, one of the leaders of the anti-Durant rebellion, resigned and was replaced by Wilfred Leland.

Nash got into carmaking on his own. With financing from Storrow, Charlie bought the Rambler automobile works in Kenosha, Wisconsin, from Thomas B. Jeffery. He called the 3,000 workers together for a pep talk: "We shall build up to a standard, not down to a price." The next year, the Jeffery name was phased out and the company renamed the Nash Motor Company. The first Nash was a 4-liter, 6-cylinder car with overhead valves, an obvious legacy from Charlie's Buick days. Sales were moderately encouraging.

Durant's power became absolute June 27, 1916, when Storrow and two fellow bankers, Emory Clark and S. F. Pryor, resigned. To make sure Walter Chrysler didn't follow Nash out the door, Durant had the chief of the Buick division fill Storrow's seat. Fred W. Warner, a former Durant-Dort salesman at the helm of the Oakland division, and William L. Day completed the sweep.

Chrysler accepted the nomination to the board graciously, but played hardball when Billy came out to Flint and told his Buick chief to forget any idea of making his own car. Walter said he would have to think about it, and get back with an answer in thirty days. They agreed to meet in the morning.

In his memoirs, Chrysler would write:

> Seven o'clock found Billy Durant right on my doorstep. I dropped into my swivel chair between my rolltop desk and my wide table; Durant seated himself on the opposite side of the table. I was going to ask him for a raise.
>
> "I'll pay you $500,000 a year to stay on here as president of Buick." He just sprang it on me that way; he did not bat an eye. I couldn't think for a few seconds.
>
> "Mr. Durant, the salary you offer is, of course, far and away beyond anything I had expected, but—"
>
> "Now, Walter [we were getting well acquainted fast] you just put aside, for the time being, all your plans of getting into business for yourself. I don't blame you for ambition, but I ask you to give me just three years of yourself."

They agreed on a three-year contract that gave Chrysler $10,000 a month plus annual profit sharing in cash or stock. Chrysler felt bold enough to ask one more thing:

> "I don't want interference. I don't want any other boss but you. If you feel that anything is going wrong, if you

don't like some action of mine, you come to me; don't go to anybody else and don't try to split up my authority. Just have one channel between Flint and Detroit, from me to you. Full authority is what I want."

Chrysler would remember how Durant beamed, touched the tabletop for emphasis, and said, "It's a deal."

Nash and Storrow were flabbergasted at what Durant was willing to pay Chrysler to retain the former locomotive mechanic.

∽∘∾

If Billy refrained from launching furious expansions, he couldn't help throwing a net wide enough to catch parts and component manufacturers. With financing from Kaufman, he set up United Motor Corporation and snared the Delco works, the Hyatt Roller Bearing Company, the ball bearing maker New Departure Manufacturing Company of Bristol, Connecticut (makers of ball bearings), and the Perlman Rim Corporation of Jackson, Michigan. With the acquisition of Delco came Charles Kettering, and with Hyatt came Alfred Sloan. Both men proved to be lasting assets. Kettering's research would benefit GM for decades, and Sloan's gift for organization would eventually make him president and CEO.

Here is Sloan's assessment of Durant as he started working for him:

> I was of two minds about Mr. Durant. I admired his automotive genius, his imagination, his generous human qualities, and his integrity. His loyalty to the enterprise was absolute. I recognized, as Mr. Raskob and Pierre S. du Pont had, that he had created and inspired the dynamic growth of General Motors. But I thought he was too casual in his ways for an administrator, and he overloaded himself. Important decisions had to wait until he was free, and were often made impulsively.

The automobile was taking on a major role in American life. Durant, his lieutenants Walter Chrysler, Arthur Mason, Wilfred Leland, and Charles S. Mott, and the moneymen Louis Kaufman, John Raskob, and Pierre S. du Pont realized, each in his own way, that mass production on the gargantuan scale demanded a new kind of supercorporation.

On October 13, 1916, the General Motors Corporation of Delaware was created and all assets of the eight-year-old General Motors Company of New Jersey folded into it. With a capitalization of $100 million, the new GM owned the entire capital stock of Buick Motor Company of Flint, Olds Motor Works of Lansing, Cadillac Motor Car of Detroit, Oakland (Pontiac) Motor Car of Pontiac, General Motors Export of Michigan, General Motors Truck Company of Pontiac, Jackson-Church-Wilcox Company of Jackson, Northway Motor & Manufacturing of Detroit, and the Weston-Mott Company of Flint. The new GM owned 62.5 percent of A.C. Spark Plug of Flint and 48.85 percent of the McLaughlin Motor Car Company (General Motors of Canada) of Oshawa, Ontario.

Net profits for 1916 were $28,800,000; net working capital was $43,664,000; and dividends totaling $11,700,000 were paid. The new corporation listed its production as Buick, 100,000 cars; Oakland, 30,000; Cadillac, 20,000; Oldsmobile, 15,000; and General Motors Truck Company, 6,000 trucks—a total of 165,000 motorcars and 6,000 trucks. And what about the Chevrolet Motor Company? Durant hesitated to bring Chevrolet into GM for fear of breaking the Clayton Antitrust Act of 1914, which outlawed business practices lessening free market conditions. Chevrolet finally became part of GM in 1918.

∽o∽

But it wasn't just cars for Durant. In Detroit one gloomy morning in 1916, Billy climbed two flights of stairs into the smelly clutter of a former organ factory to meet an inventor named Alfred Mellowes. With investing partners, Mellowes was struggling to produce a working model of an electric icebox. Billy was there on behest of one of the investors to talk the Dayton, Ohio, engineer into abandoning the idea. In two years, Mellowes had sold forty refrigerators and managed to lose $34,000.

Once inside the loft, however, Billy was his young, adventurous self. Why not electric refrigeration instead of unsanitary and inefficient blocks of ice delivered to back porches? The principle of refrigeration had intrigued inventors before Mellowes, but none had turned it into a marketable product. "I'll tell you what I'll do," Billy said. "I'll organize a company with one hundred thousand dollars new capital and give you people a quarter interest." Within months, the Guardian Frigerator Company was financed to the tune of $100,000, and Mellowes moved to an unoccupied Cadillac building on Scotten Avenue. Billy sent for A. B. C. Hardy to organize things.

Mellowes thought Durant favored the Guardian Frigerator over his automotive interests. On trips through Detroit, Billy would take a cab from the railway station to the Scotten Avenue plant. If the managers knew he was coming, they would be in at 6:30 to open the doors for the fast-paced boss. Like David Buick and Louis Chevrolet, however, Mellowes couldn't take Durant's overdrive manners. Despite promises that his brainchild would make millions, Mellowes quit one night, later saying he would have stayed if, instead of riches, Durant had offered him a few weeks off. Billy baptized Mellowes's electric icebox the Frigidaire, and once more made history. But no money. In March 1919, when he secured the GM board's approval to bring Frigidaire into the fold, GM paid him $56,266, a sum Sloan was sure was a great deal less than Billy had paid.

> You might think he had reckoned on making a big profit for himself. Not Durant. I'd bet my life he did not make a dollar for himself in that or any other similar deal. He

was not that kind. In Frigidaire, he gave the corporation the nucleus of a great industry.

The operation was turned over to Charles Kettering's Delco-Light division, whose research staff and manufacturing know-how turned Mellowes's electric icebox into a household essential.

Durant acquired the Fisher Body Company for $30 million. The Fisher family had been blacksmiths for two generations in Norfolk, Ohio, when Fred Fisher came to Detroit in 1902 and found a job as a designer with the C. R. Wilson body shop, which made bodies for the curved-dash Oldsmobile. Fred sent for his brother Charles. When Wilson turned down Fred's request for a $5 a week raise so he could get married, he and Charles both quit. Hugh Chalmers, a former National Cash Register salesman who also got into the car business, recognized the Fisher boys' ability and arranged a bank loan that allowed them to set up their own business. Fred and Charles had their brother William join them. Eventually, the four remaining brothers—Edward, Lawrence, Alfred, and Howard—worked at the Fisher Body Company. When Durant folded Fisher Body into GM, he kept the seven brothers.

Billy's 1917 foray into farm implements was a flop that would eventually cost GM $12 million. The idea sounded smart enough. Unlike Ford's tractor, which demanded that the operator ride it, the small Samson Model D tractor Durant launched was controlled with a pair of reins. An unaccompanied farmer could *walk* behind his Samson—soon renamed the Iron Horse—and bind, rake, mow, and plant his fields as he had done with a team of horses. If a farmer *rode* a tractor down his furrows, he needed a hired hand to walk or ride behind to do the sowing, raking, and binding. With the Iron Horse, the farmer could work his fields by himself. Billy loved the idea.

With full approval of his board, he acquired the Samson Sieve-Grip Tractor Company of California and several farm equipment manufacturers and merged them into Samson Tractors with headquarters in Janesville, Wisconsin. A prototype powered by a Chevrolet engine was built. In August 1919, Billy took the first demonstration model to the Wisconsin State Fair in Milwaukee, where 32 years earlier he had introduced the Flint Road Cart. Chevrolet's publicity chief Jacob Newmark staged the official Iron Horse premiere at the New Jersey State Fair in Trenton two weeks later. Here, a derby-hatted Billy was photographed plowing a stretch of field at the reins of a $450 Iron Horse. But he had no Walter Chrysler to run the Samson division. GM wrote it off as a $33 million loss in 1923, leaving Ford the only carmaker in the farm equipment business.

∽o∽

Durant was on top of his game. His contributions to the expanding auto industry were impressive. He consolidated his grip with confidential salary and bonus arrangements with his division heads. Walter Chrysler was in control at Buick, Henry and Wilfred Leland were at the helm at Cadillac. Former Buick master mechanic Edward Ver Linden, headed Oldsmobile, and Fred Warner was the manager of the Oakland plant. The Chevrolet, Buick, and Oldsmobile factories were enlarged, and a new Cadillac plant was built. E. I. Du Pont de Nemours of Wilmington, Delaware, provided much of the new money.

18

❧

Du Pont

That Willie Durant would tangle with the country's oldest industrial family was perhaps inevitable. That he would bid against Wall Street was, for a man of his financial savvy, unforgivably foolish.

History's bigger folly played out in Europe. What had started in August 1914 as autumn maneuvers with live ammunition turned into the most brutal conflict humanity had ever seen. Foresight was not among the virtues of the kaisers, czars, and kings of Germany, Austria, Russia, and a half dozen lesser monarchies who stumbled into the Great War. Their thrones vanished in the trenches of western and eastern fronts where poison gas, machine guns, aircraft, and other modern devices of destruction led to 13 million military deaths. Not that successive presidents of France and prime ministers of Great Britain and Italy were possessed of brilliant minds and clever initiatives. For four years of trench warfare, Europe's youth was sacrificed to advance, surrender, and regain once more a few hundred meters of muddy no-man's-land. As much as

179

America's April 1917 entrance into the conflict would provide untold riches for E. I. Du Pont de Nemours, the war "over there" proved detrimental to Durant.

For over a hundred years war had added to the fortunes of the Wilmington, Delaware, family. Pierre Samuel and his brother Irénée du Pont and their cousin Alfred were the descendants of the French aristocrat who in 1794 escaped the guillotine and, five years later, found it prudent to transfer himself, thirteen family members, and the family fortune to America.

Their beginnings were never humble. The ancestral Pierre celebrated his New World freedom by buying slaves for his wife. For most of the company's almost 200 years in business, making gunpowder had been a family vocation. Thomas Jefferson gave the family their first government job, to refine potassium nitrate, the chief ingredient in gunpowder. The Civil War had been especially lucrative. It was not until after a 1908 antitrust lawsuit in which Washington threatened to set up its own government plants for making gunpowder that the Du Ponts ventured into nonexplosive chemicals and discovered lacquers, celluloid, artificial leather, and synthetic dyes.

This time, profits exceeded all expectations. From their new Virginia plant in Hopewell, financed mostly by the British government, and their Old Hickory, Tennessee, factory, bankrolled by the U.S. government, the Du Ponts sold the Allies 125 million rounds of special ammunition for aircraft, 206 million black powder pellets for loading in shells, and 90 different types of gunpowder. The United States was still a neutral power in 1916 when the Du Pont de Nemours profits topped $80 million. By war's end in November 1918, the munitions business had resulted in $250 million earnings. As the company's 1918 annual report put it, "It is difficult to imagine a more satisfactory result."

The money the Du Ponts made on the war was pocket change compared to the gold the family would derive from its involvement with GM. From a $43 million investment would spring E. I. Du Pont de Nemours' greatest market. "Over $20 million in dividends were reaped every year, to say nothing of family dividends and salaries and fees as GM executives and directors, the market it provided for other companies (such as the family-controlled U.S. Rubber Company), and the enormous economic and political power such control carried," Gerard Colby would write in *Du Pont Dynasty.*

Whether John Raskob calculated that automobiles would be a new market for lacquers, celluloid, artificial leather, and as-yet undiscovered chemical by-products, he clearly saw GM's vast potential. Buying 500 shares at $70 in 1914—Pierre S. had been a bit less nimble, getting in at $82—had made him rich. By mid-1915, GM's stock had risen to $200, and after the Durant takeover, to $350. Raskob kept his ear to the ground. So did Durant. It had taken the industry from 1900 to 1914 to reach an annual output of half a million cars. Stimulated by a booming economy, the 1915 figure topped 895,000 cars, and the 1916 total reached 1.5 million. The demand was booming. In a forty-minute pep talk to 600 dealers, Hugh Chalmers disposed of his entire 1916 schedule of 13,000 cars.

Selling automobiles, however, demanded prosperity and the kind of free economy that a wartime economy would make impossible. Like most Americans, both Durant and Henry Ford were aloof from European politics. Ford hated armed conflict with such passion that he financed and led an ill-fated and much ridiculed peace mission.

In early December 1915, he chartered a Danish ship and, despite the reservations of his wife Clara and President Woodrow Wilson, sailed to neutral Scandinavia, intending to be the voice of reason and reconciliation between the Allies and the Central Powers of Austria-Hungary, Germany, Bulgaria, and the Ottoman Empire, and "to get the boys out of the trenches by Christmas." The Ford "peace pilgrims" reached Berlin, but never Paris and London. "None of the delegates had any knowledge of the history or present condition of affairs in Europe," wrote William C. Bullitt, the future U.S. ambassador to the Soviet Union who covered the Ford crusade for the *Philadelphia Public Ledger.* "None of them understood the emotions of a people at war. They believed they could 'bring the boys out of the trenches' by pouring out affectionate words. They did not think it was necessary to hammer their vague tenderness into a coherent plan of action." Hurt and humiliated, Ford returned home to tell the *Chicago Tribune* that "History is more or less bunk."

∽o∾

Durant believed that the European war was none of America's business. When the tenuous U.S.-German relations snapped in April 1917 and the United States entered the war, Albert R. Erskine, president of the Studebaker Corporation of South Bend, Indiana, wired Woodrow Wilson: STUDEBAKER FACTORIES ARE AT THE DISPOSAL OF THE GOVERNMENT. ANY ORDERS GIVEN US WILL RECEIVE PREFERENCE AND CLEARED RIGHT AWAY.

The Lelands had sold Cadillacs in Britain since 1906 and were staunchly pro-British. With America's entry into the conflict, they embraced the war effort to the point of firing German immigrants working in their Detroit factories. Old Henry had defied the threat of German U-boats and sailed to England shortly after a German submarine sank the *Lusitania* in May 1915. In London, he advised munitions boards of American capabilities, and upon his return called on Woodrow Wilson to beseech the president to prepare the country for war. Wilson was deep in his reelection campaign, and, to court the isolationist vote, wanted to keep America out of the war. To Durant, old Henry sug-

182

gested that Cadillac make airplane engines for the Royal Air Force. The British were interested in a large contract, but "our capacity to turn out automobiles is so far below the demand that I have turned each one of them down at once." Billy said no. The war would be over before any airplane engines could be built.

To Willie the war was a distraction. To the Lelands, it was a passion play that begged all full-blooded Americans to take up arms on the side of the righteous. Their clashing views of the war, if not of human nature, led to heated quarrels, to finger-pointing, to criticism, to insinuations of underhanded behavior, and, in the early spring of 1917, to Durant firing Henry and Wilfred. The Lelands had been the rock during the early years of Durant's GM, and the most charitable spin one can put on the dismissals of the father-son team is Billy's mercurial and sometimes heedless character traits.

Acting on behalf of Cadillac dealers who, Durant claimed, complained about slow and disorganized deliveries of new cars, he had found Henry and Wilfred distracted by the war. The first hint of trouble had come when he denied their requests for more inventory and longer production schedules. His decision didn't sit well with the Lelands, and on March 10, 1917, he fired them. His letter of dismissal to Wilfred Leland read:

Dear Mr. Leland:

I take this opportunity of advising you that the present arrangement will not be continued after the 1st of August 1917, and that a change in management of the Cadillac Motor Car Company is contemplated.

I trust that you will cooperate with me in any attempt to build up an organization capable of meeting the problems of the future.

Yours very truly,
W. C. Durant
President

183

The day after Congress declared war on April 6, 1917, Wilfred Leland rushed to New York City and demanded an immediate meeting. He and his father still had three months to go, and the Cadillac division had just finished a new building. For all practical considerations no airplane industry existed in the United States. Why not make airplane engines? Durant said no.

Wilfred was stunned. It was the first time Durant vetoed the Lelands' management. The way Wilfred would remember it, Durant added, "This is nonsense, this war should stop tomorrow."

"We have to help win this war," Wilfred shot back. "If it isn't won, our children will have to fight it out later. This is our war now."

"No! I don't care for your platitudes. This is not our war and I will not permit any General Motors unit to do work for the government."

Wilfred returned to Detroit. Old Henry was furious. They went to Washington and offered to build engines for Colonel George Squier, the head of the Signal Corps' aviation command. They had no plant, they explained, but they did have the know-how and resources to go into production. Although the War Department refused to give them a contract, they went back to Detroit and began organizing the manufacturing of airplane engines they were sure the government would need. They bought a small building on Holden Avenue for $300,000, and hired a Packard Motor engineer who had tinkered with an aircraft engine. Warplanes were flimsy contraptions and the challenge was to build motors that weighed less than car engines but produced more thrust.

If Wilfred had not testified to a Senate committee that Durant had fired them for wanting to undertake war work, they might still be in charge of Cadillac. Because Willie was not only rethinking firing them, but trying for a reconciliation. Old Henry, awkward on crutches for several years, was not easy to deal with, but Wilfred had been more than a loyal lieutenant. He alone had turned the bankers' thinking from liquidating GM to saving it in 1910. As an olive branch, Willie asked Wilfred to prepare a detailed recovery plan for Cadillac. Next, he went to Detroit in the hope of reaching an accommodation with father and son. The trio spent a day talking out their differences and possible corrective measures. Willie agreed to let certain GM plants take war contracts on a limited basis. Wilfred was ready to reevaluate, but Old Henry wrapped himself in patriotic indignation. They were fired, and they'd goddamn stay fired. He aired his mood at a farewell banquet that Cadillac workers and management gave him and his son. He rose, clinked his glass and told the assembly:

> "The Cadillac has been dearer to me than any other one thing in the world except my home, but there has arisen now a claim on my loyalty that is nearer and dearer still. I do not believe the people of this country realize the monumental nature of their task. The time is coming though when this realization will be forced upon us. The world's greatest need at this moment is America, and America's paramount need now is to provide means for mastery of the air."

Durant's choice to run Cadillac was Richard Collins, a former John Deere salesman whom Billy had known since the Durant-Dort days. Collins had joined the Buick sales department, and acquired the nickname "Trainload" for the quantities of cars he was responsible for shipping.

Henry Ford let his pacifism fade enough to join Durant in offering the services of his factories to the government. Buick ambulances saw action in France, and the New York National Guard showed off an armored Buick, but both Ford and GM were slow in getting government contracts. Cadillac produced 2,350 staff cars for the army, which were regular V-8s painted army olive. The division also made more than a thousand artillery tractor engines, but GM missed out on the big procurement—trucks. The U.S. Army contracted for 11,000 trucks—nearly half of the American prewar output—and the major suppliers were Mack, White, Pierce-Arrow, Diamond T, and Four Wheel Drive. General John J. Pershing had himself photographed in front of an olive-green Pierce-Arrow.

To Durant's surprise, the demand for cars did not slacken despite the drafting of the industry's best potential customers—a million young men. On Wall Street, however, speculators unloaded General Motors stock on fears of government curtailment of strategic supplies. To prop up the stock, Billy bought the slipping GM shares. He had personal lines of credit with dozens of brokers and thought nothing of it. He of all people believed the statistics that bore out the glowing confidence of a 1917 article in *Hearst's* magazine: "Never before was capital so plentiful. Never before were such profits rolled up by corporations. Never before were such wages enjoyed."

As the war effort geared up, Food Administrator Herbert Hoover launched voluntary food rationing by instituting wheatless Mondays and Wednesdays, meatless Tuesdays, and porkless Thursdays and Saturdays. "Hooverizing to beat the Hun" also meant conserving coal on heatless Mondays, and, much to the delight of prohibitionists, suspending until peacetime the manufacture of liquor. To avoid gasoline rationing, motorists observed gasless Sundays. Billy kept buying up GM stock.

∽o∾

The illusory, if romantic, allure of Henry Ford's Peace Ship and his folk-hero appeal made him run for the Senate in 1918. The instigator was Woodrow Wilson himself. "You are the only man in Michigan who can be elected and help to bring about the peace you so much desire," the president told Ford. "I wish you therefore to overcome your personal feelings and interests and make the race." His campaign was less than extravagant. He declined to make public speeches; issued no public statements, except to say he was in favor of women's suffrage; and refused to spend any money on advertising. His opponent, Truman H. Newberry, reminded voters of Ford's earlier statement that the only reason he voted was because his wife made him do it. Newberry, who belonged to a prominent Detroit family and was a former secretary of the navy, ran a dirty campaign. Ford's backers produced evidence of corruption and voter irregularities in the Newberry camp. Newberry won the election anyway. He was found guilty of election fraud, but the verdict was reversed on appeal.

President Wilson appointed Roy D. Chapin, a former Olds mechanic and test driver, chief of the Highway Transport Commission. To speed up deliveries of war matériel, Chapin bypassed the railroads and ordered recruits to truck war supplies from heartland factories to the eastern seaboard docks. At Verdun, where railroads were bombed, the French transported all men and supplies over one 35-mile-long road. And U.S. trucks arrived on the western front before the doughboys. Mechanized warfare demanded increased oil shipments, mostly from Texas, Oklahoma, and Pennsylvania fields, and petroleum freight rates between New York and Liverpool rose from $4 to $50 per ton. In the Somme victory drive, motor vehicles added an important element.

The Lelands got a government order for 10,000 Liberator airplane engines. Their plant turned out 30 engines a day. Delays in airplane deliveries, including deliveries of the Lelands' motors, led to a Senate investigation. Senator Charles S. Thomas, a Democrat from Colorado, and his aircraft subcommittee wanted to know why, and in June 1918 held hearings in Detroit. Wilfred Leland testified to sabotage at the Liberator plant that had led to wholesale dismissal of German immigrants. Prosecution had been impossible, he said, because shop floor errors could be excused as carelessness. Explaining how his father and he had resigned from Cadillac over Durant's veto of aircraft production, he said Durant had not been in sympathy with the war at the time it was declared. The younger Leland quoted Durant as saying, "The war could be stopped tomorrow and I don't want our company to take any part in war work."

Durant went on the offensive. In a telegram to Leland he asked for "the date of the meeting, where held and who was present when the statements credited to me were made."

Leland's return wire was less than forthcoming: YOUR WIRE OF AUGUST TWENTY SEVENTH RECEIVED. I DO NOT THINK A FURTHER DISCUSSION PARTICULARLY BY TELEGRAM OF THE REASONS BRINGING ABOUT OUR RESIGNATION FROM THE CADILLAC CO. WOULD BE OF MUTUAL ADVANTAGE. THE DIFFERENCES OF OPINION REGARDING POLICY WERE SUBJECTS OF DISCUSSION ON FREQUENT OCCASIONS AND IN THE PRESENCE OF SEVERAL PERSONS.

Pressed one more time to name the time, place and persons present, Leland backed down: IT IS HARDLY NECESSARY FOR ME TO SAY THAT THE PUBLICITY GIVEN TESTIMONY WAS UNFORTUNATE AND WITHOUT MY APPROVAL. IN VIEW OF ALL THIS I THINK MY PREVIOUS REPLY IS SUFFICIENT AND SHALL CONSIDER DISCUSSION BY CORRESPONDENCE OF THIS SUBJECT AS CLOSED.

Willie was less than satisfied and made public his March 10, 1917, letter dismissing the Lelands. "Their discharge had nothing to do with patriotism, the war, war contracts, or my alleged views," he said. "It was brought about for prudential business reasons, and they were so notified by me, before war was even declared."

⋙⟐⋘

The war ended on November 11, 1918. The French called the terrible four-year conflict *la dèr des dères,* desperate to convince themselves it was the last of all wars. Some Americans repeated after F. Scott Fitzgerald that "all Gods [were] dead, all wars fought, all faiths in man shaken." Others refused to worry about anything but their own business; almost everybody agreed the problems of the world were too confusing.

The war won, peace translated into soaring interest rates. In March 1919, Durant ordered an end to overtime and a return to 8-hour workdays.

When the government lifted wartime restrictions, Durant thundered ahead. He bought a surplus war plant for $1 million, and converted it to the manufacture of auto parts. Next came the $5 million acquisition of the T. W. Warner Company of Muncie, Indiana (gear manufacturers), and another body-making firm in Pontiac. A Chevrolet truck was introduced. Chevrolet continued to improve its position, but was still only a distant image in Ford's rearview mirror. The Model T, or Tin Lizzie, was still the standard by which all cars were compared.

⋙⟐⋘

When a business slump in the fall of 1920 exposed economic weaknesses, Wall Street quickly realized Ford, GM, and the rest of the auto industry had an oversupply of cars. Nevertheless, although Americans might be unsettled, they were in general cheerful, optimistic, and eager to ride in cars. Installment buying had first appeared in 1915, but relatively few financiers paid much attention. Now, buying a car on credit became the norm.

Durant and Raskob set up the General Motors Acceptance Corporation. The GMAC, which would one day be worth more than the carmaking divisions, financed the purchases of customers in lower-income groups. Hundreds of thousands responded enthusiastically to buying on credit. Henry Ford followed suit and offered a "five dollars down and five a week" plan, and his dealers quickly signed up hundreds of thousands of new customers. Ford's obsession remained mass production. He continued to produce the monotonously black Model T and was soon to learn lessons in beauty, color, and style from women consumers. In the meantime, he was the undisputed king of the industry, fabulously rich, and, with the possible exception of Charles Chaplin, the best-known American the world over.

19

⌒o⌒

Into the Roaring Twenties

The automobile transformed everything—the economy, courtship habits, family living. It was the most desired possession, striking deep roots in the 1920s psyche. "To George Babbitt," wrote Sinclair Lewis in his 1922 novel *Babbitt,* "as to most prosperous citizens of Zenith, his motorcar was poetry and tragedy, love and heroism . . . a family's motor indicated its social rank and where Babbitt as a boy had aspired to the Presidency, his son Ted aspired to a Packard Twin Six." Carmaking was the biggest industry—the largest single consumer of steel, lead, rubber, nickel, and oil. Men bought cars on reputations of technical excellence, but women took a hand in choosing them. Ford continued to say, "Let 'em have black," and the result of his color blindness was that thousands chose colored Chevrolets.

Cars acquired hydraulic, 4-wheel brakes in 1920, balloon tires two years later. The invention of fast-drying pyroxylin varnishes allowed carmakers to turn out cars in a rainbow of hues. Next came enclosed bodies and sweeping,

191

rakish fenders that made Ford's canvas tops and flapping curtains look unattractive. "Cars were never handsomer— and they were making changes in the way Americans lived, a *Time-Life* publication, *This Fabulous Century,* would note; "changes that would never be reversed." The numbers said it all. Americans bought 1,650,000 cars in 1919 and 1,905,000 in 1920, and sales reached the 2 million mark in 1923.

Durant was fifty-nine at the dawn of the decade, heavier but still a handsomely attractive man. He was in the driver's seat at GM, gunning for new hilltops, and still ready to veer through a ditch to get ahead of hay wagons. The flat-out growth was fully endorsed by the Du Pont family and, more important, by John Raskob. Pierre S., Irénée, and Henry F. du Pont owned almost a third of GM, but their minds were less than focused. Henry du Pont lacked interest in GM affairs, Irénée had his hands full running E. I. Du Pont de Nemours, and Pierre was devoting much of his time to plant research and Delaware public affairs.

They had approved the decision to increase the capital stock to $200 million for the takeover of Chevrolet in May 1918, followed by the $44 million soaking up of United Motor Corporation, the company Durant had set up in 1916 with Louis Kaufman's bank loans to absorb Delco, Hyatt Roller Bearings, and several other component manufacturers. Kaufman thought GM paid too little, and the deal led to a falling out between him and Durant. Acquisitions continued—a steel plant in Lancaster, Pennsylvania, and the remainder of the McLaughlin-owned Canadian firms. The year-end reports amply justified the growth; the 1918 figures showed sales of just under $270 million, and defense procurement neatly canceled out the slump in civilian production. "We feel fortunate in our partnership with Mr. William C. Durant, president of the General Motors Corporation and the father and leader of the motor indus-

The CEO of General Motors, 1920

try not only in the United States but in the world today," said the 1918 Du Pont de Nemours annual report.

After Durant asked for, and investment bankers sold, 5 million shares of common stock, 5 million debentures, and 200,000 shares of preferred stock, General Motors was a billion-dollar corporation. Only one other company, United States Steel, lived at this rarefied height. For the first time, GM's net sales surpassed the half billion mark ($509,676,000), while net earnings reached $60 million. It employed 86,000 people. In late January 1920, Raskob folded copies of the balance sheets since 1916 into an envelope and sent them to Durant. Over the last three-and-a-half years, they had spent $58 million, but the company now held assets worth $452 million. In a note, he added: "In other words, the General Motors Corporation of today is eight times as large as the company that the bankers were managing. This is indeed a fine tribute to your foresight."

What slowly dawned on everybody, however, was that the ruthless contraction of the auto industry into two giants made GM and Ford Motor Company too big for one-man rule. No night of long knives in the boardroom could topple Henry Ford. Suspicious and self-willed, he had bought out his original partners, turning his half-billion-dollar company into a family property. His iron grip was increasingly tyrannical. Cowardly, he asked underlings to get rid of William S. Knudsen, the Danish immigrant who built the Ford assembly plants in North America and Europe, and managed a boat-building program at Ford during the war. Henry Ford continued to rule by decree, but, imperceptibly at first, his company retreated from its earlier position of leadership. With the exception of the low-cost V-8 engine, the Ford Motor Company no longer introduced innovations.

At GM, the distance widened between Durant and Pierre S. du Pont and, more ominously, between Billy and the du Ponts' brilliant Talleyrand. What drove finance committee head Raskob and executives like Alfred Sloan and Walter Chrysler to distraction was not being able to get decisions out of Durant. They were summoned to New York City, Flint, Detroit, or wherever Billy was from Ontario to California, but had to wait hours, even days, for a meeting. In disgust, they sometimes went home without seeing him. Once, Raskob pleaded for a meeting "at some hotel where we can talk without being interrupted by telephone and otherwise." On other occasions, Raskob complained he had tried all afternoon to reach Durant by telephone or pleaded for a Saturday meeting.

Billy's management style reached the wartime *Congressional Record* when Sloan complained, with some bitterness, how he spent hours outside the GM president's office:

We scarcely felt like doing anything else until he rang the bell, so tempers soured. I was constantly amazed by his daring way of making decisions. My business experience had convinced me facts are precious things, to be eagerly sought and treated with respect. But Mr. Durant would proceed on a course of action guided solely, as far as I could tell, by some intuitive flash of brilliance. He never felt obliged to make an engineering hunt for facts.

The structure and size of General Motors bore little resemblance to the shape and proportions of the holding company Durant had hammered together in 1908. Billy seemed to sense that Raskob wanted to tie him up in bureaucracy because he resisted flattering pressures to build new GM headquarters on Detroit's Grand Boulevard and to name the command center the Durant Building. Everything in Willie's experience told him he was successful when he made the big decisions, not when a centralized bureaucracy made them. When Raskob's finance committee raised $150 million by stock sales, he objected to the cost of the proposed headquarters and to naming it after him, although he and Sloan had picked the site. In June 1919, ground was broken for the $20 million, fifteen-story building, the largest office structure in the world. The architect was Albert Kahn. Born and educated in Germany, Kahn was an innovator who, instead of building factories with bricks, used reinforced concrete. His first reinforced-concrete factory in Detroit, the 1905 Packard plant, allowed for more open floor space and expanses of windows, which instantly turned every other factory into a Dickensian prison shop. In 1909, Kahn's huge Ford plant in Highland Park had been dubbed Detroit's own Crystal Palace because it had 50,000 square feet of side and overhead windowpanes.

Over the year's construction of the Durant Building, Sloan could not get any input from the boss. On November 18, 1920, Herbert R. Lewis and his Harrison Radiator staff became the first division to conduct business in the four-winged building, which featured 30 acres of floor space.

When E. I. Du Pont de Nemours and Company assigned E. L. Bergland, an efficiency expert, to evaluate GM's operations, the dry, terse report was devastating:

> Mr. Durant, apparently, has complete charge of all of the planning and dictates largely the policies to the followed. His opinion is consulted for final decision in a great many cases as there seems to be no one else in the organization that is the final arbitrator for the various plans or for new developments. . . . When new plants are to be built Mr. Durant often personally supervises the letting of the contract and the engineering details with the engineering and contracting firm, but the details of the design receive very little attention and very little detailed information is apparently known by the members of the organization. . . . There is no system similar to our work order system for making suggestions, or no central engineering organization. There is, I think, also a certain lack of cooperative spirit between the different plants. These plants are practically independent as regards their purchasing, accounting and other organization, and as they were independent operations organizations before the General Motors Corporation was formed, and have been more or less functioning ever since as independent organizations, it is very easy to understand a feeling of this kind as there is no central organization directing them, except in the most general way.

Bergland concluded that GM's future demanded planning, and could benefit from a solid dose of the E. I. Du Pont de Nemours corporate culture. An expert from Delaware was sent to New York to teach the rudiments of centralized bookkeeping and unified assignment and supervisory procedures to the Durant staff.

The Du Pont company dug deeper into its pool of talents and assigned John Lee Pratt, another engineering graduate, to make monthly trips to New York and Detroit. Durant welcomed the appointment. He liked Pratt and asked if he could have him on a permanent basis. Pratt disarmed a lot of people by dressing simply and calling himself a "dirt farmer." He was impressed by the breadth of Durant's knowledge, and readily looked into the GM president's requests for figures on why aluminum was so expensive, what impact the automobile would have on oil reserves, and questions of whether the company should go into manufacturing plate glass and storage batteries. But Pratt also came to realize that forty or fifty individuals went directly to Durant for decisions.

A creeping unease over this one-man show set in, starting with the Du Pont allies, Messrs. J. P. Morgan & Company. The investment bankers at 23 Wall Street had maintained a position in General Motors, and in private voiced the opinion to the Du Ponts that the Durant regime was positively dangerous for an organization of GM's size.

If there was one division that brought in half the GM earnings, it was the Buick works under Walter Chrysler's leadership. But Chrysler was getting exasperated with the two sides of the Durant coin—his well-meaning interventions in Buick's affairs and his inaccessibility. Billy was congenitally incapable of keeping his word not to interfere in Walter's management. After Trainload Collins told Chrysler the boss had okayed a "branch operation" of Buick in Detroit, Walter left messages for Billy, pleading for new ground rules. A few months later, Walter was seated at a Flint Chamber of Commerce luncheon when Dallas Dort stood up and read a telegram from Durant authorizing $6 million to construct a GM plant to make body frames in Flint. At a board meeting in Detroit the next day, Walter grilled Durant. What was the cost estimate for the new plant? Who had made the calculation? How long would it take to bring the plant on line? And did Billy know that he, Chrysler, had just made a deal for frames with a

Milwaukee firm? Billy backed down. No frame factory was built in Flint, and the two men seemed to patch up their differences. But the incident was the straw that broke the camel's back. On March 25, 1920, Walter tended his resignation and walked off with $1.5 million in accumulated stock options.

Sloan almost followed. With his wife, he took a month's vacation in Europe, and while in London he decided to leave GM. Back in New York, he was ready to submit his resignation, but Billy and Catherine Durant were on vacation. Sloan sensed something that was new, gathering storm clouds perhaps, and decided to wait.

20

⋘⚬⋙

November Storm

The reason Willie Durant lost General Motors the week before Thanksgiving 1920 was not, like the first time, his heedless expansion of an industry suddenly choking on inventory. What unhorsed him were his stock speculations, GM's insatiable need for capital, and his life-long optimism.

In history's rearview mirror the recession that hit during the fall of 1920 was a classic case of overproduction meeting economic contraction following government cut-backs on wartime spending. The slump nevertheless took everybody by surprise. Car sales had declined since summer. To the surprise of Durant and Raskob, no one could tell them how many cars GM had in stock. Accountants were put to work. The divisions turned out models in a dozen different price ranges, and owned many of their suppliers. In October, the gargantuan inventory was completed. The dollar value of unsold cars and materials had risen from $137 million to $209 million, or nearly $60 million above a limit established earlier in the year.

Inventory reporting was better at Ford, and since the company made only one car, Henry Ford's team quickly adjusted production downward. Slashing prices had worked so well for Ford in 1914 that he discounted below cost, offering the Model T touring car model with a $135 markdown and the sedan with a $180 rebate. "We must, of course, take a temporary loss because the stock of materials on hand [was] bought at inflated prices," he said. "We take it willingly in order to bring about a going state of business throughout the country."

From its all-time high of $558 in September 1915, the GM share price slid to $50 and then to $25. Durant was convinced the downturn was going to be short-lived, that the automobile was headed for shimmering heights. On a gamble that the tumble was little more than a correction and that he could help prevent a further slide, he bought up dumped GM shares, found his funds running out, and began to borrow against his own GM holdings.

The Du Ponts had put a lot of money into GM. Public stock offerings over the past year had netted $37.5 million, but E. I. Du Pont de Nemours had put up nearly $55 million. Almost four years to the day after Durant had boasted of taking GM back from bankers, Pierre S. du Pont, Raskob, and the Morgan interests forced him to accept six new board members. As they always did when they acquired substantial interests in a corporation, J. P. Morgan & Company demanded board seats for themselves and those who worked with them. In June 1920, Billy accepted six new directors. William H. Woodin, president of American Car and Foundry, Owen D. Young, a General Electric vice president, and Clarence Woolley, president of American Radiator Company, represented industrial enterprises. The other three were bankers—Morgan partners Edward R. Stettinius, Seward Prosser of Bankers Trust, and George F. Baker, a First National Bank of New York vice president.

He could live with Prosser, Baker, Woodin, Woolley, and Young. The sixth new director was to be his nemesis.

Stettinius Sr. was an arrogant financier who, as assistant secretary of war, had advised the government on purchasing matters (his son, Edward Jr., would become Franklin D. Roosevelt's secretary of state and a leading figure in the formation of the United Nations). Stettinius was floating a $100 million loan for the French government when he agreed to serve on the GM board. At Raskob's suggestion, Pierre wrote a flattering letter to Stettinius, saying, "We wish you and the other new directors to feel that General Motors is an open book to you; that all questions will be considered by all of us; that no criticism or suggestion will be received in an unfriendly way." After examining the books, Stettinius thought GM's bank debt was uncomfortably large and warned that the company "requires a little watching during the next month or two."

ᔕᗜᔕ

Henry Leland, now seventy-five, announced he would create one final motorcar at the Holden Avenue plant where he and his son had made airplane engines for the government. Friends urged Henry to call it the Leland, but he said it should be named after the greatest American—Abraham Lincoln. The Lelands financed the Lincoln themselves. They were ready for the rollout when the bottom dropped out of the automobile market in September. Once more they went under. Inventories and low sales decimated other carmakers. Hugh Chalmers threw in the towel after losing a million dollars. Durant, the Du Ponts, John Studebaker, and, uncharacteristically, Henry Ford expressed interest in acquiring the Lelands' new Lincoln. Only Ford sent the Lelands a $250,000 deposit, and in February 1922

Durant, Wall Streeter

the company was his. Because the terms were so disappointing for the Lelands, Henry and Wilfred resigned. Within a few years, the Lincoln division was an important contributor to the Ford bottom line.

GM's production was all but halted in October 1920, sending the stock skidding further. John Pratt was in Durant's office when visitors from Michigan walked in and told how they had bought GM on Billy's advice, and now were facing ruin. Billy called their brokers and told them he was taking over the stock.

∽o∾

Durant's answer to the recession was an early version of mutual funds. It was an old idea of his. Why not disperse the stock so widely among installment-plan stockholders that no one, not even the du Ponts, could manipulate or control it? He had called this General Motors Stockholders'

Services Division, and made H. W. Alger, a nephew of Catherine's, an officer in the hastily formed Durant Corporation. The new company's prospectus said it would eventually offer a variety of securities, but for the time being it was making a special $18 a share offer of GM securities to people of modest means "desiring to become permanent investors rather than speculative buyers." The $18 a share offer was made possible, the prospectus explained, because the Durant Corporation had bought GM securities during "the last few days when stocks were being thrown on the market at ridiculous prices, with the consequent demoralization aided by the speculative interests." On October 7, Billy told the press there would be a fifty-share top limit, a time payment plan, and even passbooks to allow modest investors to keep track, coin by coin, of their holdings. He expected to have 300,000 stockholders on the rolls inside of five years.

The prospectus landed, among other places, at the Delaware Teachers Association. Pierre S. du Pont was a member of the Delaware state school board, and felt he had some say in stocks being peddled to public employees. In a punctilious November 8, 1920, letter, he asked Billy to desist, as it might not be clear to everyone that du Pont was not a partner in this endeavor.

The Durant Corporation bombed where Billy most wanted it to succeed, on Wall Street. However much he gift wrapped his plan as a grassroots idea, he was doing what he berated others for doing—selling GM stock. On November 10, Morgan partner Dwight Morrow asked Pierre S. whether Durant was unloading. Was this the tip of an iceberg? On October 15, the share price was $18.

As Durant had done 20 years earlier when J. Pierpont Morgan was alive and had called him "an unstable visionary," he came to 23 Wall Street. Across from him that Wednesday morning sat Pierre S., Raskob, Morrow, and George Whitney, another Morgan banker. Morrow was a man of sharp intellect and lofty demeanor who would become a U.S. senator from New Jersey. A graduate of Amherst and Columbia Law School, he had joined Morgan a year after J. Pierpont died in 1913 and during the war had worked for the Allied Transport Council. He asked Durant whether there was some larger purpose behind the Durant Corporation. Billy said no. Did he know of any "weak accounts"? Again, the answer was no. Apparently satisfied, Morrow summed up the Morgan take on the situation. GM was basically sound, he said, and its market positions certain to improve soon. In the meantime, a "stabilizing syndicate" set up by du Pont, he concluded, was strong enough to absorb any routine selling of GM stock. At the end of the meeting, Billy agreed to allow Whitney to look into the Durant Corporation accounts.

Billy asked Raskob and du Pont to have lunch with him on Thursday, November 11, the second anniversary of Armistice Day. Visibly distraught, he explained that with the stock at $15 a share, he was fast approaching the point where he could no longer meet his personal obligations. Bankers, he said, feared news of his bankruptcy might result in the collapse of GM. Pierre tried to calm him. No bankers were pressing the corporation right now.

Pierre and Raskob were in shock as they returned to Wilmington for a weekend of reflections and, with Irénée, a search for an answer. On Monday the fifteenth, they were back in New York with a solution. To prevent Durant's bankruptcy, they would invest up to $10 million in cash and extend trade credit for millions more, if that should be necessary. Billy was too immersed in long-distance conference calls to see them that afternoon. In the evening, a personal friend, who Billy only identified as representing the du Pont interests, called at his Park Avenue apartment and told him he would have to resign as president of General Motors. "The reason given," Billy later wrote Irénée, was "that I was not in sympathy with the policies of the controlling interests and would not cooperate. I must and do plead guilty to the charge."

The gloves were off.

༺•༄

On Tuesday the sixteenth, Pierre S. and Raskob demanded to know how much Durant owed. Billy said he would have to look it up.

Brokerage houses were contacted the next day to get a handle on Billy's liabilities. Raskob suggested a syndicate be set up to soak up the Durant holdings and settle all his obligations in cash, with E. I. Du Pont de Nemours infusing $8 to $10 million. That afternoon Pierre and Raskob came to Durant's office on Fifty-seventh Street. They had to wait while he dealt with the inevitable phone calls, but were finally whisked into his office an hour after the market closed. They began with the good news. The Whitney scrutiny into the Durant Corporation accounts revealed no misconduct on Durant's part. But the question that had to be answered was, how much? In June alone, Durant had signed scores of $100,000 promissory notes, mostly to Chatham and Phoenix National Bank. From penciled notes, he produced an approximation: $34 million ($277 million in today's money).

Du Pont could not fathom how anyone could owe $34 million in promissory notes. He called Irénée in Wilmington and asked his brother to come to New York City on the first morning express. Billy's assets amounted to 3 million GM shares and 1.3 million owned by unspecified "others." That night he managed to scrape together $150,000 on a margin call due the next morning. The GM stock dropped to $13\frac{1}{2}$.

The du Pont brothers and Raskob realized that unless they somehow pulled Durant out of his mess, everybody who held General Motors stock would be ruined, and the corporation itself might go under. They were not men easily given to violent emotions, but to think of how many fortunes were at risk made them seethe with anger. Cold logic, however, won out in the end. They had no choice but to buy Billy's shares at $12, only slightly under the Big Board value Thursday morning. This solution, worked out with the Morgan bankers, was presented to Durant. Billy kept his composure, saying that such a forced sale would ruin him.

At Raskob's recommendation, it was decided to firm up the GM stock with a money pool. This stabilizing pool, politely called a holding company, would issue stock, which the du Ponts would buy for a relatively modest amount of cash. It would then issue its own notes for Billy's unpaid and overdue shares; that is, give brokers du Pont–backed collateral. Brokers holding Durant's paper, however, were quick to sniff trouble and began calling Billy with new ultimatums on when and how they wanted to be paid.

Because Thursday, November 18, 1920, was so humiliating for Durant he never left a record of the events, and so we only have Pierre's account of what happened. After the market closed Durant felt he had no choice but to ask the Morgan investment bankers for help. He asked Whitney if the stabilizing pool would buy 1.1 million GM shares from him at 13. Whitney passed the request to Morrow, who called back. Surely, he said, Durant knew members of the stabilizing pool did not buy from each other. Was he in any trouble? No, not personally, Durant told him. He had, however, loaned some of his stock to friends to help them "margin their accounts." Morrow asked the hard question: Would Durant be involved in the profits or losses of those accounts? Billy answered, "Well, in certain conditions, yes."

Perhaps Morrow sensed something in Durant's voice, because although he was leaving for a long weekend at Amherst, he invited Durant to come down and discuss

things. Billy said it would be better if Morrow came uptown to the General Motors offices, because here with him
were Russell Briggs, the secretary of the Chevrolet Company, John Thomas Smith, GM's counsel, and Billy's son-
in-law Dr. Edwin Campbell, all well acquainted with the
details. Morrow said he would be there at six, and would
bring along Whitney and the latter's assistant, Thomas
Cochran.

Billy got a shock when he called Pierre and asked him
and Raskob to join the meeting. Again, we have only du
Pont's recollection, polished, no doubt, for posterity. No,
Pierre said, he could no longer be part of any deception.
Deception? Durant had been untruthful with Morrow. He
had told Morrow there were no "weak accounts." Unless
Billy admitted to the Morgan people what he had acknowl-
edged to him and Raskob on Wednesday, they would not
participate.

Durant caved in. Du Pont and Raskob agreed to come
uptown.

Before du Pont and Raskob arrived, Billy explained
the apparent discrepancy between what he had told Morrow on the tenth and the present situation by the continued slide of GM securities. What was true when the stock
stood at 15 was no longer so at 13. Morrow interrupted.
Durant better lay all the facts on the table, and never mind
last week's events.

Under the stern gazes of Morrow, Whitney, and Cochran,
and the embarrassed glances of his own people, Billy admitted he was carrying 1.5 million shares on margin, on
which he owed $15 million, and had "interests" in other
accounts also secured by GM stock. His immediate problem, however, was tomorrow morning. Before the market
opened, he needed $940,000.

Morrow realized there would be no autumnal weekend
in Massachusetts for him. He rose and announced that he,
Whitney, and Cochran would go to dinner and be back at

nine. On their way to the elevators, they ran into Pierre, Irénée, and Raskob. All six compared notes, then split, the Wilmington trio putting their heads together at one restaurant over their dinner, and the Morgan threesome huddling in another eating place. They would meet again at nine.

At the appointed hour, ten men sat down around Durant. The masters of high finance, Morrow, Whitney, and Cochran, the scions of old and new wealth, Pierre and Irénée du Pont and their brilliant Talleyrand, and Durant's own people, his son-in-law Campbell, Russell Briggs, and GM's general counsel John Thomas Smith.

It was a long night of who owed what, who paid for what, how much, and, anyway, to whom do these shares belong? A clipping in the du Pont papers quoted Morgan partner Thomas Lamont, who was not there, as saying it all came down to "corkscrewing it out of him [Durant]." *The New Shorter Oxford Dictionary* defines the verb corkscrew as a nineteenth-century locution meaning "get out of someone by devious means or with effort." The bottom line was a shade less painful than Billy's own estimate two days earlier. He owed $27 million.

Rescuers, judges, and defenders, if that is what Campbell, Briggs, and Smith were, split up and conferred in different offices. Messages passed back and forth. They needed to raise almost $1 million by breakfast, and another $26 million soon after. They modified Raskob's stabilizing pool. The Morgan men felt it was unmanageable to keep J. S. Bache, S. B. Chapin, Arthur Lipper, Dominick and Dominick, Van Emburgh and Atterbury, and Hornblower & Weeks and a dozen other brokerage houses involved as lenders. Instead, the holding company should buy the I.O.U.'s outright from the brokers. They decided Durant should have a share in the holding company, and offered him 25 percent. Because the Chevrolet Company would be called on to help raise money, Billy held out for 40 percent.

They agreed, but he was stripped of control of his stake. To prevent him from giving in to the temptation of a sellout, his share of the holding company would be frozen until a major market rally. In return for the du Ponts' $7 million in immediate cash, he gave up 40 percent of his stock at $9.50, or 4.5 points below the market. He gave up another 20 percent to various banks for loans to the holding company, no longer called the Durant Corporation but the Du Pont Securities Company. Finally, the 40 percent that was his would stay frozen in the Du Pont Securities Company, where it would stay until a major market rebound so as not to endanger anyone. In a side agreement, the du Ponts loaned Durant $1.17 million immediately—$640,000 by morning, another $530,000 by the end of the day.

At 5:30 A.M., everybody signed the draft document.

As the sun rose over Central Park that Friday morning, Durant's "baby" was no longer his. The last awkward business was his resignation. Nobody would remember asking for it. Billy would deny he himself offered to resign, although the du Ponts would suggest he did. Morrow would make no secret of his feeling that Durant was unfit to run GM. Did Billy jump or was he pushed? The metaphor his first biographer would use was the military tradition of the "suicide" gun handed an officer who has lost his honor.

The resignation would take effect December 1, seven days before Billy's fifty-ninth birthday.

21

❦

"Forget Mistakes"

Historians never found evidence of a conspiracy by the J. P. Morgan & Company and the du Ponts to destroy Durant. "Having said that, however, there is evidence that Edward R. Stettinius speculated against Durant knowing he was doomed," Richard Scharchburg, the professor of industrial history at the Kettering University, would add. "There was money to be made on Durant's miscalculations. While he [Durant] tried to keep the stock from falling, Stettinius sold shares with the intent of buying them back at a lower price."

It had happened four months before the night of final accounts. On August 1, when the stock stood at $21\frac{1}{2}$, a broker had called Willie to say 100,000 GM shares were being dumped on the market, sending the stock into a tailspin. Trading was supposed to be secret, of course, but if anyone was wired into brokers it was Durant. With a few phone calls he quickly learned the seller was his own board member, Stettinius.

Durant had kept his cool. When he heard Stettinius

was in the GM building, he called him into his office, and in his presence dictated a memo that accused him of breaking his promise to help keep the stock above 20. We do not know what response Stettinius made, but in talks with a journalist a few years later, he flatly denied any agreement to hold the price at a particular level. The incident had left both sides locked in mutual distrust, Durant knowing at least one member of his board could not be trusted, Stettinius and the House of Morgan convinced that strong economic currents were at work and that Durant was headed toward personal disaster.

"It is of course perfectly obvious that Durant has lied continuously and persistently to all of us here and to all of his associates," Stettinius wrote to an associate after the November 20 settlement. "He has apparently been trading heavily in the stock of the Company for years and continued to do so after we came into the situation, notwithstanding his repeated assurances to me that he had no interest whatever in the market. There was at first a disposition on Pierre du Pont's part to deal rather leniently with Durant and at our meeting last Sunday he suggested that Durant might take the chairmanship of the board. None of us agreed to that suggestion of course, and we all insisted that Durant would have to be eliminated from the situation. While I most certainly do not wish to pass on to anyone else the responsibility which is mine, I nevertheless cannot comprehend how it has been possible for the entire du Pont crowd to have been in such complete ignorance, as they undoubtedly were, of Durant's position."

Ironically, the du Ponts felt the same way about the Morgan people. In a letter to Irénée, Pierre wrote: "Both W. Raskob and I have felt that Morgan & Company have been ignorant of General Motors Common stock. Morgan & Company have had every opportunity to question Mr. Durant on the subject and I have not felt it my duty to pry into Durant's affairs."

GM, as analyzed by Seward Prosser and Stettinius, was already on the way to recovery. Net earnings climbed to $3 million a month, with Cadillac and Buick the first to reduce inventory, and the corporation's bank debt was estimated to be down to $50 million.

Pratt would remember a dinner at Durant's home on Fifth Avenue attended by Trainload Collins, who ran the Cadillac operations, Harry Bassett (Buick), Fred and Tom Warner (Pontiac and Oakland plants), and the Flint lieutenants Fred Hohensee, C. W. Zimmerschied, and A. B. C. Hardy. Billy ended a little pep talk to his "boys" by telling them not to be resentful of the du Pont people and to stay in their jobs. He got through the last days at the office with a stiff upper lip. What had made him try single-handedly to keep the GM stock aloft? Alfred P. Sloan believed Durant had acted out of pride and confidence in the future. "You knew he was grief-stricken," Sloan would remember, "but no grief showed in his face. He was smiling pleasantly, as if it were a routine matter." John Pratt would recall the boss as mellow, even humble, explaining that in trying to support GM he had become, well, "overextended."

Thanksgiving came with faraway tragedy for an old friend. Gaston Chevrolet was on the 150th lap at a 250-mile Los Angeles Speedway race when he struck another machine, then careened up the banked side and through a fence. He was dead when they pulled him from the wreckage.

On December 1, Durant got his hat and coat. "Well," Pratt would remember him saying, "May 1st is usually moving day, but we are moving on December 1st." With that he walked out of General Motors for the last time, went home to Catherine, and cried. When Margery saw her father, she hugged him. In her embrace, she felt his body tremble. His tears wetted her cheek. Cliff thought he should be spunky and sent a telegram: ARRIVED HOME TODAY. FULL OF PEP AND THE OLD FIGHTING SPIRIT THAT IS BOUND TO WIN. SORRY I AM

NOT WITH YOU TO OFFER CONGRATULATIONS BUT WANT YOU TO
FEEL THAT NOT ONLY MYSELF BUT ALL THE BOYS ARE WITH YOU
HEART AND SOUL. WE ARE ALL COUNTING ON YOU TO PILOT THE
SHIP AND WE WILL DELIVER THE GOODS. AM WRITING YOU TO-
MORROW. LOVE TO CATHERINE.

On Billy's birthday, December 8, Rebecca, now eighty-
eight, wrote, "My love and blessings to my boy, Willie." Uncle
William, the Crapo family patriarch in his nineties, wrote
his sister, "I see much in the papers about my nephew,
W.C.D. I hope his difficulties are not serious. His faithful
and hard work and the comfort and happiness he has freely
given to others deserves some reward. Give him my hearty
and kind regards."

If misery needed company, the slump hit others worse
than GM. Nash Motors shut down entirely, and in December
Willys-Overland, Packard, Dodge, and Studebaker followed.
On Christmas Eve, Ford closed his factory operation without setting an opening date.

The Morgan accountants compiled to the penny the
net worth of the man who only months ago had been worth
$120 million. The total value of his shares at $9.50 was
$24,045,185.45. The sum advanced to clean his slate was
$24,037,319.61, meaning his net worth was $7,865.54. The
humbling of Billy Durant lasted one week.

∽๐๏∽

He could retire and spend his golden years with Catherine
at their palatial Raymere on the Jersey shore—because
the $7,865.54 held in his name in the Morgan treasury was
not his only asset. His mother and wife still held consider-
able GM securities (Catherine alone owned 262,000 shares),
and his severance was still to be settled. He asked John
Thomas Smith, who was staying on as GM's counsel, to
negotiate the release of his frozen assets in the Du Pont

213

Securities Company. Smith, however, got nowhere because Raskob wanted the founder of GM to waive all future claims against the corporation. Billy appealed to Pierre du Pont, who had allowed himself to be elected president of GM on condition that his appointment would be temporary. In January 1921, GM agreed to pay Durant $1.5 million in cash to dispose of all outstanding claims. He surrendered his 40 percent of Du Pont Securities Company and received $230,000 of GM common stock. He was given the right to subscribe to 65,000-odd shares, meaning that on paper he possessed a modest, but secure, income— except that GM had advanced $540,000 in taxes that he now owed, plus another $250,000 for various other outlays. Not counting the portfolio in Catherine's name, this left him with some $830,000, in 1920 dollars still a tidy sum for a man contemplating retirement.

If there was one last thing he wanted to set straight, it was in regard to the building of the General Motors headquarters in Detroit. He fired off letters to R. S. McLaughlin, Alfred Sloan, A. B. C., and Hohensee, asking them to confirm he had never advocated the construction. They all wrote back saying he had not.

∽o∾

Before the recession blew over in a blizzard of consumer goods from radios and electric refrigerators to cars, shinier bathroom fixtures, even plusher burial caskets that sent the twenties roaring, Billy decided what the world needed was a new automobile. A Durant that would compete with Chevrolet, challenge Buick, and jolt Henry Ford.

On Christmas Eve, he had written letters to sixty-seven highly placed friends and GM investors who had lost money, and four days later wrote the same people asking them to invest with him in a new automotive venture. "I know that you will appreciate how keenly disappointed I am," the first letters said. "The only satisfaction I can derive is that no human being could forecast the present financial and industrial disturbance which, I think I am safe in saying, has no equal in the history of this country."

The follow-up letter went straight to the point:

> While I am not ready at this time to make the announcement (for which reason I will ask you to treat the matter in confidence), it will probably not surprise you to know that I am still interested and a firm believer in the motor industry and that I am organizing a company, controlled by myself and several of my good friends, which will be in active operation August 1, 1921.

His letters brought an amazing response and offers of stock subscriptions. "Nowhere was the reaction so great as in Flint," Lawrence R. Gustin would write. "On the day Durant Motors was announced, the Flint Chamber of Commerce said that 'strenuous efforts' were being made to induce Durant to locate his new manufacturing plants in the city. Community leaders send 'a flood of telegrams and letters' to Durant, and petitions were circulated through downtown stores and offices with the hope of sending on 30,000 names of local citizens."

By February 1921, the GM debacle was, in Durant's public utterances, a mistake. "Forget mistakes," he told a reporter. "Forget failures. Forget everything except what you're going to do now and do it."

A month later, he startled the world of finance by launching Durant Motors, capitalized with $5 million in stock. Before a factory site was even selected, Durant Motors had orders for $31 million worth of cars. The feat was remarkable not only because it showed there was no lowering of public confidence in "little Billy," but also because he tapped into the broadening of the stock market that would mark the new decade until Black Tuesday, October 29, 1929.

The beginning of the new regime at General Motors, meanwhile, was not auspicious. The Delaware dynasty's choke hold on GM stock and du Pont officials moving into top positions at GM caused rumors that Pierre S. du Pont would relocate the company to Delaware or southeastern Pennsylvania. Behind the scenes it was Sloan whose thinking guided the vast corporation, but as the new president Pierre S. was the target of resentment in the far-flung GM production towns. A few days after taking over, Pierre S. trekked across the Midwest to calm and sweet-talk mayors and city officials in company towns. To underscore GM's commitment to Flint, he authorized the financing of a new hotel named The Durant.

Accompanied by Sloan, Raskob, and several others, du Pont traveled to Dayton to inspect a new air-cooled engine that Charles Kettering and his engineers had developed. Where Durant used to tell his racing and test pilots to push cars until they broke down so engineers could discover construction flaws, the du Pont men demanded no such grueling tests of the new "copper-cooled" engine. Instead, they pronounced themselves impressed by Kettering's demonstration and talked of the engine as the means of challenging the Model T supremacy. They decided to equip the 1922 model 4-cylinder Chevrolet with the new motor, with the 6-cylinder versions for Oakland-Pontiac and Oldsmobile models to follow.

To run Chevrolet, the du Pont team hired Henry Ford's cast-off number two man, William Knudsen. Because of the shabby way Ford had fired him, the Dane's consuming ambition was to beat Ford, on the Chevrolet team. Down the corporate ladder, however, his arrival was greeted with suspicion. "Just pass the word around that I'm not bringing any Ford men here to take your jobs," he told the first executive who came to see him. Almost 20 years younger than Durant, Knudsen had much of his predecessor's style. He was always on the go, hated paperwork, wrote his own letters in longhand, and often delivered memos to a subordinate in person. He piled into a Chevy once a year and, with Richard Grant beside him, toured dealerships. Dick Grant was the quintessential salesman, a former Delco manager who was a head shorter than Knudsen, and full of tall ideas. Knudsen and Grant made it to forty-seven states, befriending dealers and listening to their complaints. He followed up with overseas travels, tripling to 80,000 the number of Chevys sold in Europe.

Knudsen thought Kettering's new engine had possibilities, and for the 1923 New York Automobile Show ordered a few copper-cooled 4-cylinder Chevrolets built. The cars at the show were a sensation.

Pierre S. wasn't sure what to do with the old-timers, and queried Durant on bonuses to Trainload Collins, Hohensee, and Ver Linden. Next, he asked Stettinius to join the GM finance committee. Stettinius agreed, and took his role seriously enough to question a $20 million general outlay and a recommendation for $5 million to bring production of copper-cooled cars to 2,000 a day. Getting decisions out of production engineers at Flint and Pontiac turned minor difficulties into major conflicts and small rivalries into turf wars, with everybody blaming everybody else.

Only 759 air-cooled Chevys of the planned 50,000-a-month production were built, and only 100 reached their customers. All were recalled. The Kettering division was swamped with complaints about noise, clutch problems, wear and tear on cylinders, and carburetor and oil pump failures. Besides blaming the corporate structure for a lack of communications between his staff and production engineers, Kettering criticized the diktats of the new "standards committee" that decreed the new car be slimmed down to compete directly with the Ford Model T. It wasn't so simple, Kettering argued. To make the Chevy light-weight, numerous components had to be redesigned.

Complaints also came down from the top. Du Pont wrote Knudsen on March 30, 1923: "It has been reported to me that copper-cooled car No IC 1187, one of the four shipped to my brother, developed trouble with the fan belt at less than 100 miles."

The cause had nothing to do with Kettering. The fan belt had been placed on the car backward. Kettering hated failure and convinced himself that if his engineers and he had been able to work out the kinks in the prototypes, the air-cooled engine would have worked. GM would wait until 1960 before trying another air-cooled engine, this time in the Corvair.

The copper-cooled engine was canceled, and with it Chevrolet nearly went, too.

∽o∽

Of the companies Durant had folded into GM, only Buick and Cadillac were making money. Oakland-Pontiac and Olds were not doing well, and the days seemed numbered for the Sheridan and Scripps-Booth nameplates. Worst of all was Chevrolet. Efficiency experts told Pierre du Pont that Chevrolet was a good candidate for the ax. Only Sloan's impassioned advocacy, continued automotive research by Kettering, and Knudsen's energetic management saved the division.

∽o∽

Durant made a ritual visit to Flint, whose citizens had responded so generously to his request for financial backing for Durant Motors. Dallas Dort was the chief hometown

Making a Durant Four in Lansing, Michigan

booster, telling the *Flint Journal,* "You may say to the good
people of the best little city in the country that one of the
plants of Durant Motors will be located in Flint."

Billy urged patience. He didn't have the luxury to build
a factory from scratch. The recession had caused Goodyear
Tire & Rubber to retrench, and Durant Motors bought two
of its plants, a $2 million facility in Long Island City, New
York, and a smaller facility in Muncie, Indiana, where
Billy installed old friends Alfred Sturt and Fred Hohensee

to design and build Durants. What Billy had in mind was "just a real good car" to match the best-selling Chevrolet Royal Mail, Baby Grand, and the Four-Ninety models of eight years earlier. The prototype was the Durant Four, which was designed and built in forty-seven days. In an interview with *Automotive Industries,* Billy put his ambition on a global scale:

> Every mile of new highway that is built created a market for many automobiles. Most countries haven't started to build roads yet. This constant talk about a saturation point is silly. Nearly everybody carries a watch, but the watchmakers are still making watches in increased quantities. The motor car business is still in its infancy. The development of the automobile is still at the experimental stage. The next twenty years will witness an expansion of the business of automobile making more marvelous by far than that of the two decades through which we have passed.

When General Motors dumped its Sheridan model and vacated the Sheridan plant in Muncie, Indiana, Durant picked it up for 75 percent of book value, incorporated Durant Motors of Indiana, a subsidiary whose 300,000 shares sold at $10 each, and announced it would make the Durant Six. Muncie, he said, would do for the Durant Six what Buick had done for Flint.

Lansing was next. In May, Durant Motors of Michigan was chartered and Edward Ver Linden, well known in town as the president of the GM Oldsmobile division, jumped ship to head his old boss's new venture. Lansing newspapers estimated between 2,500 and 3,000 workers would be hired to build the bigger Durant Six model. Next to be launched were Durant Motors of California, headed by Cliff and Norman de Vaux, and Durant Motors of Canada. Engines for the Fours were ordered from Continental Motors of Muskegon, Michigan, engines for the Sixes from

A 1924 Durant Six

Ansted Engines in Connersville, Indiana, axles from the Adams Company of Findlay, Ohio, and a year's supply of tires from Fisk Rubber in Akron. To tout the new endeavor Jake Newmark quit Chevrolet and signed on as Durant Motors' publicity chief.

A year to the date after the November night he lost GM, the investment journal *New York Curb* told its readers how more than 30,000 orders for Durant cars had been placed. Its headline read: DURANT MOTORS: CREATED OUT OF AN IDEA BY WIZARD OF AUTOMOBILE INDUSTRY. On New Year's Eve, 1921, the Prosperity Special, a freight train carrying 500 Durant Fours, left the Long Island City plant for California. The send-off was accompanied by a press release calling the 100-car train the largest single shipment of cars ever sent to one dealer, and the largest ever transcontinental shipment of any one commodity. A month and a half later, Durant Motors announced the Star, a five-passenger, 4-cylinder car with sliding-gear transmission and self-starter, to retail at $348, the price of a Model T. Henry Ford responded with a $5 rebate.

Flush with success, Willie decided to add the Star to the Durant Fours and Sixes. At a March 10, 1922, motor show in Washington, 30,000 people viewed the Star, and similar crowds thronged showroom unveilings in Philadelphia, New York City, Boston, Detroit, and Houston. Orders rolled in. But where should Durant Motors build the small, 4-cylinder Star best-seller? Billy crossed swords with Walter Chrysler and GM over a huge plant that interested him in Elizabeth, New Jersey. At the cost of $14 million, John North Willys had built the quarter-mile-long, three-story factory during the 1919 euphoria to turn out Willys-Overland automobiles. Willys had emulated Durant in building up his company, moving his headquarters from Toledo, Ohio, to New York City, and branching into making farm equipment and airplane engines. Production had peaked in 1916 and the Overland remained an expensive car, selling for double the price of a Ford or a Chevrolet. The 1920–1921 recession hit Willys hard, and the Elizabeth factory was being auctioned off to satisfy $50 million in debt.

In the hope that something could be salvaged, the Willys-Overland creditors hired miracle worker Walter Chrysler, who had left GM and, at forty-five, retired. He didn't come cheap, but the bankers, and Willys, swallowed hard and agreed to his $1 million annual salary. In a corner of the Elizabeth plant, Walter and his engineers had designed and blueprinted a "dream engine" and a completely new car that unfortunately didn't please John Willys. The designs and blueprints were now part of the receiver's sale.

Chrysler sent a representative to Elizabeth for the auction. Durant showed up in person. Chrysler's deputy dropped out at $3.1 million, GM's at $4.4 million. At $5.25 million, Billy became the owner of a plant that could produce 400 Stars and 150 Durant Fours a day. He also became the proprietor of the Chrysler's dream engine blueprints, soon to be mocked up, prototyped, and put into production as the Durant Motor's "Flint," to compete with the Buick.

During the summer of 1922, Billy announced the new Flint Six would be built in Flint. On August 30, he came out to turn over the first spade of sod at a 100-acre property on the city's south side. "It is my ambition," he told a gathering that was estimated in the thousands, "to make this the finest plant ever built. The plant is being dedicated to the best little city and the best and most appreciative people in the world." He rushed off to New York City, and was the only absentee at a parade attended by 30,000, according to the *Flint Journal*. His nonattendance didn't prevent Mayor William McKeighan from recalling how their beloved fellow citizen had created the Durant-Dort from a handful of buggies, how he had launched Buick, willed General Motors into being, overcome adversity, and risen for a second coming to make cars bearing his own name in Flint. "I do not believe that some of the dreamers who said that Flint could be a city of two hundred and fifty thousand by 1930 were so far wrong in their predictions." After the mayor, the Reverend Howard J. Clifford told the crowd that beyond financing and building cars, Billy Durant's purpose was to help workers. "He has said to me time and again 'I would rather help hundreds of thousands of people to independence than to place a library in every city in the United States.' To the credit of Flint we have one man who stands out in the industrial life of our country as a man who puts the helping of the people above the making of millions."

Billy's overview of the future of automobiles was incisive. In a 1922 interview with a trade journal, he foretold a future 20 years hence more astonishing than the 20 years since Ransom Olds's curved-dash runabout.

Most of us will live to see this whole country covered with a network of motor highways built from point to

A 1922 Mason Motor Road King, with driver Frank "Dutch" Werk-houser

point as the bird flies, the hills cut down, the dales bridged over, the obstacles removed. Highway intersections will be built over or under the through lanes and the present dangers of motor travel, one after another, will be eliminated.

In a replay of the 1908 GM acquisitions, Billy folded into Durant Motors the struggling Mason Truck Company, the Hayes Hunt Body Company, the American Plate Glass Company, the New Process Gear Company, the ignition manufacturer Warner Corporation, and the Electric Auto-Life Company. He also picked up the bankrupt Locomobile Corporation of Bridgeport, Connecticut. The Stanley brothers' Locomobile had always been a luxury car. The 6-cylinder "48" sold for $4,800, the six-passenger Berline for $6,250 (fully loaded, it could cost $12,000). The workers in Bridgeport feared Durant would try to cut corners, but the 1924 model got a much-needed face-lift and 4-wheel drive.

To run the born-again classic Willy chose George E. Daniels, a Harvard law graduate who had left the bar to become a Buick manager in the Philadelphia territory. Daniels possessed no mechanical skills, but had an eye for automobile bodies. A few years earlier, Durant had called on him to redraw the Chevrolet. "The former lawyer whipped a new body into shape which excited the admiration of the New York crowds," Jacob Newmark would remember. "Durant was so pleased with the result that he bought space in *The New York Times* to tell the industry that Daniels was responsible for the new Chevrolet body." The new Locomobile was called the Junior. It had Daniels's trim lines, but was received indifferently. It was dropped, as was the name Junior, and a new model was introduced. Nevertheless, the Locomobile lost money from the day Durant acquired it.

Durant Motors dealers pleaded for commercial models to match the Ford showrooms, which always featured light trucks. Billy obliged by building 1- to 2-ton trucks. Arthur Mason, Billy's ally from the early Buick days, headed the Mason Truck Company, which made a workhorse called the Road King. To provide additional loading space, the truck was unconventional in design. It failed to reach the critical mass of national demand. Next, Durant announced he was going after another new car, the Princeton, as a competitor to the Packard.

Billy threw a big party at the Elizabeth plant in January 1923. In the plant's 1,200-seat cafeteria, 300 lunch guests came together ostensibly to celebrate the thirty-six-year association and friendship of Durant and Fred Hohensee. During the speechmaking, a stockbroker leaned toward Billy and stage-whispered that the Durant Motors shares stood at 84. A number of Wall Street analysts thought it likely that Durant would mount another battle and once more recapture General Motors.

Seven months later Calvin Coolidge became president following the death of Warren Harding. Durant Motors was poised to thrive with the "Coolidge Prosperity." In less than two years, 75,000 Durant cars had been built and sold. Durant Motors employed 48,000 workers in ten factories with a combined capacity of over 650,000 cars and trucks a year. Durant cars were distributed in thirty-five countries. Four thousand dealers marketed the Durant Fours and Sixes, the Stars, the Flints, the Princetons, the Locomobiles, and the Road King truck. The Durant Motors Acceptance Corporation was there for installment buying and to help dealers store cars over the winter months for early spring delivery.

For Willie, the triumph was overshadowed by the death of his mother following a third stroke. Rebecca was three weeks short of her ninety-first birthday when she passed away in Flint. Catherine, who rarely traveled with Billy to the town of his beginnings, didn't accompany him to the funeral. Margery was there with her own daughter, Edwina, and would remember her father sobbing like a child at the funeral services. He locked up his mother's house. Only four years later did he accept the finality, and had his mother's furniture moved to Raymere to remind him of what had been.

22

༐༐

Feeding Frenzy

I f there was one thing that gnawed at Billy it was the memory of the November night when his enemies had taken General Motors away from him. Now his thunderous rebirth as empire builder gave him the resources to make sure it would never happen again. The idea of becoming a banker himself appealed to him, and in April 1923 he took over the abandoned charter of the Liberty National Bank. He proclaimed it a people's bank, capitalized by 300,000 stockholders, each holding one, and only one, $150 share. The Liberty National Bank was located at 256 West Fifty-seventh Street, only a few steps from Durant Motors' headquarters at 250 West Fifty-seventh Street.

Willie threw all of his energy and enthusiasm into banking reform. He named himself chairman, and in the prospectus sent to Durant Motors dealers and stockholders, announced that neither he nor the directors would draw a salary. Loans would be made without commissions, fees, or bonuses. Liberty National would make money by charging the "legal rate of interest" and "management fees." In a dig at the Morgan bankers downtown, he added that no investment company would be part of Liberty National. Robert W. Daniel, a thirty-nine-year-old bank examiner from Virginia, was named president. From Durant Motors' loyal base of dealers and small-time investors, Liberty National raised $5 million of a potential $40 million capitalization.

When the well-known business writer B. C. Forbes asked for an interview to be published in the *New York American,* Billy thought he was being asked to sit for a glamour portrait. He should have known. better. Bertie Charles Forbes had skewered George Jay Gould as a misfit in the 1917 inaugural issue of *Forbes Magazine* ("devoted to doers and doings"), and as much as he liked to heap praise on captains of industry, he was unblinking when he felt his subject deserved inquiry. B. C., as the Scottish immigrant was universally known on Wall Street, brought enterprise reporting to business journalism, uncovering market-moving information, concentrating on the human element and sharp writing backed by carefully researched facts.

Forbes asked how Durant could finance a new company six months after leaving GM, stripped of his fortune and in debt. Willy answered that a friend he wouldn't identify was helping him. The friend had "made subscriptions in my name and received the stock when issued." Forbes also asked about assets, capitalization, income figures, and management plans, and, after interviewing others, published a piece that explained how Durant had formed two companies, Durant Motors and Star Motors, which created instant paper assets by giving each other contracts. Forbes called the new companies' finances shaky, and the stock overpriced. In the first installment, Forbes lashed out at insider trading and described how Durant and his friends paid $10 a share while everybody else paid $19 or more. Billy lost his customary sangfroid and in a letter to B. C. not only accused him of distortion, but demanded to know who his informants were.

Forbes was not always ungenerous toward Durant. Three years later, when he coauthored *Automobile Giants of America,* he noted Billy's generosity:

> I personally know of many incidents illustrating Durant's unselfishness and generosity. He has done more for others than many men whose names are blazoned in the newspapers as wonderful philanthropists. I am convinced that Durant's chief ambition has never been to roll up scores and scores of millions of dollars for himself. His is not a mercenary ambition. He loves power; he constantly itches to accomplish big things.

Billy was deeply suspicious of the lords of capitalism, and saw dark forces working against him. He heard rumors that the *Wall Street Journal's* Clarence Barron was out to get him at the behest of the Chase Securities Company, which was supposedly envious of Liberty National. He asked S. S. Fontaine, the *Wall Street Journal* editor, to help him corroborate the Barron rumor, saying it would be "a wonderful addition to my already large collection . . . having to do with Wall Street methods and the operation of the Money Control."

Barron agreed to interview Durant. Their October 23, 1923, conversation turned quickly to Billy's stewardship of General Motors. To questions of his profligacy, Billy made a few points:

> I never approved of the big building in Detroit or the centralized policy for our operations. I took the Wilmington people up to Detroit and had our heads of departments meet them. To my great surprise Raskob addressed these people and told them they could have all the money they wanted for expansion. I regretted this because I had been talking economy to all of them.

The two Stars, the Flint, the expensive Locomobile, and the Road King trucks didn't repeat the Buick, Cadillac, and Chevrolet success records of ten and fifteen years ago. From the January high of 84, the Durant Motors stock slipped to 64 and was soon down to 47. Meanwhile, Sloan, Knudsen, and Grant celebrated the Chevy's thirteenth birthday on November 3, 1924. Juggling the figures for the press, the trio emphasized the "phenomenal growth" of the last three years, meaning the period since Durant had left the company. The one millionth Chevrolet had rolled off the assembly plant the year before. But the reality was that the Chevy had suffered a slump in 1924, and faced a brilliant new challenger.

Walter Chrysler had finally put his surname on an automobile. The Chrysler Six was to have been unveiled at the January 1924 New York Motor Show, but was refused because it was not yet in commercial production. Undeterred, Walter rented the lobby of the Hotel Commodore on Forty-second Street, and put the Six on display to motor show goers. The $1,250 car offered performance at a relatively low cost, a high-compression engine, and 4-wheel hydraulic brakes. The 1924 production run was 32,000. Only two years later, 170,000 Chryslers had been built. Much of the success lay in Walter's knack for picking top lieutenants, a trait he shared with Durant. K. T. Keller, who had been his right-hand production man at Buick, was in charge of production at Chrysler.

∽∘∾

The ten millionth Ford came off the Dearborn, Michigan, assembly line on June 4, 1924, with befitting fanfare. But the Model T's days were numbered. Sales dropped below the previous year's high-water mark for the first time. Cutting the price had worked before, of course, but with a

$295 sticker price on the touring car, Ford no longer had room to shave his price tag. The 1925 Model T was unchanged and had to compete with the new Sloan-Kettering-Knudsen Chevrolet that came with a one-piece windshield, a solid walnut steering wheel with a notched finger grip, automatic wipers, an improved clutch system, a new rear axle assembly, new larger brakes, and a choice of colors.

The writing was on the wall when a highly valued Ford dealer in Buffalo, New York, gave up his Ford franchise to take on Chevrolet. Nothing could persuade him to change his mind. Perhaps more galling for Ford were letters from consumers offering him advice. "Right outside my window stands a Ford, a Star and an Essex, and across the street a Chevrolet and a Pontiac," wrote B. F. O'Brien from Moline, Illinois. "The owner of each of these cars traded in a Ford. In fact, they never owned anything else but a Ford until this year, and the fellow who still has the Ford is about to buy an Essex."

Sales of the Model T dropped by 100,000 in 1925. The following year, Chevrolet came out with a new body from the Fisher brothers. Unchanged, the Model T's sales dropped 250,000 below the 1925 output. Henry Ford blamed his dealers, saying they had grown fat and lazy. He denounced Chevrolet for bringing out new cars every year. "We want the man who buys one of our products never to have to buy another," he declared. "We never make an improvement that renders any previous model obsolete."

The public could not believe "old Henry" didn't have something up his sleeve, but he didn't. Increasingly a sulking recluse, he had only yes-men under him now, as James Couzens had left with Knudsen. Planned obsolescence gave carmakers a self-renewing supply of customers, but selling a new car every few years demanded millions of dollars in design, research, and advertising.

Only one new company had begun making cars in 1923

(fourteen were crowded out). Chrysler and one other entrant started up in 1924, and fifteen fell into bankruptcy. None entered in 1925, only one the following year when the total of North American carmakers was forty-four. And there were price pressures. Roy Chapin sold his new Essex models for $900 for the touring car and only $100 more for the coach. This was the first time a 6-cylinder automobile sold for less than $1,000. Chapin created a greater stir by keeping his closed and open Hudson models at $1,500. This proved disastrous for Ford. When the price disadvantage was removed from the closed, one-body model, sales of the open car plummeted, and that hurt first and foremost the Model T. An unexpected side benefit of the closed car was that it turned the automobile into a year-round vehicle. Dealers found they could talk a prospect into making a down payment even in the late fall. Alvin Macaulay, who had gone from Burroughs Adding Machines to Packard, lopped $80 off the 1925 sedan and watched sales spurt.

ᔥ᫏ᔣ

If Ford's sin was inflexibility, Durant's was distraction. At a time when Ford should have realized his beloved Tin Lizzie was more than fifteen years old, he refused to listen to his dealers and young lieutenants who urged him to okay the development of a new car. At a time when Durant should have redoubled his efforts, he turned, imperceptibly at first, away from his newest creation. A nameplate could no longer challenge the established marques on the strength of one successful model or model year. Billy let himself be distracted by ticker tape. Perhaps the temptation—fueled by market growth—was simply too great. President Coolidge put it mildly when he declared in 1925 that "the business of America is business." Everybody was

THE SPORT ROADSTER $1025
WITH RUMBLE SEAT
Both seats upholstered in genuine leather. Standard equipment includes extra wire wheel with tire and cover, front bumper, rear bumperettes, and wind-shield wings.

A Durant roadster, 1925

spending and the economy advancing at a record clip. New techniques of mass production allowed such giants as U.S. Steel to reduce its workday from 12 to 8 hours, to hire 17,000 additional workers, to raise wages, and still show rising profits. Although no more than 1.6 million Americans were involved in the stock market during the decade, their much-publicized successes fueled the optimism, which in turn fed the happy picture of higher standards of living and stable prices. Prosperity seemed to have no ceiling.

Durant Motors' publicity chief Jake Newmark was appalled at seeing his boss neglect their enterprise. Writing with the benefit of hindsight in 1936, Newmark would remember Durant in his office at the corner of Broadway and Fifty-seventh Street initiate waves of stock purchases reaching from New York to San Francisco and principal points in between. He had good reason to worry. Willie Durant cut quite a figure on Wall Street. He knew everybody of importance, everywhere, and his word was accepted absolutely. Not only that, but he was custodian for many accounts, and had unlimited discretion; he could do what he wanted with them, buy or sell as he willed.

He made money for people when the market trend was right. But it was different when he guessed wrong. Contemporaries thought of him as one of the most dynamic figures on Wall Street, ever believing that there could be no retreat and that the country was going constantly onward to greater heights of industrialism, expansion, and corporate earnings. It is said that he never sold a share of stock short. John Pratt, the E. I. Du Pont de Nemours executive who had become Durant's assistant in 1919, said Durant thought short selling was immoral. "He didn't think it was right for anyone to sell something he didn't have," Pratt would remember. What Willie believed was that business would provide everyone with a steadily increasing share of ever-expanding prosperity. It seemed heretical to pay any heed to the likes of economist Roger Babson, who warned that a crash would come sooner or later. Billy was in one stock pool that reportedly netted him $20 million.

He bought Studebaker at 50 and saw it rise to 100, pocketing an estimated $4 million. He bought stock in the 40 percent of Fisher Body not owned by GM and followed its climb from 150 to 214. He paid $35 a share for United States Cast Iron Pipe and Foundry, the manufacturer of three-quarters of the country's gas and water meters, and saw it sprint to 100 and then, in late 1924, spurt to 138. The *New York Times* had him on the front page twice in two months, first as Wall Street's "top winner" after he bid up Cast Iron Pipe, Southern Railway, Missouri Pacific, and Radio Corporation of America (RCA), then in a follow-up story that estimated his two-day win at $2.5 million. "Say Durant's Profit Is Now $2,000,000," headlined the *New York Times* on September 9, 1924. Dividends alone brought Billy between a quarter and three-quarters of a million a year.

Who needed a car company?

Margery was a new woman. Divorcing Dr. Edwin Campbell, she easily joined the Jazz Age, cutting and bobbing her hair, and slipping into cloche hats, silk stockings, and fake jewelry. She loved music, entertainment, and travel. With Edwina on her way to Vassar College, Margery moved to Westbury, Connecticut, bought a sailboat, and had her father and stepmother up for weekends. In time she would have a plane and a pilot to fly her on adventurous jaunts.

She married Bob Daniel, the president of Liberty National Bank. Related to the Reynolds tobacco family, the dark, handsome Virginian owned an aging mansion on the James River. Margery spent part of her trust fund restoring the property. But the marriage barely outlived the restoration. Margery and Bob divorced in 1927.

Billy's relationship with his son was cordial but somewhat distant. The only thing the two had in common was their easy charm. Billy was as driven as ever. Cliff had none of the passion and talent for work that consumed his father and had given his great-grandfather a fortune.

Cliff's attention to Durant Motors of California was less than focused. As a partner with Norman de Vaux, thirty-six-year-old Cliff spent more time in Hollywood than at the Durant Motors headquarters in Oakland. Heading for his second divorce, he bought a schooner and sailed to Catalina Island, the Sunday playground for tony film people. There he sported himself with Mabel Normand, the drug-addicted fading comedienne of Mack Sennett and Chaplin one-reelers. Desperate for a semblance of a normal life, she had married Lew Cody, her costar in her first feature-length picture. Cliff rented a house in Beverly Hills, joined the airplane craze, and toyed with the idea of joining Ben O. Howard, who had discovered a profitable market building planes for bootleggers needing aircraft to bring liquor from Canadian and Mexican airstrips. Cliff

Durant in California: *(from left to right)* Norman de Vaux, Oakland Mayor Richard Davie, and Durant

bought a 26,000-acre estate in Roscommon, Michigan, by air less than 100 miles from Sault Ste. Marie, Ontario. He played the market with much of his father's skill, but with greater caution. In May 1927, Cliff advised his father he could line up good purchasing prospects. Billy wired back: BUY (WOULD SUGGEST) 3,000 GENERAL TWO SHARES FOR ONE AT NEXT MEEING WITH SIX PERCENT ON NEW STOCK AND EXTRAS. LOOK FOR DECIDED ADVANCE. BEST REGARDS. DAD.

Cliff, who didn't like New York City, had an arrangement with a young broker at Wall Street's Clarke, Childs, Inc. In jokey language, Cliff called in his orders from his mother's house, golf courses, racetracks, and hotels in Europe. His brokerage fees averaged $3,000 a month.

Willy spoiled both his children. More than any of her husbands, Pops kept Margery in style. If Cliff managed to make some money, Dad was always there in a pinch to soak up a stock market speculation gone wrong. Cliff's affection for booze led Willy to champion prohibition. In August 1928, he offered $25,000 to anyone who could come up with a practical way of enforcing the much-flaunted Eighteenth Amendment.

That year, Margery started a dope habit when she became ill during a trip to France. Whether she managed to conceal her dependency from her father is not known, but over the next twenty years she would go through $100,000 for narcotics.

Adelaide Frost Durant, Cliff's cast-off first wife, married Eddie Rickenbacker, the war ace who had shot down twenty-six German planes and was involved in several airline ventures. Addie and Eddie became fast friends of Billy and Catherine. Durant graciously opened a Rickenbacker account with the brokerage firm of Block, Maloney and Company. Billy had ten accounts with Benjamin Block, the chief broker, in his own and Catherine's name.

∽o∾

For Christmas and New Year's that winter of 1925–1926, Catherine managed to tear her husband away for a Florida vacation. They traveled down the East Coast in their private railroad car, sharing its luxury accommodations with Mr. and Mrs. Randolph Hicks. As Billy was now doing for the Rickenbackers, he was making the Satterlee and Canfield lawyer and his wife rich by skillfully managing their stock portfolio.

Like the rest of the Jazz Age rich, the Durants were captivated by the sixty miles of coastline from Palm Beach south to Miami. Addison Mizner, the "society architect," was transforming Palm Beach into a pseudo-Spanish playground for the wealthy. Everybody was making money on

Durant at age sixty-five

land. Prices had soared, and those who came to scoff often stayed to speculate. The 1926 hurricane season, which resulted in 400 dead and yachts tossed up on the avenues of Miami, had ended the rush. The Durants and the Hicks were staying at the Royal Poinciana Hotel. They were not in the same league as Marjorie Merriweather Post, whose 118-room residence was the latest "Gold Coast" addition, but caught glimpses of her and of Edward T. and Lucretia Stotesbury of the Philadelphia & Reading Railroad fortune. The Stotesburys' parties, planned with the help of seventy-five servants, were among the most sought-after affairs on the Palm Beach social calendar.

More intriguing was that Alfred I. du Pont, the black sheep of the family, was pulling his assets out of the Delaware business and moving them to Florida. Alfred had battled his cousins Pierre S. and Irénée for control of E. I. Du Pont de Nemours. At fifty-seven, he had caused a social ruckus by marrying Jessie Bell, who was twenty-one years his junior. But the blowup came when Pierre became Delaware's tax commissioner and sent a deputy to review Alfred's accounts. "I'll be damned if I'm going to have Pierre going over my books," he snapped, and moved his wealth, estimated at between $30 and $200 million, to Florida. Taking advantage of the hurricane-provoked slump in land prices, he bought hundreds of thousands of acres for a few dollars an acre.

On Sunday, January 11, the Hickses and the Durants boarded the Durants' private car, hitched to the rear of the Florida East Coast Railroad's Poinciana train, for the ride back north. They were having breakfast in their "drawing room" compartment when, during a rainstorm, the train stopped in the middle of nowhere. Catherine left the compartment and went a couple of cars ahead, perhaps to inquire about the delay. Before anyone could wonder what was causing the delay, the Overseas Limited, the train behind them, plowed into the immobilized locomotive and cars. Rescue workers pulled three dead and thirty injured from the wreck. When they reached Durant and the Hickses, blood was pouring from Billy's head. The rear-ending had sent him smashing against the compartment's forward wall, his head striking a washstand. He was bruised over much of his body, and in shock. The Hickses were shook up but otherwise unharmed. Catherine was thrown to the ground in the car ahead of the Durants. An eyewitness would remember how rescuing hands got Catherine down from the train, how she broke away from the another woman holding her hand, and in the rain ran back along the track, screaming for Billy.

A local doctor bandaged Durant, whose first thought was the market. Before he, Catherine, and the Hickses transferred to an express provided especially by the railroad, he fired off a telegram saying: WE HAD A BAD SMASHUP ESCAPED BY A MIRACLE. SOME BRUISES BUT STILL IN THE RING.

Exaggerated rumors of his injuries caused several of his preferred securities to drop. When the special pulled into Richmond, Virginia, he placed buy orders. At Union Station in Washington, D.C., he bought more choice stocks at bargain prices. Photographers got shots of Durant, his head swathed in bandages, at New York's Pennsylvania Station. When his private physician, Dr. John F. Erdmann, came to check on him at the Park Avenue apartment, he found his patient propped up in bed, on the phone. Erdmann ordered the protesting financier taken to the Post Graduate Hospital.

A week and a half after the Florida accident, Billy was credited not only with rallying a sagging market but with adding points to U.S. Cast Iron Pipe, Independent Oil and Gas, and Humble Oil. Between January 13 and January 17, the *New York Times* covered the Durant bedside and Wall Street rallies on a daily basis, and on the twenty-first reported the bears "turned tail and ran when the word was spread about the street that 'Durant is back.'"

He was the king of the bulls with every intention of remaining the pied piper leading Wall Street to ever greater heights, but the accident and its aftermath forced him to resign from Durant Motors. The February 18 announcement said he was giving up active management partly on medical advice and partly to concentrate on his investments. What wasn't said was that the company bearing his name was falling behind in the auto race.

General Motors, meanwhile, was now leading the pack.

Just over half of all cars sold in 1925 were GM and Ford models. If Billy had hoped Durant Motors would be a respectable number three, he was sorely disappointed. Walter Chrysler bought the late Dodge brothers' bankrupt firm, refurbished the Dodge, and later launched the Plymouth to compete with Chevrolet. Together, Chrysler, Dodge, and Plymouth cornered 20 percent of the market.

Durant and Dort at lunch in New York City, early 1920s

Durant and forty other carmakers shared the remaining 30 percent.

The Durant cars were also-rans compared to the Chrysler output. The Star was unable to compete in price with Chevrolet and Ford. The Princeton never went beyond two display models, a roadster and a touring car, and the Durant and Flint models lacked distinction and could not match impressive new features in the 1925 Chrysler line.

Henry Ford threw a monkey wrench into all car sales

241

in 1927 when he finally abandoned the Model T, laid off thousands of workers, and began work on the new Model A. The decision dried up the market as would-be customers put off buying until the new Ford was ready. When the Model A was first shown, police had to be called out in several cities to handle the crowds. With all its improvements, the lowest-priced Model A sold for $100 less than the Chevrolet.

Servicing Durant Motors' initial debt sucked finances from the product enhancements that would keep the Stars, the Durants, and the Locomobiles up there with the front-runners. It also left little money for advertising at a time when the automotive leaders were just discovering mammoth, nationwide advertising campaigns. Billy admitted as much in 1928 when he told the *New York Times* that "the automotive industry will eventually be composed of three or four big combinations."

23

⁓ഛ⁓

Stock Pools

Walking away from his latest "baby" was easier said than done. A year after retiring from the now skidding Durant Motors, he was back on the job. The *New York Times* carried the announcement in its March 22, 1927, edition:

> Now fully recovered from his serious illness of a year ago, he proposes to devote his entire time (with every other interest secondary) to a thoroughly constructive motor car program that will duplicate his previous and widely known accomplishment in this field.

The newspaper added that Durant would make a further statement on April 7. In anticipation, Durant Motors stock rose from 11 to $13\frac{3}{8}$, but the April 7 announcement proved less than inspiring. Billy declared he intended to form Consolidated Motors to make a new 6-cylinder Star. To minimize any conflict of interest, he was resigning his directorship in Liberty National and three other companies in whose stock he had been active. Twenty-five thousand

Durant Motors stocks were dumped on the market the next day. Two weeks later, for an immediate $2.5 million cash infusion, Durant Motors sold the Long Island City plant back to Ford. Billy tried to consolidate Durant Motors— not with a market leader like Chrysler, however, but with stragglers in even worse shape. The Durant Motors' models, he announced, would consolidate with the Moon, the Chandler, the Hupmobile, the Jordan, and the Peerless. Ten years earlier, the Peerless of Cleveland, Ohio, had been the third P (with Pierce-Arrow and Packard) of American luxury cars. Its interiors were so wildly luxurious, had written the *Automobile Trade Journal* in 1914, "as to make the fanciest limousines of our day seem like Bulgarian third-class railway cars." Like the Moon, the Chandler, the Hupmobile, and the Jordan, however, the Peerless had been going downhill for years. The merger followed the Consolidated Motors idea into oblivion.

Catherine decided a European vacation would take her husband away from it all. The great ocean liners now had radio-relayed ticker tapes to inform passengers of the additional money they would be able to spend when they reached Southampton and Cherbourg. Whether in New York, Miami, or the middle of the Atlantic, Billy was forever the bullish buyer. He was not alone. John Raskob, the Fisher brothers, and Arthur Cutten, who had made his fortune in the grain market, were fearlessly buying. With Ford's Model A delayed, they figured GM would have a record year. They also bought RCA stock in vast quantities, on the insider advice of Joseph P. Kennedy.

The father of the future president was a stock speculator in Durant's class, ruthless and brilliant with money. By issuing stock like Durant, Kennedy had bought a low-rent Hollywood studio from its British creditors, and just before Al Jolson and Warner Brothers launched talking pictures, merged it with the also-ran Pathé Pictures. Together with RCA's David Sarnoff, Kennedy was plotting

Willie and Catherine Europe-bound, 1928

the profitable merger of his movie holdings with RCA, the owner of a sound recording system that rivaled Warner's. Billy invested heavily in RCA, the speculators' favorite.

Automobiles and radio were the brightest feathers in the Coolidge Prosperity. All the markers by which the price of a promising common stock could be measured were constantly exceeded. Stocks were being bought for marginal down payments of as little as 10 percent, with the bulk of the purchase financed by brokers' credit. Kennedy, Durant, and the other bull operators were merely leading a stampede, even if thousands of speculators were selling stocks short in the expectation of a market collapse. They also knew, as Frederick Allen would write in *Only Yesterday: An Informal History of the 1920s,* that thousands of speculators "would continue to sell short, and could be forced to repurchase if prices were driven relentlessly up. And finally, they knew their American public. It could not resist the appeal of a surging market. It had an altogether normal desire to get rich quick, and it was ready to believe anything about the golden future of American business."

Stories of fortunes made overnight were on everybody's lips. Housewives were more interested in the price of RCA than the price of roast beef. Waitresses and men's room attendants in fashionable clubs, gardeners with an opportunity to loiter behind hedges on Long Island estates, taxi drivers, charwomen, anyone who could snoop, peep, or eavesdrop, had a tip. Everybody had heard about the chauffeur who had made a killing on Wall Street and retired to a country estate. Now his chauffeur was doing it.

～○～

Durant and Raskob were on opposite sides regarding politics. Billy was a lifelong Republican, Raskob a commanding voice in the Democratic Party. They were also on opposite sides of the "noble experiment" that made it a federal offense to sip a tot of whiskey. As ever more Americans flaunted the 1919 National Prohibition Act, Billy softened his stand, but maintained the federal government should control liquor.

The General Motors stock, which Durant had been forced to sell at \$9.50 that November night in 1920, stood at $139\frac{3}{4}$ on March 4, 1928, advancing in two short hours to $144\frac{1}{4}$. It gained $2\frac{1}{4}$ points the following Monday, crossed 150 on Tuesday, pushed ahead by $9\frac{1}{4}$ points at the end of the week. RCA was in the same league, leaping upward for a net gain of $12\frac{3}{4}$ points to close at $120\frac{1}{2}$. On March 26, RCA jumped 18 points and GM 5 points. Men and women jammed brokers' offices, watching as GM reached 185.

But Durant Motors was still a problem. How could it be saved? In October 1928, Billy came up with what was either a stroke of genius or a move of desperation. In a transatlantic partnership with the Société Française d'Automobile, Durant Motors would sell a snazzy French car in its showrooms in return for the Société selling Durant models in Europe. The little French Amilcar was among the decade's classic sports cars. It featured a 6-cylinder; twin-cam engine that was powerful enough to propel it to speeds of 110 mph. A contract was signed in Paris. But the idea was too little, too late.

Parts of Durant Motors would struggle on for a few more years, but at the January 1929 annual luncheon, Billy told his dealers he was once more quitting. His excuse for stepping down was that he had to attend to other, unspecified, demands. It must have sounded hollow, if not downright offensive, to his listeners to hear him say he had been terribly busy during the last year, investing over a billion dollars for banks, trust companies, and individuals—undertakings "thirty-five times greater than Durant Motors, with all its plants." He ended by saying:

> Do not for one moment gain the impression that I am retiring from business or releasing control of the company bearing my name. I am, however, delegating to the ablest group of men I could find the entire management of Durant Motors, Incorporated.

The ablest group turned out to be four executives of the Dodge Motor Company made redundant when Walter Chrysler took over that bankrupt company. Durant paid them $37,500 each a year, and the team managed to sell 75,000 cars in the boom year of 1929.

He had entered the car business twenty-five years earlier by finding financing for the nearly stillborn Buick. A few weeks after his sixty-eighth birthday, he left the business in the hope that others would somehow salvage his latest creation. The failure of Durant Motors would leave much bitterness among fiercely loyal followers. Jake Newmark was one of them. In 1936, when it was all over, he would write:

> Those who had the wisdom to stay with General Motors have had no cause to regret it while those who followed Durant have wasted ten years of their lives and, in all cases, are worse off financially than they were years ago.

∞০∽

Margery's third marriage had been as disastrous as her second, but mercifully shorter. The man was only known as "Mr. Cooper, the ginger-ale king," in family records. Shortly after their divorce, "Miss Durant," as she styled herself, met and fell in love with Fitzhugh Green, the literary collaborator and ghostwriter for the celebrity of the hour.

Green was the coauthor of Charles Lindbergh's first account of his historic transatlantic flight. We do not know whether Margery's new boyfriend introduced Billy and Catherine to Lindbergh, but they were thrilled to meet her new man. Green, an appealing outdoorsman and biographer of discoverers and explorers, was a year younger than Margery. After graduating from Annapolis, he had served as an intelligence officer in the Great War. In 1924, he had joined Richard E. Byrd's arctic team, and had since written books on polar explorers Byrd, Peary, and Bartlett.

The Lindbergh book was simply called *We,* meaning Lindbergh and the *Spirit of Saint Louis*. At the request of the Doubleday editor, Fitzhugh had written the closing chapters of what was an instant best-seller. In November 1933, Margery and Fitzhugh married—his second, her fourth.

24

~∞~

Bubble Economy

When Alfred E. Smith, a New Yorker with a fondness for wearing brown derbies, was chosen as the Democratic presidential hopeful against Herbert Hoover in 1928, Smith appointed as party chairman the ardent John J. Raskob (a choice that didn't sit well with southern party stalwarts). To give the Democratic Party a bullish address, Raskob moved the party headquarters to the General Motors Building in Manhattan.

Wall Street had a couple of scares after Hoover became the thirty-first president. To cool the market, the Federal Reserve Board tightened its own lending to member banks so that they in turn would dampen speculative credit. Billy was incensed. The creation of the Federal Reserve Bank itself was an abomination, he said, an undue burden on commerce. His alternative was to make Liberty Bonds legal tender.

Sitting on a fortune while the rest of Wall Street was in ruin made Joe Kennedy realize it would be easier for less fortunate people to forgive his riches if he claimed it was a hunch that had saved him, not his ability to analyze a situation in the most clearheaded way or his refusal to be swept along on the tides of opinion. Shrewdly, he began telling of how, elbowing his way into a broker's office during the summer of 1929, he momentarily gave up and surrendered instead to a shoeshine boy in the lobby. "The boy who shined my shoes didn't know me," Joe would tell *Newsweek* the year his son John F. Kennedy became president. "He wasn't looking for a market tip, but he told me precisely what was going to happen to various stocks on the market that day. I listened silently as I looked down on him and when I left the place I thought: 'When a time comes that a shoeshine boy can tell you what's going to happen in the market and be entirely correct, there's something the matter with me or the market.' And I got out."

Durant had no shoeshine boy to make him stop and think. During the spring he had applauded the decision of several New York banks to counter the Federal Reserve's attempt to let some air out of the financial bubble. Anything was better than a panic, reasoned Charles E. Mitchell, president of National City Bank. Durant joined right in: "Any group of eight men with, or assuming, power which, by careless or intentional action, succeeded in destroying credit and confidence—the basis of our great prosperity—will be subject to criticism by every sensible businessman," he told the *New York Times* on February 28, 1929. President Hoover had been in office five weeks when Durant asked for, and received, an invitation for a late-night White House meeting. Rushed into the Oval Office at 9:30 P.M. for what turned into a wide-ranging, one-hour conversation, Billy beseeched the president to rein in the Federal Reserve.

The threat of asset-price inflation, and its consequences, was only vaguely understood, and even the Fed
hesitated. Its minutes that spring read: "There is no means
of knowing beyond question how far this recent rise in
stock prices represents excessive speculation." Which was
another way of saying the Fed didn't want to be blamed if,
as a result of its interest hikes, the bubble imploded into
a recession. Hoover had campaigned on prosperity for
all, and his Republican administration had no intention of
dabbling in interventionist ideas. While neither Hoover
nor Durant would leave detailed accounts of the meeting,
we can assume that the industrialist millionaire's warn-
ings of an out-of-control Federal Reserve fell on receptive
presidential ears.

Hoover owed much of his election to the bull market.
His endorsement by party leaders had only been lukewarm,
but on the day of his nomination, Wall Street gained its
balance. The defection of southern Democrats from the Al
Smith ticket had assured Hoover's election, but many progressive Republicans distrusted him. What Durant told
Hoover that April 3, 1929, evening was that by curbing
credit, the Fed might bring about the collapse it kept saying it was trying to avoid. When the aftermath of the
stock market crash was a spreading worldwide crisis and
reporters asked Billy if it was true he had foretold a "financial disaster of unprecedented proportion" to the president, he replied, "I intimated as much to him."

∽o∾

Durant rode the market for all its worth. He had over
thirty brokers working for him, some of them with mul-
tiple accounts for him, for Margery, for old Buick and
Chevrolet dealers, for Trainload Collins, for Durant Motors vice president George McLaughlin, and for a number

of subcontractors. He made daily calls to almost all the brokers, ordering them to buy here, sell there, juggling Columbia Gramophone, American Can, Anaconda, and U.S. Steel. Unlike Joe Kennedy, who after his shoeshine incident sold his 75,000 RCA shares at $50 a share, Billy rode the stock up. On September 5, RCA stood at 505. In one ten-day span, he invested $400,000 and earned $145,855.

While GM and Ford went from strength to strength, Durant Motors was failing largely because it was underfinanced. Wall Street market gyrations didn't bother Ford. He considered stockholders to be parasites and preferred to plow profits back into the business. "The stockholders had already received a great deal more than they had put into the company," Ford told John Dodge. When Dodge suggested Ford should buy out his fellow stockholders, Henry dismissed the suggestions. He already had control. What he paid attention to was technical leapfrogging by GM. When William Knudsen introduced a 6-cylinder Chevrolet in the fall of 1929, Ford immediately ordered work to start on a new V-8 engine. Thirty different V-8s were designed, built, tested, and rejected by Henry. To get it right, he gave the go-ahead "to spend money until it hurts."

Alfred Sloan paid attention to the stock market. GM's stock, which Willie had been forced to give up at $9.50 to cover his $27 million debt, stood, on September 3, 1929, at $181\frac{7}{8}$. Du Pont, Raskob, and the Morgan bankers were making out, on his hunches and audacity. The 1.5 million shares he had surrendered to cover his margins that November night in 1920 were now worth more than a quarter billion dollars. And even his chief antagonist was now in a stock pool with him. Raskob had joined a syndicate whose other heavy hitters included Charles Schwab, Percy Rockefeller, Mrs. David Sarnoff, and—who would have guessed—the one-time locomotive cleaner from Ellis, Kansas, Walter Chrysler. "The way to wealth," Raskob wrote in a *Ladies Home Journal* article entitled "Everybody Ought to be

Rich," "is to get into the profit end of wealth production in this country."

Billy bought time for a fifteen-minute radio address over New York's WABC station on April 14. The speech earned him the headline he expected in the next morning's *Times:* W.C. DURANT DEMANDS RESERVE BANK KEEPS ITS HANDS OFF BUSINESS.

There were letters from small-time investors, wrenching letters asking for advice on how to recover losses on Durant Motors stock. The market emboldened Billy to put $5 million in a kind of conscience fund. Copy was written for a *Saturday Evening Post* ad offering a list of serial numbers of securities that "W.C. Durant wishes to buy." The advertisement never ran because lawyers told him that if challenged, no court would allow him to redeem one stockholder and not another. He would have to pay off all holders submitting their shares.

Billy and Catherine sailed on April 19 aboard the *Aquitania* on a second trip to Europe. In London and Paris he spent the afternoons on the transatlantic telephone with his brokers. To keep up with the action on Wall Street, he ran up a record $1,409 phone bill. On May 31, he gave a lecture to members of the American Club in Paris, saying that U.S. prosperity rested on three pillars—affordable automobiles, the value of labor, and "our ability to raise enormous sums of money for industrial development." To his own rhetorical question of where the money came from, he answered that it came in part from wealth accumulated by intelligent and energetic people.

"Say what you will, confidence—not halfway confidence but 100 percent confidence (with a small portion of conservative optimism) is the real basis of our prosperity. With all the wealth in the world, confidence lacking, we never could have reached the position we occupy today, and this great asset, confidence, should not be destroyed.

That is the reason why the businessmen of America are almost a unit against the present policy of the Federal Reserve Board."

He added that credit was America's lifeblood, that margin buying was a way of capitalizing the future, and that brokers' loans were proof of prosperity. Because the Federal Reserve could not see the error of its ways and did not have the courage to reverse its tight credit policy, the result might indeed be "fear, trembling and destruction of confidence."

On June 18, Billy and Catherine returned to New York aboard the *Majestic* as stock prices rose out of all proportion to earnings, indicating the market's willingness, as one broker later put it, to discount not only the future but also the hereafter. Brokerage houses came up with a wondrous proliferation of holding companies and investment trusts that existed to hold stock in other companies, and these companies often existed to hold stock in yet other companies. Pyramiding, it was called. Three hundred million shares were estimated to be carried on margin.

Like Joe Kennedy, Durant was rarely identified as a buyer, but he was such a known presence that he figured in newspaper doggerels:

We are lost! The Captain shouted
As he staggered down the stairs.
"I've got a tip," he faltered,
"Straight by wireless from the aunt
Of a fellow who's related
To a cousin of Durant."
At these awful words we shuddered
And the stoutest bull grew sick
While the brokers cried "More margin!"
And the ticker ceased to tick.

The Federal Reserve tightened its lending to member banks in August. The medicine had its intended effect. Higher interest rates calmed the roiling market, and pushed stock prices down. In a switch, National City's Mitchell declared that this correction had done "an immense amount of good by shaking down the market." On October 22, Mitchell had new assuring words: "I know of nothing fundamentally wrong with the stock market or with the underlying business and credit structures." Durant asked for congressional control of the eight Federal Reserve members. To create momentum for muzzling the Fed, he sent reprints of his Paris speech to a long list of corporate presidents. This was no time to get cold feet, he repeated to anybody who would listen.

∽o∾

A week later, Durant's edifice, honeycombed with speculative credit, crumbled with the rest of the market. The voices rising from the stock exchange floor became a roar of panic. Sixteen million shares were dumped on Tuesday, October 29. Market-wise pundits struggled to describe the horror on the stock exchange floor. With a measure of irony, broker Fred Schwed was to write, "Like all life's rich emotional experiences, the full flavor of losing important money cannot be conveyed by literature." There were rumors that Durant, like Kennedy and financier Bernard Baruch, had sold out before the bottom fell out, and that he reentered the security market too soon.

As stocks careened ever lower, his $18 million in paper fortunes were lost by November 1. Brokers who carried him on credit sold his holdings at pitiful fractions of their purchase value. Six months earlier, he had placed $6 million of bonds in a safe deposit vault for the purpose of providing himself with an annuity. After Black Tuesday, he put up the entire $6 million in response to margin calls.

The president of Union Cigar, stunned when his company's stock plummeted from $113 to $4, fell or jumped to his death from the ledge of a New York hotel. But Durant refused to show panic. As with earlier misfortune in his life, he forced himself to see the positive side, and, in public, to be on the side of the angels. America would survive, he asserted to anyone who asked, because Americans were optimistic, progressive, and living in "an age of big things." He believed the Federal Reserve's meddling in the natural rhythms of market confidence was to blame, and faulted President Hoover for not taming the Fed. When a Wall Street reporter asked him if it was true that because he couldn't come up with $5 million to cover a margin call, he had lost $20 million, he answered, "Some people like to spread harsh tales when it is just as easy to spread friendly ones. I'm the richest man in America—in friends." The boast would be sorely tested in the months to come.

25

⌒o⌒

A Lion in Winter

O ne candid admission would reach posterity through the son of Durant's lawyer friend from the GM days, John Thomas Smith. Years later, Gregory Smith would remember his father telling him how one night he and Gregory's mother had shared a ride up Fifth Avenue with Billy and Catherine Durant. The women were in the backseat, and Billy and John Thomas faced them on flip-down seats. As the darkened limousine glided up the avenue, Billy gently put his hand on his friend's knee and said, "John Thomas, I'm wiped out."

On November 13, 1929, stocks skidded to the year's lowest level. In less than two months, $30 billion worth of securities had gone down the drain. A shell-shocked Durant changed his tune. With the rest of the country, he turned to President Hoover for action, for expressions of confidence to prevent the damage from spreading further. His indignant demands that the government keep its hands off the natural rhythms of supply and demand were replaced by pleas for government guarantees of savings.

While he was not among the business leaders Hoover consulted, he became a sponsor and the chief of an organization called the Bank Depositors' League. As banks across the country collapsed—the ill-named Bank of United States in New York was the largest failure in American history— he paid $1,000 a month to rent a Washington, D.C., office and hire staff for a lobbying effort for federal bank deposit guarantees.

By New Year's 1930, 3 million men had lost their jobs, but Wall Street seemed to collect itself. Spring saw stock trading reach the previous summer's fever pitch, with leading stocks regaining more than half the ground they had lost. But in April commodity prices began to slide, followed by declining production, followed by another stock market tumble.

"We have now passed the worst and with continued unity of effort we shall rapidly recover," said President Hoover in early May. On May 28, he was reported predicting business would be normal by fall. "The grim face went on, the physicians uttering soothing words to the patient and the patient daily sinking lower and lower—until for a time it seemed as if every cheerful pronouncement was followed by a fresh collapse," Frederick Allen would write in 1935. "Only when the failure of the treatment became obvious to the point of humiliation did the Administration lapse into temporary silence."

There was a positive note for Billy, who had the satisfaction of seeing newspapers, a newsreel, and two wire services back away from claims that he had helped swindle a wealthy divorcée. He was a partner with a friend and broker Samuel Ungerleider in the investment trust Ungerleider Financial Corporation. After shares owned by Elizabeth C. Hudson collapsed while she was touring South America, she told reporters, Durant and Ungerleider had let her stock fall to $50, sold large blocks to a dummy buyer, then bought the assets back at $52.

Elizabeth Hudson was the wronged woman, according to the tabloid headlines. The escapades of her former husband, Percy K. Hudson, at his palatial Long Island mansion with his actress inamorata, Vida Whitmore, had won Elizabeth a divorce decree and a $200,000 alimony that she claimed Durant and associates had pillaged. She had been in Valparaiso, Chile, when her Wall Street broker wired her that unless she produced $100,000 in cash by 10 A.M. the following morning, she would lose every dime.

Billy's answer was a $40 million libel suit—the largest sum for a libel suit to date—against the *Washington Herald,* the New York *Daily News,* the *New York Evening Telegram,* the *New York Evening Journal,* the *Chicago Herald & Examiner,* the *San Francisco Examiner,* the *Los Angeles Examiner,* King Features, and International Newsreel Corporation. The divorcée's attorneys and lawyers for the news organization discovered that her accusations were unfounded and backed away with abject apologies. Graciously, Durant dropped the matter, and, with Catherine, sailed for Europe.

Other lawsuits ended on less gallant notes. Billy owed Ben Block, the broker who had carried sixteen accounts—ten for Billy, one each for Catherine, Randolph Hicks, Eddie Rickenbacker and three for Durant Motors associates—$2.4 million, secured by stocks now worth much less. Billy sued Block to enjoin the broker from selling the collateral. After three years of legal maneuvering, Billy lost. Sailing W. Baruch, another broker, sued Durant for a past-due balance of $4,681. Billy countersued for $70,000, claiming a member of the Baruch firm had knowingly given him a false tip. He lost that case, too.

In August 1930, Billy once more took over the reins of Durant Motors. Once more there were plans to manufacture a small foreign car, the French-built Mathias. Nothing happened. He sold off some parts suppliers and merged others. When he placed orders with several parts

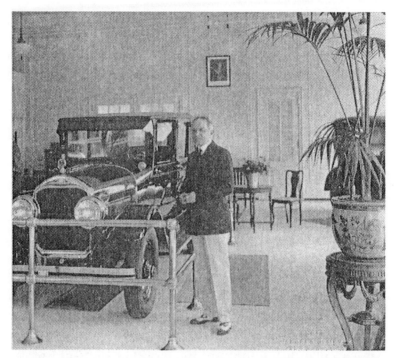

Willie showing off a Durant R55 in Asbury Park, New Jersey

manufacturers in February 1931, he was denied credit. By April, receivers removed fixtures at the Durant Motors headquarters. There were no bidders on the Lansing plant. It and the remaining properties were forfeited or sold, mostly to General Motors.

The depression took its toll on the rest of the industry. By year's end, 6 million Americans were out of work. New car buying dropped to one-third the 5.3 million cars and trucks sold in 1929. Investors stubbornly expected the tide to turn, but in early 1931, the stock market plunged to below the November 1929 lows. The auto industry was hit hard. By 1932, production dropped to a low of just over 1.0 million vehicles. While output began to climb after that, the 1929 figure was not to be surpassed in peacetime for more than twenty years.

Liberty National Bank collapsed. Durant owed it $402,000 himself, and the bank itself was $50,000 behind in rent. In his tussles with bankers, he had learned a good deal, and during the spring of 1931 he mounted intricate deals for changing collateral, shifting notes, and purchasing stocks at arbitrarily set values. By June, Liberty National's remaining assets were liquidated for a fraction of their value.

Billy's finances were a quagmire. His millions had melted away, but Catherine and he managed to hide their reduced circumstances, if not from themselves, at least from others. The owners of the Park Avenue apartment building let them slip behind in rent—tenants for $1,375 a-month luxury apartments were no doubt hard to come by. The prospect of an infusion of cash was dashed in 1932. Satterlee and Canfield informed him that the law firm had negotiated down his tax liability for the years 1923–1927. He had a refund coming of $116,431. Attorney fees, however, amounted to $300,000, but in view of "present conditions," Satterlee and Canfield would only take his refund. He pleaded with them, and offered a larger fee if he could have $31,000 in cash. Herbert Satterlee, who back in 1908 had attended the birth of General Motors, answered personally: "I trust that upon further reflection you will realize that our firm has made all the concessions that can reasonably be asked of it."

A young Italian couple with an infant daughter came into the Durants' existence in 1933. Aristo and Mathilde Scrobogna were from Trieste. An uncle had brought Aristo to America with a pledge to pay for his medical school. The promise had evaporated with the depression, and the Scrobognas were happy to work at Raymere as caretaker and housekeeper. The association of the young immigrant couple and the maturing Durants became a lasting one. Catherine and Willie became little Estelle's quasi-grandparents.

"Mrs. Durant was a wonderful woman," Scrobogna would remember fifty years later. "She was a great support to Mr. Durant."

Scrobogna would one day become the custodian of Durant's papers.

∽o∾

Lady aviators were all the rage at the time. Margery was right behind Amelia Earhart, Amy Lovell, and Bessie Coleman, the Californian flyer who had to go to France to get licensed because no American aviation club would certify a black woman. Earhart crossed the Atlantic solo in 1932, while Britain's Lovell made a round-the-world flight and also broke the altitude record (Katharine Hepburn played her in *Christopher Strong* in 1933).

Newspapers followed Margery's flight when she left for Africa in the spring of 1932. She set out from Le Bourget airfield in Paris in January, and, via Marseilles, crossed the Mediterranean. She was delayed in Kampala, in British East Africa, by propeller trouble, then continued south. In May, she arrived safely back in Paris.

Her father, meanwhile, campaigned for federal deposit insurance. On behalf of his league, he sent out thousands of telegrams to elected officials, corporate officers, educators, and opinion makers asking for their endorsement. President Hoover's popularity declined along with prices and profits. The Republicans' June 1932 convention in Chicago was, in the opinion of H. L. Mencken, "the stupidest and most harrisome ever heard of . . . a convention of country postmasters, federal marshals and receivers in bankruptcy. Unemployment and depression were seldom mentioned."

After the Democrats chose Franklin D. Roosevelt as their presidential candidate a week later, Durant caused something of a stir by announcing his intention to vote for the challenger.

∽∘∾

On October 25, FDR gave his "four horsemen" speech in Baltimore. "Destruction, delay, deceit and despair" were the horsemen of the Republican leadership. Hoover was so unpopular that mounted police had to protect him in Detroit. Traveling in a fleet of limousines provided by Henry Ford, the presidential party drove down streets lined with glum and silent people. Democratic stalwart Joe Kennedy campaigned with FDR and at whistle stops sought out local financial leaders to explain why Roosevelt was the man to save capitalism. Pierre S. du Pont spent millions trying to prevent Roosevelt from becoming president while his daughter, Ethel du Pont, married FDR's son, Franklin Jr. Durant thought there was altogether too much partisanship, and asked 500 business leaders to join him in decrying "reckless preaching of the gospel of fear by thoughtless partisan politicians."

Roosevelt won forty-two of the forty-eight states. The popular vote was 22.8 million for Roosevelt and 15.7 million for Hoover. It was twelve years since William Woodin had sat on Durant's GM board (imposed by Raskob and du Pont along with Edward Stettinius and four others). Now, however, the president-elect tapped the American Car and Foundry chief to be his secretary of the treasury. Billy asked a number of CEOs what they thought the new administration should focus on first. The answer he got was, not surprisingly, the banking crisis.

A day after Roosevelt took office on March 4, 1933, the new administration decided to stop the run on banks and the hoarding of gold by proclaiming a three-day bank holiday and calling for a special session of Congress. Tackling the economic issues led to an appointment for Joe Kennedy. At the recommendation of Bernard Baruch, Roosevelt made Joe the chairman of the new Securities and Exchange Commission. Some thought the appointment grotesque, but FDR saw it as a brilliant stroke. Who would be better to clamp down on illicit practices than an insider who had made his pile?

Knowing Kennedy and Woodin was as close as Durant came to the power center of the New Deal. His lobbying for federal deposit insurance meant little, since there was virtually no congressional opposition to the 1933 legislation establishing the Federal Deposit Insurance Corporation (FDIC). His influence faded with his wealth.

To ward off irrelevance and hold on to self-respect, Willie protested too much, veering embarrassingly from pleas and righteous explanations to unfocused jabs at windmills. Always impeccably attired, he still stayed in the best hotels when he traveled—Catherine and he were in Germany in May 1933. "You'd never know he was broke," said stockbroker John Anderson after seeing Billy in Detroit. Behind the facade there was a discreet move from the opulent Fifth Avenue apartment to a smaller Park Avenue flat. Parts of his property were put in Catherine's name, but these assets, too, melted fast in the relentless downward slide. The Durants had paid $830,000 in taxes in 1920; now they fought the Internal Revenue Service over the last crumbs. Their 1933 tax filing listed $9,478 in gross income and a net of $3,731. Billy grossed $15,171 in 1934, then dropped again to $4,528 the following year. His net income for 1936 was $5,428.

On February 8, 1936, the full dimension of Durant's ruin became a matter of record. A personal note accompanied his bankruptcy petition in New York's federal district court:

My petition in bankruptcy, filed today, is due to frequent and repeated court proceedings instituted by a few creditors, representing less than 5 percent of my total obligations, who have attempted to obtain a preferential position. Action by the creditors referred to has prevented me from giving my best effort to rebuilding my fortune, and I no longer propose to be harassed and annoyed. I wish to state that all creditors will be treated alike, and if fortune favors me all will be paid in full.

His declared debt was $914,000, mostly in judgments to brokers and landlords. He owed $409,000 to five brokerage firms, $30,000 to the owners of 907 Fifth Avenue, and $120,000 claimed by the 1767 Broadway Corporation for office space. There was a judgment of $105,000 to E. E. C. Mathis, the Parisian carmaker founded by Emile Mathis, whose handsome sedans were to have saved Durant Motors. Two banks were owed $50,000, and there was a scattering of obligations to individuals. To satisfy his creditors, he listed his assets as $250 worth of clothes.

いのい

The Durants no longer lived at Raymere and could barely afford Scrobogna to look after the Jersey shore home. The depression made it difficult to sell luxury residences. Indeed, as unemployment figures reached 13 million, it was considered bad taste to even look rich, and fashion and Hollywood adjusted downward to plain dresses and comedies about smart chambermaids fooling silly millionaires. Metro-Goldwyn-Mayer might be paying Joan Crawford $100,000 a year, but the studio publicity department ordered her to say how much she envied Plain Jane secretaries who had the freedom to go shopping on their lunch hour. When Billy and Catherine couldn't find a buyer for Raymere, Meredith Galleries of New York organized an auction that lasted five days.

Through it all, Billy stood at the front door watching buyers cart away their purchases. A Louis XVI suite in the master bedroom went for $359, a Sheraton bedroom suite for $250. Buyers picked over the contents of the library, the billiard room, and the reception rooms for a total of $6,823. The property itself sold for $44,000, giving the Durants' creditors a grand total of $111,778. Reporters from the *Asbury Park Press* wanted to do the story of the fallen founder of General Motors who had owned factories, assembly lines, and commanded a hundred thousand workers. But he refused to play the part of the crestfallen has-been. He was relieved to be rid of Raymere, he told them. Selling it allowed him to use his resources for projects he was not yet at liberty to disclose.

The local newspaper wrote about him again six months later when he leased the Durant Motors showroom in Asbury to a food court. On the eve of the grand opening, Billy was there to show employees how to keep the food mart spotless. This gave the *Asbury Park Press* photographer an idea. Would Mr. Durant show how best to wash a dish? He was pleased to oblige, and the next day readers were treated to a photo of the former millionaire, dishcloth in one hand, and a saucer in the other, apparently reduced to working as a dishwasher. The photo made newspapers across the country.

Going to Flint hurt. The Vehicle City of his youth and his triumphs was an early victim of the hard times, full of boarded-up windows and locked gates. And it was full of people who had believed in him and had poured their earnings into his dreams. Dallas Dort had died in 1925, and the town was no longer the preserve of optimistic, close-knit families. Besides his grandnephew Sidney Stewart and Ralph Workman, a onetime Durant sales executive, nobody had time for him, even people he had made millionaires.

Billy came and went quietly, primarily to oversee the

Pomeroy-Day Company. During the high-flying 1920s when his annual income was over $5 million, he had barely paid attention to the $20,000 a year the property holding had given him. In his reduced circumstances, the income loomed large, and in 1935 he took back management from Bert Pomeroy and Melzor Day. To give Aristo Scrobogna an income, he put his erstwhile caretaker on the Pomeroy-Day payroll.

❧

News of the bankruptcy brought comfort in the form of letters from people Durant didn't know. From Cincinnati came a note from John Corcoran on the stationery of the Corcoran Manufacturing Company, Sheet Metal Products. The company no longer existed, explained Corcoran, adding that he was currently "bossing a W.P.A. gang. I am telling you this to let you know a man can take a good licking and still make good. Cheer up, Billy, and things will work out all right." Thad Preston wrote, "I would make any sacrifice possible to assist you." A letter from W. J. Kellogg said, "You have the courage, honesty and the guts and friends to stage the big comeback." "The automobile and the refrigerator," wrote J. P. Fiske, "would not be what they are today except for your outstanding pioneer work."

Alfred Goebel, an elevator operator in the Gotham building with whom Durant had played checkers, wrote that he hoped and prayed things weren't as bad as the newspaper reports had it:

> Although twenty years have passed, it can never be erased from my memory, not alone the playing of checkers, but your wonderful kindness to all the employees of the building, and on that Saturday, when the firm moved to the Fisk building, there was genuine sadness

on the face of each, and every elevator operator. Some years ago I tried ever so hard to see you at the Post Graduate Hospital, but was unable to get past the desk, but I kept myself posted on the progress of your condition through the daily papers, and words cannot explain how glad I was to read that you had fully recovered from your injuries. Please excuse me for writing this letter, and I do hope, Mr. Durant, that you are in the very best of health.

He was going on seventy-eight, and ready to try again.

Although nothing came of it, he offered to go to work for Samuel Rosoff, a friend and subway construction millionaire who found himself the owner of a Brooklyn brewery, as a beer salesman for 5 percent of the profits. Willie paid special attention to people suggesting marketing schemes. The holder of a patent to a power-driven scooter called the Motor Glide wrote to suggest a partnership. Someone else wrote to ask for help in financing a "remote control unit for radio."

Durant went into business with three veterans of the early days of the A. C. Spark Plug Company. Archibald Campbell, R. B. Vessey, and G. G. Somers had formed CVS Manufacturing to make spark plugs, and in 1935 Durant joined them as vice president. Crown Points Products, one of Billy's numerous companies, was revived, and the automobile products were sold through Crown Points' marketing.

Nothing had changed in Durant's attitude and approach to business since the days when Pierre du Pont, John Raskob, and Alfred Sloan despaired of getting a meeting with him. Campbell, who was treasurer of CVS, found his vice president impossible to nail down. The Durant archives hold letters from Campbell pleading for attention to accounts past due, price changes, orders not filled, and manufacturing problems. Billy was incapable of focusing on details. His ingrained optimism made him order increased production even though 10,000 spark plugs sat unsold on shelves. In vain, Campbell begged Win Murphy, Billy's private secretary since 1909 and now an officer in Crown Point, to deliver his boss to a February 1938 directors' meeting that would decide the fate of the venture. Without Durant's presence, the directors decided to go out of business.

There was a touching, affecting nobility of manner in the aging Durant that Campbell found irresistible. When Durant was in Flint and staying at his namesake hotel, he would call on Campbell on Sundays and ask him to come down and write letters for him. Campbell, Vessey, and Somers might have lost substantial sums on the spark plug venture, but Arch Campbell found it unthinkable not to show up at the appointed hour at Durant's hotel room.

Others felt equally obligated. Durant defaulted on a $30,000 loan that Charles S. Mott, former Flint mayor and investor in GM, advanced in 1936. Alfred Sloan "contributed" $20,000 to a Durant investment that turned into a loan that was never repaid. Charles Kettering was tabbed for $2,100 for a former Buick racing team manager's investment in a western mine. There are no records, but there is a suggestion that Walter Chrysler also contributed to a mining scheme in Nevada. The mother lode of the mine in Goldfield, Nevada, was cinnabar, the sulfide that is the principal ore of mercury. Like quartz, the vermilion cinnabar has a high refractive power. Durant was sure the government would subsidize the mine in case the country was dragged into a war in Europe.

∽o∾

In New York City, Billy and Catherine moved into a modest apartment at an elegant address: 45 Gramercy Park North. One venture of his turned into a viable business and a source of pride. In 1939, he persuaded a contractor to turn an empty Pomeroy-Day garage into an eighteen-lane bowling alley. Billy supervised the conversion himself—the soda counter, the blue-and-red equipment, the cream-colored walls, uniforms for the waitresses. Women would be welcome, and their presence would help lift bowling from its spit-and-sawdust days toward social self-improvement, he told the Flint press a few days before the opening. Soon there would be a second alley, which might be the "first unit of a chain of recreational centers."

"I haven't a dollar, but I'm happy and I'm carrying on because I find I can't stop," he told a *Detroit News* reporter a year after the opening. "Many people value money too highly; I'm trying now to do good for as many people as possible. After all, money is only loaned to a man; he comes into the world with nothing, and he goes out with nothing."

Together with the story and photo of Billy showing the *Asbury Park Press* photographer how to wash a dish, the bowling alley venture would add to the posthumous legend that the founder of GM ended up as a dishwasher. In a proposal for a Durant television documentary in 1996, James Morrison wrote that Durant "died broke, working as a fry cook in a bowling alley in Flint, Michigan."

❧

Overweight and alcoholic, Cliff died of a heart attack in his Beverly Hills home in October 1937. He was forty-seven. Obituaries listed the younger Durant as a sportsman, financier, businessman, and racecar driver. Willie soldiered on, becoming more and more Henry Crapo's grandson and William Clark Durant's son. Like grandfather Henry Crapo, who couldn't let go of business, and ill-starred William Clark Durant, who couldn't stay away from the stock market, Billy bought a seat in the Chicago Board of Trustees. His principal associate in this small organization of private stock speculators was Joseph Buchhalter, the author of the *Buchhalter Plan of Trading*.

Speculating in grain futures, Buchhalter and his associates obtained from their investors the power to execute buy and sell orders. Any movement in price, usually by no more than a cent or two, and Buchhalter would execute a contract on which there was a profit, inform the customer of his winnings, deduct a commission, and leave the other, or losing, position "open." On March 15, 1939, the Department of Agriculture's regulatory agency for the grain market accused Buchhalter, Billy and Catherine, and another partner of fraud. The partners informed their customers of their profits, but left them unaware of countervailing losses until much later. After a year of hearings, they were all banned from the commodities market.

꙳

Like Joe Kennedy, Roosevelt's ambassador to the Court of St. James's since 1937, Durant wanted to keep the United States out of any new European war. The country should concern itself with its own people and "trade only with Canada." One Sunday in 1939, after Britain and France declared war on Nazi Germany, Campbell was summoned to Durant's hotel room and asked to hand out antiwar leaflets at Flint churches. The handbills inveighed against President Roosevelt's demand that Congress repeal the Neutrality Act so as to allow the Allies to buy American weaponry and munitions. Campbell dutifully distributed the leaflets.

Alfred Sloan invited Durant to Flint for the rollout of General Motors' 25 millionth car, a Chevrolet, in January 1940. Sloan, who was now the chairman of GM and William Knudsen president, led Billy by the hand to the front of the platform and introduced him to the crowd.

Durant and Aristo Scrobogna, 1940

Two months later, Sloan lost Knudsen when Roosevelt tapped him to become the government's defense coordinator. Crippling disease had forced Walter Chrysler to hand over the reins of the Chrysler Corporation to K. T. Keller in 1938. Chrysler died on August 18, 1940.

Keller would remember Knudsen's unmistakable Danish accent asking him on the telephone from Washington one Sunday morning, "K.T., do you want to make tanks?"

"Sure," said Keller. "Where can I see one?"

Knudsen arranged for Keller and several Chrysler engineers to study the army's latest tanks at the Rock Island, Illinois, Arsenal on the Mississippi River.

∽o∾

Durant turned eighty on December 8, 1941, the day the United States entered the war. There were hundreds of cards and messages, flowers and gifts, including subscriptions to a fund for publishing his autobiography. There were telegrams from Charles Kettering, Adelaide and Eddie Rickenbacker, Herbert Satterlee, and Charles Fisher for his brothers and himself. The biggest bouquet came from Sloan, who wrote that it expressed "for myself personally and more particularly for the great organization of which I am part, our appreciation and gratitude to you, our first leader."

Pearl Harbor filled the headlines, but the *Detroit News* published a feature story on William C. Durant that brought loving well wishes from people he had affected. Wrote a former worker at the Tarrytown, New York, Chevrolet plant: "I got one of the greatest kicks out of life when one morning you came through the body plant and walked along holding my arm and giving us boys credit for putting over the 619 model at small cost." He concluded: "So just thought I would drop you a line congratulating you on being eighty years old, and hoping there are many more birthdays in store for you."

While Catherine quietly sold off her possessions, including a double string of pearls, Billy turned to introspection. It was time to write his life story, and the man to help him was Aristo Scrobogna. This Italian immigrant had graduated to fellow dishwasher, investment adviser, and personal secretary.

Willie prepared himself punctiliously for work on the

autobiography by dictating to Scrobogna. In notes to himself in the margin of Scrobogna's typescript, Willie scribbled: "Presentation must be: clear, pleasant, not drag. Too full of clichés. Make a proposition—negotiate for control. Select paper for book. Number of sheets, size, width of margin top, bottom and sides." He wrote to Charles Nash asking for confirmations on details of joint endeavors. Nash was living in Los Angeles and in his pleasant reply told his former boss his doctors had condemned him, in the aftermath of a heart attack, to a retirement during which he would "rust out." Alfred Sloan's 1941 autobiography, *Adventures of a White-Collar Man,* gave Billy a chance to recall the thrill of GM's early days. Reading excerpts in the *Saturday Evening Post* was an unalloyed pleasure, Billy wrote the GM chairman.

> I do wish, Mr. Sloan, that you had known me when we were laying the foundation—when speed and action seemed necessary. You are absolutely right in your statement that General Motors justified an entirely different method of handling after the units had been enlisted. To sum up, the early history reminds me of the following story. General Wheeler, who came up from the ranks, met Major Bloomfield, a West Pointer, at the Chickamauga [Tennessee] battlefield. . . . In speaking of the engagement General Wheeler said, "Right up on the hill there is where a company of infantry captured a troop of cavalry." Major Bloomfield said, "Why, General, you know that couldn't be, infantry cannot capture cavalry." To which General Wheeler replied, "But, you see, this infantry captain didn't have the disadvantage of a West Point education and he didn't know he couldn't do it, so he just went ahead and did it anyway."

Sloan was diplomatic in his book as behooves the chief of the nation's largest single producer of weapons and war materials. He avoided personal references that might create unhappiness, he wrote, inviting Durant to a preview of GM's 1941 line at the Waldorf Astoria.

ᴄᴏᴏᴄ

The war halted new car production in February 1942— gasoline rationing was imposed a month later. Detroit switched from carmaking to building tanks, trucks, and airplanes, just as Daimler-Benz in Germany built 100,000 of its aeronautical engines, the workhorse of the Luftwaffe, and diesel engines for tanks and military trucks. The war effort showed the might of General Motors. Its engineers designed 72 percent of the items the firm made under government contracts, from tanks and armored cars to aircraft engines. GM's factories built fighter planes, bombers, and machine guns.

For an eighty-one-year-old man to travel to the Nevada desert in September was ill advised, but Billy insisted on visiting the mine in Goldfield, a bone-dry, one-street western hamlet between the Montezuma and Lone Mountain peaks seventy miles across the state line from California's Death Valley. Temperatures there often reached 115 degrees Fahrenheit. He had persuaded Chrysler and Kettering to invest in the mine, but only copper was stimulated by defense needs, and the cinnabar quarry went into bankruptcy.

The trip was exhausting for Billy. Upon his return to Flint, he was felled by a massive stroke. From New York, Catherine hurriedly reached his bedside at the Hurley Hospital. Scrobogna arrived from Goldfield.

The recovery was slow and only partial, and complicated by the removal of his prostate. Willie showed his determination to get better by tossing an empty water tumbler from one hand to another. As he told a nurse who caught him in his glass tossing, "Just trying to see what I can do."

On December 15—one week after his eighty-first birth-day—he left by ambulance for Detroit and a train ride back to New York City. The *Flint Weekly Review,* the official publication of the American Federation of Labor, saluted the departure, saying: "He had made no complaint. He never has."

True to form, he muted his complaints as cardiac after-shocks slowly robbed him of alertness. To Ralph Workman, the former Durant sales executive who was also seriously ill, he wrote: "Take the 'Old Man's' advice and go easy. I have been trying to recover my old form and have not suc-ceeded exactly as I would like although have been on the retired list for eighteen months and the plan of winning the bowling championship of the State of Michigan is being postponed from day to day."

"Keep working" was his advice to others and to himself. When W. H. Washer, a Flint inventor, wrote in November 1943 asking about patents for cement posts and telephone lenses, Billy wrote back that he was all for setting up a small plant after the war where "we might possibly com-bine two or three industries." In a follow-up letter, he wrote:

> A little later I will be in a position to take a large order of cutting tools and kindred appliances at prices that will meet any reasonable competition. I look for two or three years of activity after the terminal of the war, when-ever that may be. My advice to you and all others is to "keep working."

Durant continued to rise at 7:30 each day. He became restless if Scrobogna was late for work on the autobiogra-phy. "Why don't you rest, Willie," Catherine asked him. "We are not given enough time, Mama," he would answer. On his eighty-fifth birthday he sat in a wheelchair, dressed in a gray suit, for an interview. Visits from Win Murphy, the secretary he had hired in 1909, became shorter.

He lapsed into a coma on March 15, 1947. Catherine summoned a doctor. Billy died in his sleep in his apartment at 45 Gramercy Park early the next morning.

After the funeral at the Episcopal Calvary Church, he was buried next to his mother. Twelve years later Margery's ashes were placed in the tomb next to her grandmother and Pops. Catherine lived to be eighty-six. When she died in 1974, she joined Willie, her mother-in-law, and step-daughter at the Woodlawn Cemetery in the Bronx.

26

༄ঽ০ঽ৽

Afterimages

Death spared Billy the ignominy of seeing Margery arrested on narcotics charges. Six months after her Pop's passing, Margery and Fitzhugh Green were charged with running a drug ring for their own use. In New Haven, Connecticut, Fitzhugh pleaded innocent while Frederick P. Deisler, a private detective and drug runner for the couple, pleaded guilty. Margery was not in court for the pleading on September 26, 1947. She was a patient at a private hospital, but the indictment said she had been an addict since 1926 while her husband had used drugs "for many years." Federal agents said a South American diplomat had received $13,000 from the Greens to obtain drugs for them. Testimony before a grand jury, wrote the New York *Daily News*'s New Haven correspondent, "unfolded a story of drug addiction and craving that leads into the Mafia dope ring centered in 107th Street of Manhattan's Harlem district. The Greens, however planned to expand their sources of heroin and morphine and paid the South American officials at least $13,000 for dope which was never delivered."

2 Socialites Seized On Narcotics Charge

(Special to The News)

New Haven, Sept. 26.—Comdr. Fitzhugh Green, 59, noted author and explorer, and his socialite wife, Mrs. Margery Durant Green, 60, four-times-wed heiress daughter of the late W. C. Durant, multimillionaire motor magnate, were named in Federal Court today as central figures in a sensational narcotics-peddling case.

Accused with them was Frederick P. Deisler, a private detective, of 7 E. 44th St., New York. All three were charged with receiving and concealing narcotics and with knowledge of their unlawful importation.

The Greens, both named as drug addicts, had paid more than $100,000 for narcotics in the last two years, the indictments charged.

Ring Believed to Be in Action.

Federal officials said that existence of an organized dope ring was indicated in records found in Deisler's hotel room in New York. Among those involved, according to agents, are a prominent South American diplomat stationed in New York, a Manhattan attorney and two New York doctors. They were not identified.

Green pleaded innocent when arraigned today and was ordered to trial Oct. 27. Deisler pleaded guilty. Mrs. Green was not in court. She is a patient at a private hospital at Hartford, but U. S. Attorney Adrian Maher said she would be arraigned Oct. 27 if physicians permitted.

Deisler, according to the Government, was hired through a prominent attorney as a go-between to obtain drugs for the Greens. Mrs. Green has been an addict since 1928, and her husband has used drugs "for many years," the indictments said.

Green, retired naval officer, is an Annapolis graduate who served as an intelligence officer in both world wars. He was a member of polar expeditions and co-author with transatlantic flier Charles A. Lindberg of "We."

The South American diplomat entered the picture, federal agents said, when he received $13,000 from the Greens on his promise to obtain drugs for them.

Green and Deisler were released in $2,500 bond. Deisler will be sentenced after Green's case is disposed of.

Comdr. and Mrs. Fitzhugh Green.

From the New York *Daily News,* September 16, 1947

Until they were both patients at the New York Hospital in Manhattan the year before—Margery for a gallbladder operation, Fitzhugh for various ailments—they had obtained drugs from a number of doctors. At the hospital, however, their supply was cut off and they had to resort to having deliveries smuggled in to them. When the hospital learned of the dope traffic, they were asked to leave. It was while they recuperated at the fashionable Hampshire House in New York that a doctor supplied them with drugs and introduced them to the diplomat. Margery was a very sick woman when she caught Fitzhugh with a nurse. "Harsh words followed," Scrobogna would remember. "Fitzhugh tumbled to the bottom of the stairs. When people rushed to him he was dead." Margery died of a heroin overdose. Instead of sharing a grave with her last husband, her will demanded that her ashes be buried next to the remains of her father and grandmother.

∾o∾

Two years after Durant's death, the federal government brought an antitrust suit against E. I. Du Pont de Nemours, claiming the company monopolized trade in cellophane— one of the vast range of products Du Pont invented. The case dragged on for years. In a pretrial brief dated October 15, 1952, government lawyers wrote that from the beginning of the Du Pont–Durant relationship, "it is clear the Du Pont group was planning to oust Durant when the opportunity was ripe and of taking over sole and complete control of General Motors." The government based its case, in part, on a 1917 letter written by John Raskob recommending investing in GM:

Mr. Durant should be continued as president of the company, Mr. P.S. du Pont will be continued as chairman of the board, the Finance Committee will be ours and we will have representation on the Executive Committee as we desire, and it is the writer's belief that ultimately the Du Pont Company will absolutely control and dominate the whole General Motors situation with the entire approval of Mr. Durant, who, I think, will eventually place his holdings with us, taking his payment therefore in some securities mutually satisfactory.

Durant did not get around to writing his version of the events. Intriguingly, he had planned to cover the subject in his autobiography. Among the headings of his planned chapters are:

When General Motors Stock Was Cornered—a Startling Incident in the New York Stock Exchange.
The Invitation Extended to the Du Ponts to Become Interested in General Motors.
How I Retired from General Motors in 1920 and the Reason.

Although this did not totally exonerate Willie, Catherine went to her grave believing the 1920 collapse of the GM stock was engineered by forces hostile to her husband. In the early 1970s, Aristo Scrobogna told Durant's first biographer, Lawrence Gustin, that he remembered Durant once saying that there had been moments when he had been a blundering fool. The admission was seared in Scrobogna's memory because it was so out of Durant's character to admit he was wrong.

∽∘∾

A century after William Crapo Durant turned Durant-Dort Carriage Company into the leading North American cart builder, there are no Durant relatives in Flint and few reminders. The only descendant is grandson William Durant Campbell, who lives as a recluse in New York City. The Durant School on Flint's Third Avenue is—perhaps ironically—situated across from Kettering University.

Within a month of his death, a William C. Durant Memorial Association was formed to erect a monument in a downtown park. Nothing came of it. Charles Mott didn't think it was right. In 1958, the white-haired Mott, who thanks to Durant and his own perseverance had become one of the wealthiest men in Flint, stood with GM President Harlow H. Curtice and a handful of other dignitaries on top of a marble slab for the dedication of the Durant Plaza memorial. Under 1861 WILLIAM CRAPO DURANT 1947—FOUNDER OF GENERAL MOTORS 1908, the inscription read:

In the Golden Milestone Year of the Corporation Its Proud Birthplace Dedicates This Plaza in Lasting Appreciation of What His Vision, Genius and Courage Contributed to His Home City and to the Renown of American Industry.

Mott had the last word:

I want to call your attention to the fact that in spite of all the mistakes and other things that have been said about Durant, you guys [General Motors] and I would not be here today if it hadn't been for Durant. Durant should be recognized as one of the big men that started to build Flint—Flint would have been a bush town if it hadn't been for Durant . . . I take my hat off to him for having the idea and the accomplishment.

In 1988, a statue of Durant was erected at the footbridge between the Flint Riverfront Hotel and Carriage Town. Four years later, a statue of J. Dallas Dort was placed besides Durant's, allowing both men to look down the street at the restored Flint Road Cart Company factory, now a national historic building, and Charles Nash's house when he was D & D's superintendent, now a state historical site. A decade later, a distant relative, William Durant Radebaugh of Battle Creek, Michigan, found a voice recording W. C. Durant had made on New Year's Day, 1931. Apparently the result of his investment in U & I Broadcasting Systems that year, Willie had sent Catherine's great aunt, Ella Day, the 5-inch disk. When *Fortune* magazine placed Durant in its Business Hall of Fame on April 25, 1996, the recording was played during acceptance remarks by Buick General Manager Ed Mertz.

⌘

As General Motors approached its 100th birthday, the carmaker was the world's largest company in sales and shares of global economic output. Microsoft was the darling of a public in love with the stock market, its stock nearly six times the value of GM's shares. Yet GM had 608,000 employees and its $166 billion in sales were fifteen times greater than Microsoft's. Compared with GM, Microsoft's sales were tiny because its most popular product sold for about $90 apiece while cars and light trucks sold for $20,000 each.

The giant was, again, facing Darwinian lessons. After a number of Durant's successors sought sweeping solutions costing billions of dollars, the integrated structure that Willie had started and Sloan had perfected was seen as an out-of-date obstacle to the company's well-being. GM's shares underperformed on Wall Street by 70 percent for a decade. The management culture that worked for Sloan and his successors into the 1970s, when GM's North American market share reached 60 percent, was backfiring in the global economy. The latter-day Morgans, investors, and stock analysts saw the plants stretching from Warren and

Dayton in Ohio through Anderson and Kokomo in Indiana to Flint and Detroit and Oshawa, Ontario, much like Durant had bought them, as so many dinosaurs. Durant and Sloan had reasoned that the more components GM made itself, the greater the returns and the advantages whenever it made a technological breakthrough. Where Durant and Sloan had devised economies of scale, end-of-century management gurus saw outmoded organizing philosophies. Wall Street analysts calculated that Albert Champion's old A.C. factory in Flint, renamed Delphi East, produced spark plugs at costs 25 to 35 percent above competitive prices. Why should anybody make cars in Flint when assembly lines in Mexico could muster a workforce for less? And if Mexicans got too expensive, move your plant down the food chain. If Chinese workers got too expensive, "Think Bangladesh" was the reigning philosophy.

Frank Briscoe's argument in 1908 for a union partially won out over Durant's "states' rights" ninety years later, when the company took a leaf from Ford and combined the marketing (but not purchasing and engineering) of the Buick, Cadillac, Oldsmobile, and Pontiac-GMC divisions. After a crippling eight-week strike by the United Auto Workers in 1998 that began in Flint, GM said it would build a new generation of plants in the United States, using fewer workers to assemble large chunks of vehicles built by outside suppliers. The Ford Motor Company, however, had no intention of building new plants. Close cooperation between workers and management was the rule at Ford, where the strategy was to pursue lots of little efficiency improvements in each factory. At GM, workers had been seen as a liability for decades. Back in 1943, when Peter Drucker wrote *The Future of Industrial Man* and invented management theory, he criticized GM for treating its workers as a feudal cost center instead of an asset.

We can only wonder what Willie, Henry Ford, Walter Chrysler, old Henry and Wilfred Leland, Charlie Nash, and

Louis Chevrolet would think of the "hollowing out" of industrial America. They wanted to see a car in every garage. But how can Americans buy cars if the logic of outsourcing pushes their incomes to the level of Bangladeshis? Willie's successors high up in Detroit's Renaissance Towers don't want to hear of any worldwide glut of carmaking capacity. Living with the consequences of decades of insular management, poor business decisions, and hostile labor relations, they might wish for a resurrected William Crapo Durant ready to steer into a ditch to get around a hay wagon and down the road to catch the future.

Notes on Sources

Interviews with Aristo Scrobogna, the last surviving collaborator of William C. Durant (1861–1947), and with Richard P. Scharchburg of the Kettering University/GMI Alumni Foundation Collection of Industrial History in Flint and several other automotive professionals are the sources of this book. The author has read most of the biographies on the automobile pioneers and has used such sources as zeitgeist and examples of the nascent industry. Several individuals, archives, and libraries helped in the research. The William C. Durant Papers are at the Kettering University in Flint. They include a selection of letters by Rebecca Crapo Durant to her son, WCD, his fewer return letters, as well as the surviving correspondence of Grandfather Henry Crapo. Also in the Durant Papers is WCD's "Autobiography," an unpublished and fragmentary manuscript written during his declining years and never finished. A few letters have been consulted at the Papers of P. S. du Pont, Eleutherian Mills Historical Library in Wilmington, Delaware. Documentation supporting quotes in the narrative are cited below:

The Funeral

Details of William C. Durant's funeral and the mourners in attendance taken from an article in the *New York Times,* March 21, 1947, and Lowell Thomas's broadcast, March 18, 1947. W. W. Murphy, "What was that?" attributed to Richard P. Scharchburg, General Motors Institute, 1972. Malcolm W. Bingay, "The world for him," quoted in Andrew Whyte, *The Century of the Car, 1885–1985,* page 34. J. P. Morgan on WCD as "an unstable visionary," quoted in Stanley Jackson, *J. P. Morgan,* page 228. Alfred P. Sloan, "Too often we fail to recognize," quoted in Alfred Sloan with Boyden Sparkes, *Adventures of a White-Collar Man,* pages 126–127.

1. The Man

Louis E. Rowley, "There are no harsh lines," quoted in *Detroit Saturday Night,* September 4, 1909. WCD's hanging to a windowsill quoted in the "Autobiography." Arthur Pound, "He would lead his staff," quoted in Arthur Pound, *The Turning Wheel: The Story of General Motors through 25 Years, 1908–1933,* page 95. Jacob Newmark, "What a man," in Jacob Newmark, "My 25 Years with W. C. Durant," *Commerce and Finance,* May 16, 1936. WCD, "My work," in "Autobiography."

2. Rebecca's Boy

Notes on Flint and the "advanced ideas" of its citizens detailed in *The Golden Jubilee of Flint,* page 183. Henry Crapo, "When Durant was here," Durant Papers, May 19, 1865, R. G. Dun & Co. entry quoted in Bernard A. Weisberger, *The Dream Maker,* page 36. Henry Crapo, "He has been so intoxicated," Durant Papers. Rebecca C. Durant, "A quick little chap," recollection in a letter to WCD, September 18, 1916. Henry Crapo, "My dear little grandson," H. H. Crapo to W. W. Crapo, August 13, 1863, Durant Papers. W. W. Crapo, "Full of excuses," from letter to Rebecca Durant, September 2, 1872. W. C. Durant,

"Very anxious," letter to W. W. Crapo, October 8, 1877, Durant Papers.

3. Testing the Waters

Bernard A. Weisberger, "If it was considered": Weisberger, *The Dream Maker,* page 26.

4. D & D

Alfred Sloan, "He was as steady," in Sloan, *Adventures,* page 8. Richard Crabb, "By sharpness of intellect," in Richard Crabb, *Birth of a Giant: The Men and Incidents that Gave America the Motorcar,* page 121. A. B. C. Hardy, "Get out of the carriage business," quoted in Lawrence R. Gustin, *Billy Durant: Creator of General Motors,* page 73. Arthur Pound, "He was a mighty seller," in Arthur Pound, *The Iron Man of Industry: An Outline of the Social Significance of Automatic Machinery,* page 121.

5. Madison Square Garden

WCD, "I was mighty provoked," quoted in Crabb, *Birth of a Giant,* page 120. Hugh Dolnar, "Dr. Hills has driven," quoted in Terry B. Dunham and Lawrence Gustin, *The Buick,* page 44.

6. David Buick

"Fame beckoned to David Buick," quoted in Beverly Rae Kimes, "Wouldn't You Rather Be in a Buick," *Automobile Quarterly,* summer 1968. David Buick, "I had one horsedrawn," quoted in Dunham and Gustin, *The Buick,* page 13. Alexander Winton, "As I came down Broadway," quoted in *U.S. News & World Report,* June 9, 1967. Walter Marr, "Showing the way," quoted in Crabb, *Birth of a Giant,* page 130.

7. Private Lives

Rebecca Durant, "My dear, dear boy," in letter to WCD, December 8, 1901, and WCD's response, Durant Papers. Rebecca Durant, "Dear Rosie," letter of May 3, 1903, Durant Papers. Details from Rosy's death certificate, in Archives of Bureau of Vital Statistics, New York City Department of Health. Rebecca Durant, "My dear, dear boy," letter to WCD, May 17, 1903, Durant Archives.

8. Carmaking

Meetings at Durant home "emitting an unending stream of facts," taken from Margery Durant, *My Father,* page 57. The *Flint Journal*'s stay-in-Flint stipulation was spelled out in the *Flint Journal,* September 11, 1905. Arthur C. Mason, "Start it up," quoted in Kimes, "Wouldn't You Rather Be in a Buick." WCD, "After a short visit," in his "Autobiography." Arthur Pound attributing Buick's upsurge to WCD found in Pound, *The Turning Wheels,* page 87. Richard Crabb, "The record growth," found in Crabb, *Birth of a Giant,* page 146.

9. The Selden Cartel

The Selden Group's response to James Couzens taken from Crabb, *Birth of a Giant,* page 219. James Couzens "It may take years," quoted in ibid., page 220. Frederic Coudert, "Your honor," quoted in Peter Collier and David Horowitz, *The Fords,* page 55.

10. Competition

Ransom Olds, "After a long, sleepless," quoted in Karl Ludvigsen and David Burgess Wise, *The Complete Encyclopedia of the American Automobile,* page 132. Anonymous reporter, "Durant sees," quoted in George May, *A Most Unique Machine,* page 176. Charles Nash, "Dallas, Billy's crazy," quoted in WCD letter to Nash, January 29, 1942, Durant Papers. WCD, "Mr. Buick wishes," in letter to John Carton, undated, Durant Papers.

11. Affair of the Heart

Margery Durant, "Don't go so fast," taken from Durant, *My Father,* page 157. Details of Catherine Lederer's secretarial work for WCD in 1905 told to author by Aristo Scrobogna, July 1998. Rebecca Durant, "It's hard to see," in letter to WCD, March 30, 1908. Margery Campbell, "Dearest Pops," letter to WCD, May 24, 1912.

12. Checkered Flags

Terry Dunham and Lawrence Gustin on the lack of rigid discipline in the Buick team taken from Dunham and Gustin, *The Buick,* page 357. Walter Chrysler, "She said nothing," quoted in Ludvigsen and Burgess Wise, *The Complete Encyclopedia of the American Car,* page 45. Alfred Sloan, "I recall," Sloan, *Adventures,* page 21. Henry Leland, "You must grind," quoted in Crabb, *Birth of a Giant,* page 117. Charles Mott, "He was one hell of a gambler," quoted in May, *A Most Unique Machine,* page 218.

13. Thinking Big

WCD, "I suggested," quoted in Keith Sward, *The Legend of Henry Ford,* page 62. Francis Stetson, "The greatest living promoter," Jackson, *J. P. Morgan,* page 288. WCD, "Mr. Satterlee said," in "Autobiography," Durant Papers. WCD, "That's exactly what I want," Mrs. Henry M. Leland with Minnie Dubbs Millbrook, *Master of Precision,* page 97. Lee Dunlap, "There wasn't any plan," Pound, *The Turning Wheel,* page 95. J. Pierpont Morgan, "They *couldn't* do it," Jackson, *J. P. Morgan,* page 12.

WCD, "Had a long session," letter to Carton, Carton papers, Michigan Historical Collection. Fred Smith "Durant saw," Fred Smith "Motoring Down a Quarter of a Century," *Detroit Saturday Night,* December 2, 1928. WCD, "They say I shouldn't," Lawrence H. Seltzer, *A Financial History of the American Automobile Industry,* page 157.

14. Darwinian Lessons

"Henceforth," in *Detroit Saturday Night,* January 22, 1910. The analysis of General Motors in 1909 is detailed in Seltzer's *A Financial History of the American Automobile Industry,* pages 160–163. John Anderson "We thought we were in great jeopardy," Allan Nevins and Frank Earnest Hill, *Ford: The Times, the Man, the Company,* vol. 1, page 424. Ford, "We will fight," ibid., page 421. WCD, "By May 1st," in "Autobiography" notes, 1910, Durant Papers. A. B. C. Hardy's memories of the Elkhart, Indiana, stopover and "Durant shook Goss," taken from Dunham and Gustin, *The Buick,* page 82. "The directors' table," quoted in Leland and Millbrook, *Master of Precision,* page 106. "In each instance," Leland Family records, Wilfred C. Leland Memoirs. Henry Leland, "After all," quoted in Crabb, *Birth of a Giant,* page 286.

15. A "New Baby"

Margery Durant, "It was nothing new," in Durant, *My Father,* page 77. John Carton, "Billy never thought," quoted in Arthur Pound, "General Motors' Old Home Town," *Michigan History,* March 1936. Unnamed New York banker quoted by James Storrow in Henry G. Pearson, *Son of New England: James Jackson Storrow, 1846–1926,* pages 138–139. Henry Leland, "Lay all the other," quoted in Leland and Millbrook, *Master of Precision,* page 130. WCD, "Do not think," quoted in Sloan, *Adventures,* page 53.

16. Back in the Saddle

Walter Chrysler, "I cannot hope," Walter Chrysler, *Life of an American Workman*, page 143. Louis Chevrolet, "I sold you," Lawrence R. Gustin, *Billy Durant: Creator of General Motors*, page 146. WCD, "Grownup people," "Autobiography" notes, Durant Papers. WCD, "It occurred to me," in letter to A. G. Bishop, May 2, 1914, Durant Papers. WCD, "Eventually, we can use," in "Autobiography" notes, Durant Papers. Henry Ford, "Every piece of work," quoted in Garet Garrett, *The Wild Wheel: The World of Henry Ford*, page 85. WCD, "We have orders," Beverly Rae Kimes and Robert C. Ackerson, *Chevrolet: A History from 1911*, page 20. Arthur Pound, "So great was the demand," in Pound, *The Turning Wheel*, page 148. WCD to Willson, "Hold every share," quoted in Gustin, *Billy Durant*, page 168. "Everything coming fine," WCD to Ed Campbell, quoted in Durant, *My Father*, pages 181–182. "Now, er, Mr. Durant," quoted by Booton Herndon in *True* magazine, December 1958. "I'm in control," WCD to Storrow, quoted in Gustin, *Billy Durant*, page 170. WCD, "I Took General Motors," quoted in Kimes and Ackerson, *Chevrolet*, page 22.

17. A Different Animal

Bernard Weisberger, "Powerful people," in Weisberger, *The Dream Maker*, page 215. Rebecca Durant, "My dear boy," letter to WCD, September 18, 1916, Durant Papers. "Well Charley, you're through," WCD to Nash, quoted in Weisberger, *The Dream Maker*, page 198. Walter Chrysler on his argument with Charles Nash and WCD's compensation can be found in Chrysler, *Life of an American Workman*, pages 140–141. WCD, "I'll tell you what I'll do," quoted in William Hollingsworth Whyte, *The Organization Man: Alfred P. Sloan*, page 215. Alfred Sloan, "I was of two minds," in Sloan, *Adventures*, page 25. Sloan on GM acquisition of Frigidaire in ibid., pages 109–110.

18. Du Pont

Gerard Colby, "Over $20 million," Gerard Colby, *Du Pont Dynasty,* page 232. William C. Bullitt, "None of them," in *Philadelphia Public Ledger,* December 19, 1915. Henry Ford, "History is more or less," quoted in the *Chicago Tribune,* May 25, 1916. Henry Leland, "Our capacity to turn out," Henry Leland to WCD, October 14, 1916. WCD's letter dismissing the Lelands dated March 10, 1917, in "Autobiography" notes, Durant Papers. Wilfred Leland, "We have to win," Leland and Millbrook, *Master of Precision,* page 174. Henry Leland's speech to the Cadillac farewell banquet quoted in the *Detroit Journal,* June 18, 1917. WCD, "Never before," in *Hearst* magazine quoted in Time-Life, *This Fabulous Century, 1910–20,* page 23. Wilfred Leland quoting WCD as saying "The war could be stopped," in *Detroit Free Press* and *New York Tribune,* August 27, 1918. Woodrow Wilson, "You are the only man in Michigan," quoted in Nevins and Hill, *Ford,* vol. 2, page 118. WCD pressing Wilfred Leland for time and date of remarks and Leland's responses of August 28–30, 1918, can be found in the Durant Papers.

19. Into the Roaring Twenties

"Cars were never handsomer," in Time-Life, *This Fabulous Century, 1920–30,* page 256. John Raskob, "We feel fortunate," letter to WCD, January 28, 1920, Durant Papers. Alfred Sloan, "We scarcely felt," quoted in *Congressional Record,* Sixty-fifth Congress, Third Session, 1918, page 888.

20. November Storm

Henry Ford, "We must of course," quoted in Crabb, *Birth of a Giant,* page 385. Edward R. Stettinius's assessment of GM's bank debt is in a letter to Morgan partner Thomas Lamont, quoted in John D. Forbes, *Stettinius Sr., Portrait of a Morgan Partner,* page 128. WCD, "The reason given," in Weisberger, *The*

Dream Maker, page 287. Thomas Lamont on "corkscrewing" facts out of WCD found in a clip from an undated *New York Evening Mail,* Durant Papers. Weisberger's metaphor of loaded gun in Weisberger, *The Dream Maker,* page 272.

21. *"Forget Mistakes"*

Richard Scharchburg, "Having said that," Richard P. Scharchburg to author, July 1998. Stettinius, "It is of course," in Forbes, *Stettinius Sr.,* page 131. Alfred Sloan, "You knew," in Sloan, *Adventures,* pages 125–126. John Pratt's remembering WCD's last days in Richard P. Scharchburg, *W. C. Durant, "The Boss,"* page 53. Lawrence R. Gustin, "Nowhere was the reaction," in Gustin, *Billy Durant,* page 224. WCD's Christmas Eve letters to subscribers, December 24, 1920, in Durant Papers. WCD, "Forget failures," Kimes and Ackerson, *Chevrolet,* page 28. Pierre du Pont, "It has been reported," Papers of P. S. du Pont, Eleutherian Mills Historical Library. WCD, "Every mile of new highway," quoted in *Automotive Industries,* October 5, 1922. WCD, "Most of us," quoted in Clarence Walker Barron, *They Told Barron,* page 110. Walter Chrysler, "He brought it out," in Chrysler, *Life of an American Workman,* page 180.

22. *Feeding Frenzy*

B. C. Forbes published his interview and commentary on WCD in the *New York American,* May 15, 1923. WCD, "I never approved," quoted in Barron, *They Told Barron,* pages 102–103. WCD letter to *Wall Street Journal* editor S. S. Fontaine dated May 15, 1923, Durant Papers. Jacob H. ("Jake") Newmark's "My 25 Years with W. C. Durant" was published in installments in *Commerce and Finance,* May 16–October 17, 1936. B. F. O'Brien to Henry Ford, "Right outside my window," December 7, 1926, quoted in Robert Lacey, *Ford: The Man and the Machine,* page 290. John Pratt, "He didn't think," quoted in Gustin, *Billy Durant,* page 211. WCD stock recommendations to Cliff Durant, May 9, 1927, Durant Papers. WCD, "The automotive industry," quoted in the *New York Times,* June 2, 1928.

23. Stock Pools

Frederick Allen's comments on speculators in Frederick Allen, *Only Yesterday: An Informal History of the 1920s,* page 46. Jacob Newmark, "Those who had the wisdom," in Newmark, "My Twenty-five Years with W. C. Durant."

24. Bubble Economy

Joseph P. Kennedy's anecdote of escaping the 1929 crash quoted in Axel Madsen, *Gloria and Joe: The Star-Crossed Love Affair of Gloria Swanson and Joe Kennedy,* page 252. WCD on his meeting with President Hoover appeared in the *New York Times,* December 14, 1929. Henry Ford, "The stockholders had already received," quoted in Nevins and Hill, *Ford,* vol. 2, page 90. Henry Ford, "Spend money until it hurts," quoted in Charles E. Sorenson with Samuel T. Williamson, *My Forty Years with Ford,* page 229. WCD, "Say what you will," quoted in the *New York Herald-Tribune,* Paris edition, June 1, 1929. The Durant doggerel quoted in John K. Galbraith, *The Great Crash, 1929,* insert page.

25. A Lion in Winter

WCD, "John Thomas," quoted in Weisberger, *The Dream Maker,* page 332. Frederick Allen, "The grim face," in Allen, *Only Yesterday,* page 284. Herbert Satterlee, "I trust," in letter to WCD, January 3, 1933, Durant Papers. H. L. Mencken, "The stupidest," quoted in Madsen, *Gloria and Joe,* page 291. WCD causing stir with possible Roosevelt vote in the *New York Times,* October 8, 1932. Aristo Scrobogna, "Mrs. Durant," told to author by Aristo Scrobogna, July 1998. WCD's bankruptcy petition published in the *New York Times,* February 9, 1936.

Letters from John Corcoran, Thad Preston, and J. P. Fiske to WCD, February 21, 1936, in Durant Papers. Alfred Goebel, "Although twenty years," in letter to WCD, February 9, 1936. WCD, "I haven't a dollar," quoted in *Detroit News,* April 27, 1941. James Morrison's speculations on WCD dying broke in a letter to Richard Gagnon, May 7, 1996. Clarence [Kaye?], "I got one of the greatest kicks," in letter to WCD, December 7, 1941, Durant Papers. WCD, "I do wish," in letter to Alfred Sloan, December 8, 1941, Durant Papers. *The Flint Weekly Review* assessment of WCD appeared on May 12, 1974. WCD, "A little later," in letter to W. H. Washer, November 25, 1945.

26. *Afterimages*

Aristo Scrobogna on Margery Durant Green and death of Fitzhugh Green, told to author by Aristo Scrobogna, July 1998. The story of the Greens' arrest on narcotics charges appeared in the New York *Daily News,* September 27, 1947. John Raskob, "Mr. Durant should be continued," in letter from Pierre S. du Pont to Irénée du Pont, November 20, 1920.

Bibliography

Allen, Frederick L. *Lords of Creation.* London: Harper Bros., 1935.

———. *Only Yesterday: An Informed History of the 1920s.* New York: Harper & Row, 1964.

Barron, Clarence Walker. *They Told Barron.* New York: Harper's, 1931.

Beasley, Norman. *Knudsen: A Biography.* New York: McGraw-Hill, 1947.

Blattner, Jean-François. *Emile Mathis.* Paris: Edifree, 1990.

Brooks, John. *The Great Leap: The Past 25 Years in America.* New York: Harper & Row, 1966.

Burlingame, Roger. *Henry Ford: A Great Life in Brief.* New York: Alfred A. Knopf, 1964.

Chrysler, Walter. *Life of an American Workman.* New York: Dodd, Mead, 1937.

Cohn, David L. *The Good Olds Days.* New York: Simon and Schuster, 1940.

Colby, Gerard. *Du Pont Dynasty: Behind the Nylon Curtain.* Secaucus, N.J.: Lyle Stuart, 1984.

Collier, Peter, and David Horowitz. *The Fords: An American Epic.* New York: Summit, 1989.

Crabb, Richard. *Birth of a Giant: The Men and Incidents that Gave America the Motorcar.* Philadelphia: Chilton, 1969.

Dunham, Terry B., and Lawrence Gustin. *The Buick: A Complete History.* Kutztown, Pa.: Automobile Quarterly Publications, 1987.

Durant, Margery. *My Father.* New York: G. P. Putnam, 1929.

Executive Committee, Golden Jubilee. *The Golden Jubilee of Flint, Michigan, 1855–1905.* Flint, Mich.: 1905.

Forbes, B. C., and O. D. Foster. *Automotive Giants of America.* New York: Forbes Publishing, 1926.

Forbes, John Douglas. *Stettinius Sr., Portrait of a Morgan Partner.* Charlottesville: University of Virginia Press, 1974.

Galbraith, John K. *The Great Crash, 1929.* Boston: Houghton Mifflin, 1988.

Garrett, Garet. *The Wild Wheel: The World of Henry Ford.* London: Cresset Press, 1952.

Gustin, Lawrence R. *Billy Durant: Creator of General Motors.* Grand Rapids, Mich.: William B. Eerdmans, 1973.

———. *A Pictorial History of Flint.* Grand Rapids, Mich.: William B. Eerdmans, 1976.

Herndon, Booton. *Ford: An Unconventional Biography of the Men and Their Times.* New York: Weybright and Talley, 1969.

Hornung, Clarence P. *Portrait Gallery of Early Automobiles.* New York: Harry N. Abrams, 1968.

Jackson, Stanley. *J. P. Morgan: A Biography.* New York: Stein and Day, 1984.

Kimes, Beverly Rae, and Robert C. Ackerson. *Chevrolet: A History from 1911.* Kutztown, Pa.: Automobile Quarterly Publications, 1986.

Lacey, Robert. *Ford: The Man and the Machine.* Boston: Little, Brown, 1986.

Langworth, Richard M. *Chrysler and Imperial: The Postwar Years.* Minneapolis: Motorbooks International, 1976.

Leland, Mrs. Henry M., with Minnie Dubbs Millbrook. *Master of Precision: Henry M. Leland.* Detroit: Wayne University Press, 1966.

Leslie, Stuart W. *Boss Kettering: Wizard of General Motors.* New York: Columbia University Press, 1983.

The Life History of the United States. New York: Time-Life Books, 1964.

Ludvigsen, Karl, and David Burgess Wise. *The Complete Encyclopedia of the American Automobile.* Secaucus, N.J.: Chatwell Books, 1979.

McCaughey, William H. *American Automobile Album.* New York: E. P. Dutton, 1954.

Madsen, Axel. *Gloria and Joe: The Star-Crossed Love Affair of Gloria Swanson and Joe Kennedy.* New York: Arbor House, 1988.

May, George. *A Most Unique Machine: The Michigan Beginnings of the Auto Industry.* Grand Rapids, Mich.: William B. Eerdmans, 1975.

Nault, William H. "William C. Durant." *World Book Encyclopedia.* 1982 ed.

Neal, A. D. *The Antitrust Laws of the USA.* London: Cambridge University Press, 1970.

Nevins, Allan, and Frank Earnest Hill. *Ford: The Times, the Man, the Company.* New York: Charles Scribner's Sons, 1957.

Pearson, Henry G. *Son of New England: James Jackson Storrow, 1846–1926.* Boston: Thomas Todd, 1932.

Pound, Arthur. *The Iron Man in Industry: An Outline of the Social Significance of Automatic Machinery.* Boston: Atlantic Monthly, 1922.

———. *The Turning Wheel: The Story of General Motors through Twenty-five Years, 1908–1932.* Garden City, N.Y.: Doubleday, Doran, 1934.

Rickenbacker, Edward V. *An Autobiography.* Englewood Cliffs, N.J.: Prentice-Hall, 1967.

Rogliatti, Gianni. *Great Collectors' Cars.* New York: Grosset and Dunlap, 1973.

Scharchburg, Richard P. *W. C. Durant, "The Boss."* Flint, Mich.: General Motors Institute, 1973.

Schlesinger, Arthur J. *History of U.S. Political Parties.* New York: Chelsea House, 1973.

Sedgwick, Michael. *Antique Cars.* New York: Exeter Books, 1981.

Seltzer, Lawrence H. *A Financial History of the American Automobile Industry.* Boston: Houghton, 1928.

Sloan, Alfred P., with Boyden Sparkes. *Adventures of a White-Collar Man.* New York: Doubleday, Doran, 1941.

———. *My Years with General Motors.* Garden City, N.Y.: Doubleday, 1964.

Smith, Martin, and Naomi Black. *America on Wheels.* New York: William Morrow, 1986.

Sorensen, Charles E., with Samuel T. Williamson. *My Forty Years with Ford.* New York: W.W. Norton, 1956.

Stein, Ralph. *The American Automobile.* New York: Ridge Press/ Random House, 1975.

Sward, Keith. *The Legend of Henry Ford.* New York: Reinhart, 1948.

Weisberger, Bernard A. *The Dream Maker: William C. Durant, Founder of General Motors.* Boston: Little, Brown, 1979.

Whyte, Andrew. *The Centenary of the Car, 1885–1985.* London: Octopus Books, 1984.

Whyte, William Hollingsworth. *The Organization Man: Alfred P. Sloan.* New York: Simon and Schuster, 1956.

Winans, Christopher. *Malcolm Forbes.* New York: St. Martin's, 1990.

Index

303

Index

Index

309

Index

Printed in the United States
29040LVS00004B/51